First World War
and Army of Occupation
War Diary
France, Belgium and Germany

33 DIVISION
100 Infantry Brigade
Queen's (Royal West Surrey Regiment)
1st Battalion
1 January 1916 - 31 January 1918

WO95/2430/1

The Naval & Military Press Ltd
www.nmarchive.com
Published in association with The National Archives

Published by

The Naval & Military Press Ltd

Unit 10 Ridgewood Industrial Park,

Uckfield, East Sussex,

TN22 5QE England

Tel: +44 (0) 1825 749494

www.naval-military-press.com

www.nmarchive.com

This diary has been reprinted in facsimile from the original. Any imperfections are inevitably reproduced and the quality may fall short of modern type and cartographic standards.

© **Crown Copyright**
Images reproduced by permission of The National Archives, London, England, 2015.

Contents

Document type	Place/Title	Date From	Date To
Heading	WO95/2430/1 1 Battalion Queen's (Royal West Surrey Regiment)		
Heading	33rd Division 100th Infy Bde 1st Bn Queen's Roy West Surrey Regt. Jan 1916-Jan 1918 From 21 Div 5 Bde To 19 Bde 33 Div		
Heading	1 R.W. Surrey Regt Vol XVIII XXXIII (100)		
Heading	100th Bde 33rd Div 1/R.W. Surrey Jan Vol XV		
War Diary	Bethune	01/01/1916	31/01/1916
War Diary	Annequin Fosse	01/02/1916	07/02/1916
War Diary	Beuvry	08/02/1916	14/02/1916
War Diary	A1	15/02/1916	29/02/1916
War Diary	Mad Bethune	01/03/1916	04/03/1916
War Diary	Bethune	05/03/1916	08/03/1916
War Diary	Beuvry	09/03/1916	11/03/1916
War Diary	Trenches Auchy Left	12/03/1916	15/03/1916
War Diary	Beuvry	16/03/1916	20/03/1916
War Diary	Trenches Auchy Left	20/03/1916	22/03/1916
War Diary	Auchy Left	22/03/1916	24/03/1916
War Diary	Bethune	25/03/1916	31/03/1916
Map	Auchy Left Sector		
War Diary	Bethune	01/04/1916	04/04/1916
War Diary	Le Quesnoy	05/04/1916	05/04/1916
War Diary	Cuinchy Left	06/04/1916	09/04/1916
War Diary	Le Quesnoy	10/04/1916	13/04/1916
War Diary	Cuinchy Left	14/04/1916	17/04/1916
War Diary	Bethune	18/04/1916	25/04/1916
War Diary	Auchy Left	26/04/1916	29/04/1916
War Diary	Beuvry	30/04/1916	03/05/1916
War Diary	Auchy Left	04/05/1916	08/05/1916
War Diary	Beuvry	08/05/1916	13/05/1916
War Diary	Auchy Left	14/05/1916	15/05/1916
War Diary	Bethune	16/05/1916	28/05/1916
War Diary	Fouquereuil	28/05/1916	31/05/1916
Miscellaneous	General de Wignacourt Commanding the Sub-Division of Arras Bethune to General London Commanding 33rd Division Appendix XXVIII	27/05/1916	27/05/1916
War Diary	Fouquereuil	01/06/1916	08/06/1916
War Diary	Beuvry	09/06/1916	12/06/1916
War Diary	Auchy Left	13/06/1916	16/06/1916
War Diary	Village Line	17/06/1916	20/06/1916
War Diary	Cuinchy Left	21/06/1916	24/06/1916
War Diary	Village Line	25/06/1916	30/06/1916
Heading	100th Inf. Bde. 33rd Div. War Diary 1st Battn. The Queen's (Royal West Surrey Regiment) July 1916		
War Diary	Cuinchy Left	01/07/1916	03/07/1916
War Diary	Le Quesnoy	03/07/1916	06/07/1916
War Diary	Busnettes	07/07/1916	07/07/1916
War Diary	Lillers	08/07/1916	08/07/1916
War Diary	Saleux	09/07/1916	09/07/1916
War Diary	Saint Saveur	09/07/1916	09/07/1916

War Diary	Daours	09/07/1916	10/07/1916
War Diary	Morlancourt	11/07/1916	12/07/1916
War Diary	Bicordel	13/07/1916	14/07/1916
War Diary	Fricourt	14/07/1916	14/07/1916
War Diary	Bazentin	15/07/1916	15/07/1916
War Diary	West of Highwood	15/07/1916	16/07/1916
War Diary	Bazentin	16/07/1916	16/07/1916
War Diary	Mametz Wood	17/07/1916	20/07/1916
War Diary	High Wood	21/07/1916	21/07/1916
War Diary	Bicordel	22/07/1916	23/07/1916
War Diary	Near Albert	23/07/1916	31/07/1916
Miscellaneous	Appendices XXIX XXIX XXX XXXI		
Miscellaneous	G.O.C. 33rd Division Appendix XXIX	10/07/1916	10/07/1916
Miscellaneous	Fourth Army. Special Order of The Day Appendix XXIX (a)		
Map	Appendix XXX		
Map	Appendix XXXI		
Heading	100th Brigade. 33rd Division. 1st Battalion The Queen's Royal West Surrey Regiment August 1916		
War Diary	Near Albert	01/08/1916	07/08/1916
War Diary	Bazentin Le Grand	07/08/1916	08/08/1916
War Diary	High Wood	09/08/1916	13/08/1916
War Diary	Bivouacs Between Becordel of Meaulte	13/08/1916	13/08/1916
War Diary	Bivouacs Becordel	14/08/1916	19/08/1916
War Diary	Pomier Trenches Near Mametz Village	20/08/1916	20/08/1916
War Diary	Pomier Trenches	21/08/1916	22/08/1916
War Diary	Trenches West of Delville Wood	23/08/1916	25/08/1916
War Diary	Fricourt Wood	26/08/1916	27/08/1916
War Diary	Bivouacs Becordel	28/08/1916	29/08/1916
War Diary	Becordel More To Ribemont	30/08/1916	30/08/1916
War Diary	Billets Ribemont None To Mirvaux	31/08/1916	31/08/1916
War Diary	Billets Mirvaux	31/08/1916	31/08/1916
Miscellaneous	List of Officers In 1st Battalion The Queens Regt Appendix XXXII	00/08/1916	00/08/1916
Miscellaneous	A Form. Messages And Signals.		
War Diary	??	01/09/1916	01/09/1916
War Diary	Heuzecourt	02/09/1916	03/09/1916
War Diary	Burbers Sur Canche	04/09/1916	04/09/1916
War Diary	Siracourt	05/09/1916	05/09/1916
War Diary	Averdoingt	06/09/1916	07/09/1916
War Diary	Halloy	08/09/1916	09/09/1916
War Diary	Souastre	10/09/1916	12/09/1916
War Diary	Front Trenches (Left Bde) Infront Of Gommecourt	13/09/1916	15/09/1916
War Diary	Front Trenches	16/09/1916	16/09/1916
War Diary	Gommecourt	16/09/1916	17/09/1916
War Diary	Trenches Gommecourt	18/09/1916	20/09/1916
War Diary	Fonquevillers	21/09/1916	26/09/1916
War Diary	Hombercamp	27/09/1916	27/09/1916
War Diary	Warlozel	28/09/1916	28/09/1916
War Diary	Sus St. Leger	29/09/1916	29/09/1916
War Diary	Brevillers	30/09/1916	19/10/1916
War Diary	Merricourt	20/10/1916	20/10/1916
War Diary	Meaulte	21/10/1916	21/10/1916
War Diary	Monsel Camp	22/10/1916	24/10/1916
War Diary	Bernafay Wood	25/10/1916	30/10/1916
War Diary	Guillemont	31/10/1916	02/11/1916

Type	Description	Start	End
War Diary	Lesboeufs	03/11/1916	05/11/1916
War Diary	Ox Trench	06/11/1916	06/11/1916
War Diary	Carnoy Citadel	07/11/1916	10/11/1916
War Diary	Liercourt	11/11/1916	29/11/1916
Map	33rd Div No 18		
Operation(al) Order(s)	100th Infantry Brigade Order No. 154	03/11/1916	03/11/1916
Miscellaneous	Operation Order No. by Lieut. Colonel S.T. Watson. D.S.O. Commanding 1st Battalion "The Queen's" Regt.		
Miscellaneous	Warning Order.	04/11/1916	04/11/1916
Operation(al) Order(s)	100th Infantry Brigade Order No. 155	04/11/1916	04/11/1916
Miscellaneous	Operation Order No. by Lieut. Col. S.T. Watson D.S.O. Commdg. 1st Batt. "The Queen's" Regt.		
Map	Not To Be Taken Beyond Battn HD. Qrs		
War Diary	Liercourt	01/12/1916	04/12/1916
War Diary	Vaux	05/12/1916	05/12/1916
War Diary	Morlancourt	06/12/1916	06/12/1916
War Diary	Camp III	07/12/1916	07/12/1916
War Diary	Camp 107	08/12/1916	08/12/1916
War Diary	Maurepas	09/12/1916	09/12/1916
War Diary	Rancourt	10/12/1916	11/12/1916
War Diary	Maurepas	12/12/1916	14/12/1916
War Diary	Camp III	14/12/1916	22/12/1916
War Diary	Camp 17	23/12/1916	28/12/1916
War Diary	Bussus Bussuel	29/12/1916	20/01/1917
War Diary	Bray	21/01/1917	23/01/1917
War Diary	Camp 19	24/01/1917	27/01/1917
War Diary	NE Clery	28/01/1917	31/01/1917
War Diary	Road Wood	01/02/1917	05/02/1917
War Diary	N.E. Clery	06/02/1917	08/02/1917
War Diary	Camp 19	09/02/1917	16/02/1917
War Diary	Frise Bend	17/02/1917	20/02/1917
War Diary	N.E. Clery	21/02/1917	24/02/1917
War Diary	Frise Bend	25/02/1917	28/02/1917
War Diary	N.E. Clery	01/03/1917	05/03/1917
War Diary	Camp 19	06/03/1917	06/03/1917
War Diary	Corbie	07/03/1917	02/04/1917
War Diary	Villers Bocage	03/04/1917	03/04/1917
War Diary	Beauval	04/04/1917	04/04/1917
War Diary	Neuvilette	05/04/1917	05/04/1917
War Diary	Grenas	06/04/1917	07/04/1917
War Diary	Souastre	08/04/1917	08/04/1917
War Diary	St. Amand	09/04/1917	12/04/1917
War Diary	Mercatel	13/04/1917	15/04/1917
War Diary	Hamlincourt	16/04/1917	22/04/1917
War Diary	Hamincourt	20/04/1917	22/04/1917
War Diary	Between Fontaine & Croisille Raily Cutting T 27 A	23/04/1917	25/04/1917
War Diary	Berles Au-Bois	26/04/1917	30/04/1917
Operation(al) Order(s)	Battalion Order No. 59 by Lieut. Colonel C.F. Watson C.M.G. D.S.O. Comdg. 1st Battalion The Queen's" Regiment. Saturday 31st March 1917	31/03/1917	31/03/1917
Operation(al) Order(s)	Battalion Orders No. 60 by. Lt. Col. C,F, Watson. C.M.G. D.S.O. Comdg. 1st Battalion The Queen's Regt. Monday 2nd April 1917	02/04/1917	02/04/1917
Miscellaneous	Time Table of Artillery Barrage To Accompany 100th Infantry Brigade Order 221		

Type	Description	Date From	Date To
Operation(al) Order(s)	Battalion Orders No. 61 by Lieut Col C.F. Watson Cmg. DSO To Queen's	03/04/1917	03/04/1917
Operation(al) Order(s)	Battalion Order No. 62 by Lieut. Col. C.F. Watson C.M.G. D.S.O. Comdg Bn The Queen's Regt Wednesday	04/04/1917	04/04/1917
Operation(al) Order(s)	Battalion Order No. 64 by Lieut. Col. C.F. Watson C.M.G. D.S.O. Comdg Bn. "The Queen's Regt	06/04/1917	06/04/1917
Map	Printed by No.3 Advanced Section		
Operation(al) Order(s)	Operation Order No. 1 by Lieut. Col. L.M. Crofts. D.S.O. Comdg. Bn. The Queen's "Regiment	22/04/1917	22/04/1917
Miscellaneous	Report on Operations	23/04/1917	23/04/1917
Miscellaneous	A Form. Messages And Signals.		
Miscellaneous	Furnace		
Miscellaneous	The A Mask Stated Went The		
Miscellaneous	Furnace		
Miscellaneous	Furnace Situation		
Miscellaneous	Furnace		
Miscellaneous	A Form. Messages And Signals.		
War Diary	Berles Au Bois	01/05/1917	01/05/1917
War Diary	Blaireville	02/05/1917	02/05/1917
War Diary	Boiry St Martin	03/05/1917	11/05/1917
War Diary	Near Croisilles (T 22 A)	12/05/1917	15/05/1917
War Diary	Moyenneville	16/05/1917	19/05/1917
War Diary	Croisilles Vicinity of	20/05/1917	21/05/1917
War Diary	Trenches	22/05/1917	23/05/1917
War Diary	Moyenneville	24/05/1917	26/05/1917
War Diary	W of St Leger (T 28 C.2.5)	27/05/1917	28/05/1917
War Diary	Croisilles Vicinity of	29/05/1917	31/05/1917
War Diary	Moyenneville	01/06/1917	01/06/1917
War Diary	Berles-Au-Bois	02/06/1917	20/06/1917
War Diary	Moyenville	21/06/1917	24/06/1917
War Diary	Front Line Trenches	25/06/1917	26/06/1917
War Diary	Moyenneville	27/06/1917	28/06/1917
War Diary	Front Line Trenches N.E. Croisilles	29/06/1917	29/06/1917
War Diary	Front Line Trenches	29/06/1917	29/06/1917
War Diary	Moyenneville	29/06/1917	29/06/1917
War Diary	Front Line Trenches	28/06/1917	30/06/1917
Miscellaneous	O.C. 1st Queen's. 222 F. Co. R.E. (For Information)	26/06/1917	26/06/1917
Operation(al) Order(s)	Battalion Order No 3 by Lt. Col. L.M. Crofts D.S.O. Comdg Bn The Queen's Regt	28/06/1917	28/06/1917
War Diary	Berles Au Bois	01/07/1917	05/07/1917
War Diary	Picquigny	06/07/1917	30/07/1917
Operation(al) Order(s)	Battalion Order No. 128 by Lieut. Col. L.M. Crofts D.S.O. Comdg Bn The Queens" Regiment.	30/07/1917	30/07/1917
Diagram etc			
Miscellaneous	Right of Nebus		
War Diary	Prequiring	01/08/1917	01/08/1917
War Diary	Coudekerque Branche	02/08/1917	03/08/1917
War Diary	Ghyvelde	04/08/1917	15/08/1917
War Diary	Beach Near Frontier Chyvelde	16/08/1917	18/08/1917
War Diary	Coxyde	19/08/1917	27/08/1917
War Diary	Ghyvelde	28/08/1917	28/08/1917
War Diary	Coudekerque	29/08/1917	31/08/1917
War Diary	Wormhoudt	31/08/1917	31/08/1917
War Diary	Coudekerque	31/08/1917	31/08/1917

Type	Description	Date From	Date To
Operation(al) Order(s)	Battalion Orders No. 129 by Lieut. Colonel. L.M. Crofts D.S.O. Comdg Bn The Queen's Regt.	02/08/1917	02/08/1917
Operation(al) Order(s)	Battalion Order No. 142 by Lieut Col L.M. Crofts D.S.O. Comdg Bn The Queens Regt.	17/08/1917	17/08/1917
Miscellaneous	Demands Made On This Sheet Should Consist of Personnel Required From The Base Only And Should Not Include Any Demands For Personnel Which Can Be Completed by Promotions Or Appointments Within The Unit.		
Operation(al) Order(s)	Battalion Order No. 153 by Lieut Col L.M. Crofts D.S.O. Comdg Bn The Queens Regt.	30/08/1917	30/08/1917
Heading	War Diary		
War Diary	Bayenghem	01/09/1917	15/09/1917
War Diary	Buysscheure	16/09/1917	16/09/1917
War Diary	Steenvoorde	17/09/1917	17/09/1917
War Diary	Berthen	18/09/1917	19/09/1917
War Diary	Near Reninghelst	20/09/1917	28/09/1917
War Diary	Scottish Wood	28/09/1917	28/09/1917
War Diary	La Belle Hotesse	29/09/1917	30/09/1917
War Diary		24/09/1917	25/09/1917
War Diary	Menin Road Near Veldhoek	25/09/1917	25/09/1917
War Diary	Veldhoek	25/09/1917	28/09/1917
Operation(al) Order(s)	Battalion Order No. 166 by Lieut. Col L.M. Crofts D.S.O. Comdg Bn The Queens Regt	14/09/1917	14/09/1917
Operation(al) Order(s)	Battalion Order No 167 by Lieut. Col. L.M. Crofts D.S.O. Comdg. Bn The Queens Regt.	15/09/1917	15/09/1917
Operation(al) Order(s)	Battalion Order No. 168 by Lieut Col L.M. Crofts. D.S.O. Comdg Bn The Queens Regt	16/09/1917	16/09/1917
Operation(al) Order(s)	Battalion Order No. 171 by Lieut. Col. L.M. Crofts D.S.O. Comdg. Bn The Queens Regt.	19/09/1917	19/09/1917
Operation(al) Order(s)	Battalion Order No. 175 by Lieut. Col. L.M. Croft. D.S.O. Comdg Bn The Queens Regiment	24/09/1917	24/09/1917
Map	Message Map		
Miscellaneous	Message Form.		
War Diary	La Belle Hotesse	01/10/1917	05/10/1917
War Diary	St. Martin Au Laert	06/10/1917	06/10/1917
War Diary	Aldershot Camp S W of Neuve Eglise	07/10/1917	14/10/1917
War Diary	Bristol Castle E S.E. of Wulverghem	15/10/1917	22/10/1917
War Diary	Kortepyp 'A' Camp	23/10/1917	31/10/1917
Operation(al) Order(s)	Battalion Order No. 130 by Lieut Col L.M. Crofts D.S.O. Comdg Bn The Queen's Regt	04/10/1917	04/10/1917
Miscellaneous	War Diary		
Diagram etc	Appendix 3		
Map	Message Map Appendix (2)		
Miscellaneous	Message Form.		
Map	Trench Operation Map		
Miscellaneous	Message Form		
Operation(al) Order(s)	Battalion Order No 189 by Lieut Col L.M. Crofts D.S.O. Comdg Bn The Queens Regt.	14/10/1917	14/10/1917
Miscellaneous	Translation of Captured German Order Appx 5	24/09/1917	24/09/1917
Miscellaneous	The Attack On 33rd Division Between Polygon Wood And Menin Road September 25th 1917 Appx 6	25/09/1917	25/09/1917
Miscellaneous	Special Order of The Day by Major-General P. Wood C.B., C.M.G. Commanding 33rd Division. Appx 7		
Miscellaneous	Special Brigade Order Appendix 8	30/09/1917	30/09/1917
Miscellaneous	G.O.C. And All Ranks, 33rd Division.	08/10/1917	08/10/1917

Type	Description	Date From	Date To
Miscellaneous	Bar To The Military Medal		
War Diary	Kortepyp 'A' Camp	01/11/1917	07/11/1917
War Diary	Trenches U 5	08/11/1917	11/11/1917
War Diary	Bristol Castle T 6 D	12/11/1917	13/11/1917
War Diary	Neuve Eglise	14/11/1917	18/11/1917
War Diary	Toronto Camp	18/11/1917	25/11/1917
War Diary	E of Ypres I 9a 3.2	26/11/1917	30/11/1917
Operation(al) Order(s)	Battalion Orders 203 by Major H.E. Ire Monger Comdg 1st Bn The Queens Regt	06/11/1917	06/11/1917
Miscellaneous	Additions To Battalion Order 203 Paragraph 9		
Operation(al) Order(s)	Battalion Orders No 209 by Lieut Col Crofts D.S.O. Comdg Brig Regt.	17/11/1917	17/11/1917
Miscellaneous	Report On Raid Night of 10/11th November	11/11/1917	11/11/1917
Miscellaneous	Patrol Order To Each Recipient Orders On Raid On Night 10/11th November	07/11/1917	07/11/1917
Miscellaneous	Barrage Table To Accompany 24th D.A. O.O. No. 133		
Operation(al) Order(s)	14th Divisional Artillery Operation Order No. 133 by Lieut Colonel L.J. Osborn V.D.	09/11/1917	09/11/1917
Miscellaneous	Orders for Raid To Be Carried Out by 1st Battalion "The Queen's" Regt on Night 10/11th November 1917	10/11/1917	10/11/1917
Miscellaneous	Patrol Order-To Each Recipient of Orders on Raid On Night 10/11th November	07/11/1917	07/11/1917
Miscellaneous	Supplementary Orders For Raid On Night of 10/11th November 1917	10/11/1917	10/11/1917
Miscellaneous	War Diary 2 Copies No 4 & 5		
Operation(al) Order(s)	Battalion Order No. 216 by Lt. Col. L.M. Crofts. D.S.O. Comdg Bn The Queens Regt.	24/11/1917	24/11/1917
Operation(al) Order(s)	Battalion Order No. 220 by Lieut. Col. L.M. Crofts D.S.O. Comdg Bn The Queens Regt	29/11/1917	29/11/1917
War Diary	Seine (D. 16 D 15 40)	01/12/1917	03/12/1917
War Diary	Front Line S of Passchen Daele	04/12/1917	06/12/1917
War Diary	E of Ypres I 9a 3.2	07/12/1917	07/12/1917
War Diary	Toronto G.18a 6.5	08/12/1917	09/12/1917
War Diary	Toronto Camp	10/12/1917	10/12/1917
War Diary	N of Steenvoorde K 25c 9.9	11/12/1917	13/12/1917
War Diary	Poperinghe	14/12/1917	21/12/1917
War Diary	N of Steenvoorde K 25 C 9.9	22/12/1917	31/12/1917
Operation(al) Order(s)	Battalion Orders No. 222 by Major H.E. Iremonger Comdg The Queens Regt	09/12/1917	09/12/1917
Operation(al) Order(s)	Battalion Order No. 224 by Lt Col L.M. Crofts DSO Comdg Bn The Queens Regt	13/12/1917	13/12/1917
Operation(al) Order(s)	Battalion Orders No. 231 by Major H.E Iremonger Comdg Bn The Queens Regt	20/12/1917	20/12/1917
Heading	War Diary		
War Diary	N of Steenvoorde K 25 C 9.9	01/01/1918	04/01/1918
War Diary	Toronto Camp G 18a 6.5	05/01/1918	05/01/1918
War Diary	Seine	06/01/1918	09/01/1918
War Diary	Hamburg	10/01/1918	13/01/1918
War Diary	Toronto Camp	14/01/1918	17/01/1918
War Diary	St Jean Camp I 3 B 3.6	18/01/1918	28/01/1918
War Diary	Setques	29/01/1918	31/01/1918
Operation(al) Order(s)	Battalion Orders No. 4 by Lieut Col Lt. B.R. Sladen Comdg The Queens Regt	03/01/1918	03/01/1918
Operation(al) Order(s)	Battalion Order No 5 by Lieut Col Lt. B.R. Sladen Comdg The Queens Regt	11/01/1918	11/01/1918

Operation(al) Order(s)	Battalion Order No. 6 by Lieut B.R. Sladen Comdg The Queens Rgt	07/01/1918	07/01/1918
Operation(al) Order(s)	Battalion Order No. 7 by Lieut Col. B.R. Sladen Comdg The Queens	12/01/1918	12/01/1918
Operation(al) Order(s)	Battalion Order No. 22 by Major H.E. Iremonger Comdg The Queens Regt	27/01/1918	27/01/1918

WO/95/2430/1

1 Battalion Queen's
(Royal West Surrey Regiment)

33RD DIVISION
100TH INFY. BDE

1ST BN (QUEEN'S)
ROY. WEST SURREY REGT.

JAN 1916 - JAN 1918.

FROM 2 DIV
  S. BDE

To 19 BDE   33 DIV

1/33

1 R.W Surrey Regt

Vol XVIII

XXXIII (100)

1/R. W. Sweeney
106th Bde 33rd Div.

vol ~~XXX~~ XL

Jan 18
Jan 16

WAR DIARY or INTELLIGENCE SUMMARY

Army Form C. 2118

1/5th Surrey

Place	Date 1916	Hour	Summary of Events and Information	Remarks and references to Appendices
BETHUNE	1st Jan		Nil	
	2 Jan		Battalion paraded by Coys at 1.35 pm and marched to Festubert Area. 16th KRR in right or leading and left Groups and later in two Groups and both in left on Casualties wounded. Gun Boat H.Q. and POINT FIXE was relieved on our turn.	
	3 Jan		Quiet up to 3 pm. Casualties 1 killed.	
	4		Quiet day. Casualties 3 Other Ranks killed, 2 wounded.	
	5		" 1 Other Rank killed	
	6		2Lt Buchan proceeded to a trench mortar course at CEVENANT. Casualties nil	
	7		Relief by 2' Worcesters commenced at 3pm and completed at 5pm. Bat. went into Billets at ANNEKIN (V)	
	8		Bathing and ordinary Routine with 420 men on fatigue. Casualties 1 Other Rank wounded	
	9		350 men on working parties.	
	10		Relieved 16th K.R.R. in A. Sector starting at 4.45 pm — 98th Brigade now on Right and 2 Coys Bn in Left.	
	11		Quiet except heavy shelling of BRADDELL POINT and main LABASSEE Road.	
	12		10 Cadets joined for 48 hours attachment in trenches. Lieut. J BURTON killed.	
	13		C.S.M. LARKIN killed and 2 Other Ranks wounded.	

Army Form C. 2118

WAR DIARY
or
INTELLIGENCE SUMMARY
(Erase heading not required.)

Instructions regarding War Diaries and Intelligence Summaries are contained in F. S. Regs., Part II. and the Staff Manual respectively. Title Pages will be prepared in manuscript.

Place	Date	Hour	Summary of Events and Information	Remarks and references to Appendices
	14/5/15		Captain Boyd left for General Staff 2nd Division. Lieut I.W.S. SPMONS assumed the duties of adjutant.	
	15th		Quiet day. Except for relief of BRADDELL post. Relieved by 18.R.F. Relief Started at 5.30 and finished by 7.30 pm. We marched back to BETHUNE at 7th & respectively and Rue de Hichels.	
BETHUNE	16th		Ordinary Routine 2nd Lieut BENNETT went to a Brabin Course.	
	17th		Bathing. Fatigue party of 100 men and one officer to R.E. yard. 2 Lieut I.S.S. Munition force to a machine gun Course	
	18th		Ordinary Routine	
	19th		" "	
	20		" "	
	21		Bat. Parade ordinary Routine	
	22		" Routine	
	23		" "	
	24		Bat. Relieved 1st Coy of 18.R.F and 1 Coy A Surrenders. in 21. Relief Complete at 7.40. Started at 5.30 p.t.	
	25th		Nothing in nothing one wounded, orders to be Relieved by K.R.R. (6)	?
	26th		Relief Completed. Attack feared. Shelling all day night by our guns. Heavy fulls Retaliation.	

WAR DIARY
or
INTELLIGENCE SUMMARY

(Erase heading not required.)

Army Form C. 2118

Place	Date	Hour	Summary of Events and Information	Remarks and references to Appendices
	27th		Specks attack. Bulwarks on both sides. Relieved by K.R.R. Platoons at 12 in finished at 4.30 pm. Went back to FACTORY TRENCH.	
	28th		In support to HORSE SHOE WORDS. Being heavily shelled.	
			Very heavy bombardment from 10 am to 5 pm. Standing by for cavalry attached but knock held their own. Interchangeable Riddle, heavily shelled. Also own mgf. (3 killed 3 wounded)	
	29th		Relieved 2 Worcesters. (K.R.R. on right, 19.3 on left) Bombing Raid on Crater at night, this had sanity Repulsed by 13 Coy.	2 Lt. SKENE left top kitch Enfant Royal Santa Kay Am.
	30th		Slight shelling, nothing to Report. HQrs at Maison Rouge.	
	31st		Relieved by 2d Worcesters - went back to HANNEQUIN FARM.	

Fymond
Major
/Queen's Regt.

WAR DIARY or INTELLIGENCE SUMMARY

Army Form C. 2118

Place	Date	Hour	Summary of Events and Information	Remarks and references to Appendices
PONT du FASSE	1 Feb		Ordinary Routine.	
	2		Relieved 2nd Middlesex Cavalry in Rifle Brigade K.R.R. in L/F. We are in Z.O. — nothing to report.	
	3		Nothing to report. (1 killed) Quiet.	
	4		Bombing on L/F.	
	5		Very quiet. Little shelling in L/F of Bat. 1 Or at Railway Icet P. (2 wounded)	
	6		Relieved by 2nd R.W.F. went to BEUVRY. (2 killed 3 wounded)	2/Lt. Blumer killed
	7		Nothing to report.	
BEUVRY	8		Ordinary Routine	
	9		" "	
	10		" "	
	11		" "	
	12		" "	
	13		Moved up to trenches in A.1 - 16 Ar on L/F - 19 B2nd on Rifle Ham.	
	14		Relieving during day — quiet at night.	
			Very quiet — during capture aeroplane — Raid proposed — 1 killed	

WAR DIARY or INTELLIGENCE SUMMARY

Army Form C. 2118

Place	Date	Hour	Summary of Events and Information	Remarks and references to Appendices
A1	15th	—	Very quiet – Lot of patrolling – 1 Killed –	
	16th		Quiet ampaink [?] active during night – 1 killed –	
	17th		B. Coy relieving D – C Coy relieved by A. – Good patrols are by 2/Lts Delagh & Ruff – using to Rifinf – Enemy were reported the mg posts and made men by snipers – man – Capt Brittain T. 10th joined Bn. in trenches from Base – Mr	
	18th		Relieved by ????	
	19th		Shelling (several at about 10.30 p.m.) by enemy from by trench first which we know (Inchies) for 1 hour. P.M. Recommended for brain an wiring nr. Glanor. Under heavy Mih & M.G. fire – 2 Killed 10 wounded – F. Coy attached for instruction – 2 killed F. Coy 8 L Minimators then relieve C Coy. Some explodes on left opposite Cogan 3rd in F. Coy Brick stacks Knocks enemy crater – 1 wounded. A Listing Wt Sunk	
	(20th)		a Lt of patrols	
	21st		Ste on Left - 19th B re on Right	

Army Form C. 2118

WAR DIARY
or
INTELLIGENCE SUMMARY
(Erase heading not required.)

Place	Date	Hour	Summary of Events and Information	Remarks and references to Appendices
A.1	22		t/over Relieved - in quiet - Evening had	
	23		att took handicaps by huns - patching things at - chased 6th	
			Sergt - for reserves party arrived in rifle -	
	24		16th Scottish Rifles join B⁺ - 16 M's leave B⁺ - 1 wounded (suicide)	
	25		Nothing to report	
	26		Wire netting with tunnel venture	
	27		Tunnel venture active in left sector	
	28		In quiet - attempted raid - failed owing to wire -	
	29		quiet -	
			Relieved by 1/5 Scottish Rifles - 2 wounded	
Transit	1st			
BETHUNE	2		Cleaning up in Billets	
	3		Army Routine	
	4		Army Routine	

Army Form C. 2118

WAR DIARY
INTELLIGENCE SUMMARY
(Erase heading not required.)

Place	Date	Hour	Summary of Events and Information	Remarks and references to Appendices
BETHUNE	Mch 5th		Ordinary Routine - Reserve line of Pailly to Brewere examined by C.O. & Coy Commanders in view of occupying them in Case of hostile attack.	
	6th		Draft of 47 joined Bn. Good quality + up to average.	
	7th		Ordinary Routine	
	8th		Bn Route march of about 9 miles	
BEUVRY	9th		Bn moved up to BEUVRY as Bde Reserve.	
	10th		Working parties 350 strong all day: by Commanders up to trenches to see the line	
	11th		Working parties. Beery cellars -	
Trenches AUCHY LEFT.	12th		Bn - to trenches - Relieved KRR 16th - 4th Suffolks on left. 2nd Worcesters on right - all quiet.	
	13th		Int. by Relief - a little shelling.	
	14th		quiet	
	15th			
BEUVRY	16th		Relieved by 16 KRR - Bn to BEUVRY.	
	17th		Lt W R Cardale to be assistant adjutant.	

Army Form C. 2118

WAR DIARY
or
INTELLIGENCE SUMMARY
(Erase heading not required.)

Instructions regarding War Diaries and Intelligence Summaries are contained in F.S. Regs., Part II. and the Staff Manual respectively. Title Pages will be prepared in manuscript.

Place	Date March	Hour	Summary of Events and Information	Remarks and references to Appendices
BEUVRY	18th		Raid practiced by C Coy. Half the battalion on fatigue. Capt. Brookhurst Hill took over A Coy.	
	19th		Church parade for men not on fatigue the night before. Raid practiced.	
	20th		Bombing accident while practising raid – 7 wounded – one died of wounds since. Relieved 16th K.R.R. in AUCHY LEFT.	
Trenches AUCHY LEFT	21st		Quiet day; no casualties; good patrol by Lt. Symons. Lt. Carlisle took over front of acting adjutant.	
	22nd	8.0 p.m.	Quiet day; no casualties. In evening; raid carried out on German front line just S. of MINE POINT. Complete success. 2/Lt. Lukyn + 2/Lt. Morris started out with 32 men; wire previously cut by artillery – 2/Lt. Morris wounded by chance bullet; 2/Lt. Lukyn took his place – trenches entered, 1 sentry killed, 1 escaped wounded. 4 dug-outs full of Germans bombed & blown in. Party returned intact with German gas-helmet, after remaining 15 to 20 minutes in enemy trench. Barrage of T.M.s, rifle grenades & Mills bombs on both flanks. Following messages of congratulation received:— (1) From Corps commander (General Hacking C.B.) "Congratulations on successful raid." (2) From army commander (General Sir Charles Monro)	Appendices XXVII

1875 Wt. W593/826 1,000,000 4/15 T.R.C. & A. A.D.S.S./Forms/C. 2118.

WAR DIARY or INTELLIGENCE SUMMARY

Army Form C. 2118

Place	Date March	Hour	Summary of Events and Information	Remarks and references to Appendices
AVCHY LEFT.			"Please convey to my old regiment the pleasure it gives me to hear of their successful raid last night." (3) From Brigadier General AWF. Baird, C.M.G., D.S.O. "Congratulate you & your platoon on success." Promoted for gallantry in the field, no. 11246 L/Cpl Geering. Recommended for immediate awards :- 2/Lt. Lobwyn, Military Cross, 2/Lt Geering, Mention, no. 3467 Pte. Paterson, no. 11246 Cpl. Whaley, no. 3705 Cpl. Geering and no. 9290 Cpl. Brie for D.C.M.s.	
	23rd	4.30 p.m.	Left company at MINE POINT trench mortared in morning. Heavy bombardment for 1½ hours of front & support line. One killed. Small mine near MIDNIGHT crater. Two wounded by bombs at night. No damage. Colonel Croft granted 4 days leave to England.	
	24th		Quiet day; heavy snow. Repair of damage done by yesterday's bombardment. One wounded.	
	25th		Fine day; quiet. No casualties. At 7.0 p.m., relieved by 1st. Cameronians (19th. brigade) & went back to billets at MONTMORENCY BARRACKS, BETHUNE.	
BETHUNE.	26th		Battalion billeted at École des Jeunes Filles. Ordinary routine, cleaning up, etc.	

Army Form C. 2118

WAR DIARY
or
INTELLIGENCE SUMMARY
(Erase heading not required.)

Instructions regarding War Diaries and Intelligence Summaries are contained in F. S. Regs., Part II. and the Staff Manual respectively. Title Pages will be prepared in manuscript.

Place	Date March	Hour	Summary of Events and Information	Remarks and references to Appendices
BETHUNE	27th		Ordinary routine. All Officers met Corps Commander, General Hakeing, at 2.30 at Vacant, when he explained the present situation, etc. 2.1.t. Pearey Bottomley joined the battalion.	
	28th		Ordinary routine. Colonel Croft returned off leave.	
	29th		Ordinary routine. Wiring parties of 2 Officers & 200 men at work at Beuvry & Rt Reg.	
	30th		Battalion route march round Hinges & Avelette.	
	31st		Ordinary routine.	McFarlane Lt Major

AUCHY LEFT SECTOR.

Path taken by raiding party →→→
French raided marked ———

Army Form C. 2118

WAR DIARY or INTELLIGENCE SUMMARY

(Erase heading not required.)

11 Queen's Regt.

April, 1916

Place	Date	Hour	Summary of Events and Information	Remarks and references to Appendices
BETHUNE	1.		Ordinary routine. Mixing party of 100 men at Le Prol. Awards: 2/Lt. Schoper, Military cross; 9240 ep. Bru, 3705 Cpl Gearing, 3467 Pte. Paterson, D.C.M.	
	2.		Church parade in morning. Afternoon, moved from MONTMORENCY BARRACKS to ECOLE DES JEUNES FILLES, relieving 1/4 Suffolks	4 1/K.R.R.
	3.		Ordinary routine; practice of bombing attacks & new bayonet fighting course.	
	4.		Ordinary routine, as yesterday.	
	5.		C.O. & Os.C. Coys. reconnoitred new CUINCHY left in morning. Afternoon, moved to billets at LE QUESNOY.	
LE QUESNOY	6.		Working party of 100 men in morning. 70 at night. Relieved 16th. K.R.R. in CUINCHY left.	
CUINCHY LEFT	7.		Quiet day; a few L.H.V. shells in brickstacks. 1 killed, 2 wounded.	
	8.		Two Coys. 17th. K.R.R. attached for instruction.	
	9.		Some heavy T.M. bombs near brickstacks. Light shelling with 77 m.m. 1 killed, 1 wounded. Usual light shelling; very quiet on whole. No reply to our rifles or rifle grenades. 1 killed, 1 wounded. Good patrol by 2/Lt. BUCKNER & 6251 MITCHELL. Two Coys. 17th. K.R.R. left after instruction.	Official Lt. Symons awarded leave to England, admitted to hospital; had not joined by end of month.
LE QUESNOY	10.		Quiet day. 1 Wounded. Relieved by 16th. K.R.R. & proceeded to billets in LE QUESNOY.	MBL
	11.		Cleaning up & ordinary routine. Working parties of 160 in evening. 4 officers & 8 R. Coys attached to 17th. K.R.R. in Cuinchy Right to give instruction.	

Army Form C. 2118

WAR DIARY
or
INTELLIGENCE SUMMARY
(Erase heading not required.)

1/Queen's Regt.   April, 1916.

Place	Date	Hour	Summary of Events and Information	Remarks and references to Appendices
	12.		Ordinary routine. Working parties of 140 again in evening. Battalion had bath.	
	13.		Working parties normal to night; total 150 men. Company commanders conference to settle programme of work for Brigade rest.	
CUINCHY LEFT.	14.		Working party of 60 in morning. Relieved 16th K.R.R. in morning. Relieved 16th K.R.R. in CUINCHY LEFT; 1/6 Scottish Rifles on right. 4 officers & 2 N.C.O.'s completed duty with 17th K.R.R.	
	15.		Quiet day. 1 killed, 1 wounded. A few 5.9" shells in Cuinchy Village.	
	16.		Quiet day again. 1 wounded. A few 5.9" into Cuinchy Village again in evening.	
	17.		Quiet day. 2 wounded. In evening, party of D coy made reconnaissance of S crater with mining officer, to look for suspected mine shaft. No shaft found; on mining officer being killed; 4118 Pte. Jones & 4737 Pte. Edwards showed much gallantry in recovering his body from crater.	18th April. Capt. Nicholas (3rd Buffs) admitted to hospital with shell shock.
BETHUNE.	18.		Quiet again, a wet. In evening, C.Q.M.S. Longhurst (C Coy) & 1 man killed, & 2 other ranks wounded in billets in Montmorency Barracks, Bethune. Relieved by 1st Cameronians, & proceeded to billets in Montmorency Barracks, Bethune.	22nd April. 2/Lt Crooks formerly MBE
	19.		Baths & cleaning up all day.	
	20.		Ordinary routine. Riding school started for young officers.	
	21.		Ordinary routine.	
	22.		Ordinary routine; no proper parades owing to rain.	
	23.		Church parade in morning. Rugger match, officers of Queen's & Worcesters V. A.S.C., who won.	

Army Form C. 2118

WAR DIARY
or
INTELLIGENCE SUMMARY
(Erase heading not required.)

11 Queen's Regt.   April, 1916

Place	Date	Hour	Summary of Events and Information	Remarks and references to Appendices
	24.		Short battalion route march in morning. Afternoon, inspection of battalion by Army Commander, General Sir Charles Monro, who addressed Battalion.	
AUCHY LEFT.	25.		Ordinary routine. C.O. & Company commanders inspected trenches of AUCHY LEFT.	
	26.		Ordinary routine in morning. Evening, relieved 4th King's Regt. in AUCHY LEFT by 2nd Worcesters on right. 2 wounded.	
	27.		Gas attack at 6.0 a.m.; gas drifted up to us; helmets worn for 1 hour. Rest of day quiet. No casualties. We fired many rifle grenades, as enemy were active with them. Good patrol by 2/Lt. Rouquette.	
	28.		Usual exchange of rifle grenades & T.M.'s round R.W.F. crater. A little shelling on communication trenches. 1 killed, 3 wounded. In evening, gas reported on both flanks, but nothing came of it.	
	29.		Heavy bombardment of Fishing alley in morning. 8m 5"9", L.H.V. & T.M. activity during day. German sniper brought down on our right.	
BEUVRY	30.		Much quieter day. 1 wounded. Relieved by 16th K.R.R. & returned to billets in BEUVRY. Working parties of 2 officers & 70 men at night. Draft of 144 other ranks joined regiment today.	MDR

L. M. Crofts H Col
Comdg 11 Queens

WAR DIARY
or
INTELLIGENCE SUMMARY

Army Form C. 2118

1/Queen's Regt.

May, 1916

Vol 19

Place	Date	Hour	Summary of Events and Information	Remarks and references to Appendices
BEUVRY.	1.		Battalion had baths all day. 4 officers & 180 men on working parties. Conference of officers & platoon sergeants in afternoon.	
	2.		Working parties of 2 officers & 200 men. Divisional Commander, General Strickland, inspected horses & transport in afternoon.	
	3.		Ordinary routine. Working parties of 325 men.	
	4.		Working parties of 110 men in afternoon. Relieved 16th K.R.R. in Auchy Left, after dusk. 2/Lt. Matter relinquished post of Brigade Intelligence Officer & took over temporary command of A coy.	
AUCHY LEFT	5.		Quiet day. 1 wounded. Our T.M.'s did good work on R.W.F. craters.	
	6.		At 5.55 a.m. enemy mine blown S. of BABY craters; 2 men buried in left-hand in EASTERN TWIN crater. Barrage of 77mm & 4.2" shells for half an hour, & again after an hour. Party of B coy occupied far lip at once, & prevented enemy from leaving his trenches by rifle fire & bombs; 2/Lt. Crichton, 8867 Sgt. Elderkin, 8814 L/Cpl. Wyber & 981 L/Cpl. Harding did very well, 2/Lt. Crichton being slightly wounded (at duty) by shell-fire. 2/Lt. Crichton recommended for Military Cross, the other three ranks for Military Medal. Work on crater all day. Light shelling & heavy minnies about mid-day & in afternoon; heavy bombardment with L.H.V. 4.2" & minnies for an hour at dusk. Day's casualties, 4 killed, 8 wounded, (2 at duty) & Lt. Crichton wounded (at duty). New crater called QUEEN's crater.	

Army Form C. 2118

WAR DIARY
or
INTELLIGENCE SUMMARY
(Erase heading not required.)

1/Queen's Regt.   May, 1916.

Place	Date	Hour	Summary of Events and Information	Remarks and references to Appendices
	7.		Quieter day; very little shelling or T.M. fire, but bombing round QUEEN'S craters all night. 5 wounded; 1 wounded at duty yesterday admitted to hospital.	
	8.		Quiet day. An O.P. knocked out by direct hit in morning. 1 killed, 3 wounded. G.O.C. Division (General Hunton) complimented B Coy on their quick action in preventing occupation of QUEEN'S crater by the enemy. Relieved by 16th K.R.R., & returned to billets in BEUVRY.	
BEUVRY.			2/Lt. Brust joined battalion this evening.	
	9.		Batln all day. 180 men out on working parties.	
	10.		Ordinary routine. Working parties of 120 men again.	
	11.		Ordinary routine. Working parties of 150 men. Concert in evening in Cinema Hall.	
	12.		Ordinary routine. Working parties of 215 men.	
	13.		Ordinary routine. Working parties of 120 men. Detachment at 1st Army All Gas (Aisne) was changed today.	
AUCHY LEFT	14.		Church parade in morning. All officers attended new meeting. Working parties of 90 men. After duty relieved 16th K.R.R. in AUCHY LEFT. mine near Midnight crater put after our advanced party took over; eleven of the enemy [strikethrough] accounted for by rifle & M.G. fire	

Army Form C. 2118

WAR DIARY
or
INTELLIGENCE SUMMARY
(Erase heading not required.)

1/Queen's Regt.   May, 1916

Instructions regarding War Diaries and Intelligence Summaries are contained in F.S. Regs., Part II. and the Staff Manual respectively. Title Pages will be prepared in manuscript.

Place	Date	Hour	Summary of Events and Information	Remarks and references to Appendices
	15.		Very quiet day; 1 wounded. At 10.0 p.m. a Bless rum near "Midnight" crater, & party of 16th K.R.R. attempted raid, but lost their way, & got into our own trenches, coming out of our dug-outs, & wounding stretcher bearer (afterwards died of wounds). Heavy artillery & T.M. barrage from 10.0 to 10.30 p.m. on both sides.	
BETHUNE.	16.		Very quiet day; 1 wounded. Relieved by 20th R.F.'s after dark, & proceeded to billets at MONTMORENCY BARRACKS, BETHUNE.	
	17.		Cleaning up all day. Company commanders conference in evening	
	18.		Baths all day, & ordinary drills. Lt.-Col. Crofts granted 10 days leave to England. Major Parnell in command.	
	19.		Ordinary routine; companies went out to Oblinghem for parade. 2/Lt. Crichton granted Military Cross; no. 8667 Sgt. Elleston; no. 981 L.Cpl. Harding & no. 8814 L.Cpl. Nyther granted Military Medal for action on blowing of QUEEN'S crater on 6th May.	
	20.		Ordinary routine. Lecture to battalion signallers by divisional signals officer in morning, cautioning against German listening apparatus.	

Army Form C. 2118

WAR DIARY
or
INTELLIGENCE SUMMARY
(Erase heading not required.)

1/Queen's Regt. May 1916.

Place	Date	Hour	Summary of Events and Information	Remarks and references to Appendices
BETHUNE	21		Church parade in morning. C.O. & Company commanders carried out tactical scheme at Choques.	
	22.		Battalion parade at Choques in morning. Ordinary routine.	
	23.		Brigade route march via Oblinghem, Gonnehem, Choques & Vendin; started 6.15 a.m. back at 10.45 a.m. Lecture to all officers on "Discipline" by E.G.C.M.,i Battalion boxing contests at Annequin in evening. some very good fighting.	May 23 2/Lt. BOWER joined battalion
	24.		Ordinary routine. C.O. Capt. Godfrey & Adjutant on Brigade Staff Ride all morning.	
	25.		Ordinary routine, & Guard of Honour practised. Finals of Brigade Boxing tournament in Theatre.	May 25 2/Lt. ROBINSON joined battalion
	26.		Ordinary routine in morning. Regiment found Guard of Honour under Capt. Brockhurst Hill & General Monro for presentation of medals to French General in the Grand Place. A very smart turn-out, & very steady on parade.	
	27.		Working party of 3 officers & 100 men in morning, & similar party in afternoon. C.O. & Adjutant attended Bayonet fighting Demonstration in morning. In afternoon, C.O. & company commanders reconnoitred the line in Cuinchy Left.	Vide Appendice XXVIII

WAR DIARY
or
INTELLIGENCE SUMMARY

Army Form C. 2118

1/Queen's Regt. May, 1916.

(Erase heading not required.)

Place	Date	Hour	Summary of Events and Information	Remarks and references to Appendices
BETHUNE.	28.		In evening move for next day suddenly cancelled. Col. Croft returned from leave, & resumed command of battalion. Church Parade in morning; the C.O. & 2 coy. commanders inspected Village line behind 15th. Division in morning, owing to expected German attack on Loos Salient. At 4.30 p.m., received sudden orders to move, & proceeded to billets in FOUQUEREUIL. Col. Croft took over command of 100th Brigade owing to absence on leave of the Brigadier-General.	
FOUQUEREUIL	29.		Major Parnell & 2 coy. commanders reconnoitred Village line behind 15th. Division. Ordinary routine for the troops. The battalion was ready to move at short notice.	
	30.		Ordinary training all day. Major Parnell & 2 coy. commanders inspected Village line behind 16th. & 1st. Divisions. In evening, Col. Croft returned from the Brigade, & resumed command of the Battalion. Complimentary memo. received from Division regarding Guard of Honour on 26th inst.	Appendix XXVIII.
	31.		In morning, battalion practised artillery formation in the Bois des Dames. A draft of 15 other ranks joined battalion; first batch of Derby recruits were amongst them; rather a poor lot physically.	

Army Form C. 2118

WAR DIARY
or
INTELLIGENCE SUMMARY

1st Queen's Regt.   May 1916.

(Erase heading not required.)

Place	Date	Hour	Summary of Events and Information	Remarks and references to Appendices
FOUQUEREUIL	31 (cont.)		The battalion was mentioned in General Haig's dispatch for period Dec. 19th 1915 to May 19th 1916 as follows:— "While many other units have done excellent work during the period under review, the following have been specially brought to my notice for good work in carrying out or repelling local attacks or raids:— × × × × × 1st Battalion the Queen's Regiment. × × × × × " The following message was sent to H.M.S. Excellent for the Glorious First of June:— "All ranks 1st Queen's hope the luck of this day may soon be repeated." Whilst 33rd Division ~~took up the line~~ Battalion now at 2 hours notice, as German attack seems not so imminent — J. M. Crofts Lt.Colonel Cmdg. 1st Bn The Queen's	

Appendix XXVIII

AC.36/76.
33rd Divn.

BETHUNE, 27th May 1916.

General de WIGNACOURT,
    Commanding the Sub-Division of ARRAS)BETHUNE.

to General LANDON,
    Commanding 33rd Division.

I beg to thank you for the honour you have done to our gallant wounded and mutilated soldiers in sending a detachment of your troops to the ceremony of presentation of "Medailles Militaires" and "Croix de Guerre".

Seeing your brave soldiers marching past, looking so high-spirited and stalwart, your old English motto "Je Maintiendrai" was brought back to my memory, and I could not help saying to myself that in these days of heroic feats, there was not a man amongst them who was not ready to put this proud "devise" into practice to the very utmost of his power.

Will you please tell them that when one sees such soldiers, one has the impression that no adversary, however "Boche" he may be, can overome them.

(signed) WIGNACOURT.

To All Units, 33rd Division.

The above is a copy of a letter received by the G.O.C., in connection with Friday's (May 26th) presentation of French and British Decorations.

The G.O.C. has great pleasure in publishing the above letter to all ranks of the Division, and at the same time wishes to express to all ranks who took part in the ceremony, his approval of their turn-out, smart soldierly appearance, and the highly satisfactory manner in which they handled their arms.

Lieut. Colonel,
A.A. & Q.M.G.
33rd Division.

1 RW Survey 2/13

1st-Queen's Regt. June, 1916.

Vol 20

6 1/RWS

WAR DIARY
or
INTELLIGENCE SUMMARY
(Erase heading not required.)

Army Form C. 2118

Place	Date	Hour	Summary of Events and Information	Remarks and references to Appendices
FOUGEREUIL	1.		Ordinary routine. Training carried on by companies in Bois des Dames, where range was available.	
	2.		Ordinary routine. Training in Bois des Dames. Following message received from H.M.S. Excellent; "Captain and Officers and Ship's Company of H.M.S. Excellent send congratulations to the Queen's on Glorious First of June, & wish them best of luck in the present campaign."	
	3.		Ordinary routine. Cricket match, Officers v. Sergeants in afternoon. The Sergeants won.	
	4.		Church Parade in an orchard. Lt. Col. Crofts took over command of 1st-5th Bde. during absence on leave of Brig. Gen. Baird; Major Parnell assumed command of battalion. Draft of 72 other ranks of 1st. Royal Fusiliers arrived to-day, bringing battalion up to or under strength; the majority had been previously wounded, & average age was higher than usual; four of them afterwards rested P.B.	

Army Form C. 2118

WAR DIARY
or
INTELLIGENCE SUMMARY

(Erase heading not required.)

1st Queen's Regt.

June 1916

Instructions regarding War Diaries and Intelligence Summaries are contained in F. S. Regs., Part II. and the Staff Manual respectively. Title Pages will be prepared in manuscript.

Place	Date	Hour	Summary of Events and Information	Remarks and references to Appendices
FOUQUEREUIL	5.		Battalion route march about 9 miles, near Marles & Bruay in morning. In afternoon Officers played sergeants at cricket & beat them; both teams had tea on the field. 2/Lt. J.S. Milner joined today; posted to D Coy.	
	6.		Ordinary routine. 2/Lts. C.E.D. Shrubb & W.C. Butterworth joined today; posted to A and C Coys respectively.	
	7.		Ordinary routine. All officers visited model of German trenches opposite divisional front in Bethune.	
	8.		Training carried on as usual. Twenty six recommendations for the Military Medal submitted, taken from N.C.O.s & men who had been longest in the country.	
BEUVRY	9.		Had Baths all day at Ecole des Jeunes Filles. In evening marched to Tillett at BEUVRY, relieving 16th K.R.R. Lt. G.A. Pillow & 2/Lt. H.P. Foster joined the battalion today; bringing officers' strength up to 38, including M.O.	
	10.		Ordinary routine; 180 men on fatigue during the day.	

Army Form C. 2118

WAR DIARY
or
INTELLIGENCE SUMMARY
(Erase heading not required.)

1st Queen's Regt.   June 1916

Place	Date	Hour	Summary of Events and Information	Remarks and references to Appendices
BEUVRY	11.		Church parade in morning. 210 men on working parties. 2/Lt H.P. Foster took over command of A Coy. vice 2/Lt (Temp Capt) O.S. Flinn	
	12.		Ordinary routine. 300 men on fatigue during day. C.O. & Company Commanders reconnoitred trenches in "Auchy Left" subsection in morning	
AUCHY LEFT.	13.		Relieving for trenches. 180 men on fatigue. At 9.30 p.m. relieved 16th K.R.R. in AUCHY LEFT sector.	
	14.		Slight rifle grenade & T.M. activity all day. M.G's very active at night. 1 wounded (died of wounds.) At 1.30 a.m. we carried out brief bombardment with rifle grenades & T.M's.	
	15.		Quiet day; a few 5-9" shells. 1 killed. Capt. GODFREY proceed to Staples on 2 months course of training recruits; 2/Lt P. GURREY took over command of C Coy.	
	16.		Considerable T.M. activity all day; "minnie" active. One O.P. knocked out. Casualties 9 wounded (1 died of wounds.)	

Army Form C. 2118

WAR DIARY
or
INTELLIGENCE SUMMARY
(Erase heading not required.)

1st Grens. Regt.   June 1916

Place	Date	Hour	Summary of Events and Information	Remarks and references to Appendices
VILLAGE LINE	17.		At 2.0 a.m., enemy shelling heavily bombarded Brickstacks, enemy retaliated strongly, centre company coming in for part of it. Relieved by 16th K.R.R. in evening & went into reserve in VILLAGE LINE and Keeps. No casualties. The AUCHY & half CUINCHY sectors amalgamated Today & named CUINCHY sector. General work on communication trenches. 150 men on carrying parties.	
	18.			
	19.		Battn. at ANNEQUIN NORTH for half the battalion. 50 men on carrying parties.	
	20.		Battn. for remainder of battalion. 100 men on carrying parties.	
CUINCHY LEFT	21.		Usual work in trenches. 50 men on carrying parties. Relieved 16th K.R.R. in CUINCHY LEFT in evening.	
	22.		We exploded mine in R.W.F. crater at 9.30 p.m. Enemy exploded very large mine at DUCKS BILL (GIVENCHY) & shelled our reserve positions & canal bank with heavy shells. Some T.M. activity. Casualties 9 wounded. (1 died of wounds.) Lt. H.P. FOSTER promoted temporary Captain with effect from 11th inst.	

Army Form C. 2118

WAR DIARY
or
INTELLIGENCE SUMMARY
(Erase heading not required.)

1st Queen's Regt.
June, 1916.

Place	Date	Hour	Summary of Events and Information	Remarks and references to Appendices
CUINCHY LEFT	23.		Considerable T.M. & rifle grenade activity. We exploded mine at R.W.F. crater at midnight. Heavy rain flooded trenches in afternoon. British aeroplane brought down behind "the Dump" at 8.0 a.m. Casualties, 2 killed, 3 wounded. 2/Lt. J BURRELL rejoined battalion from 5th Bn. M.G. Corps.	
	24.		Our artillery cut enemy wire in afternoon, & our heavy T.M.'s did same thing in evening. Enemy retaliated strongly. Casualties, 2 wounded.	
VILLAGE LINE	25.		Considerable activity by our artillery all day; otherwise quiet. Were relieved in evening by 16th K.R.R., & went into VILLAGE LINE and the Keeps. Mine exploded near MIDNIGHT bombardment afterwards. 2/Lt. GURREY promoted Temporary Captain with effect from 15th inst.	
	26.		All quiet. 1 man accidentally wounded.	
	27.		Quiet day; no casualties. We exploded 2 mines between 11.0 p.m. & 12.0 midnight, & 9th H.L.I. carried out very successful raid in Cuinchy Right, bringing in about 16 prisoners & 2 machine guns.	

Army Form C. 2118

WAR DIARY
or
INTELLIGENCE SUMMARY
(Erase heading not required.)

1st. Queens Regt.   June 1916

Instructions regarding War Diaries and Intelligence Summaries are contained in F.S. Regs., Part II and the Staff Manual respectively. Title Pages will be prepared in manuscript.

Place	Date	Hour	Summary of Events and Information	Remarks and references to Appendices
VILLAGE LINE.	28.		General work on Trenches. Wet day. No casualties. between MIDNIGHT & IPSWICH craters by enemy	A mine exploded
	29.		Quiet day. Clearing up trenches after rain. In evening, relieved 16th K.R.R. in CUINCHY LEFT. New deep dug-outs occupied in Btn. Hd. Qs. in VILLAGE LINE. Some T.M. activity in evening.	1 wounded.
	30.		Fairly quiet day. We bombarded enemy front line successfully with 18 pounders in afternoon. Mine exploded just on our right in R.W.F. centre at 4.10 p.m. Enemy strafed heavily with L.H.V. shells, T.M.s & rifle grenades from 11.0 to 11.30 p.m. Draft of 13 other ranks arrived to-day. Casualties: 1 wounded.	

J.M. Cutbill
Capt. 1/Queens

1875. Wt. W593/826 1,000,000 4/15 J.B.C.&A. A.D.S.S./Forms/C. 2118.

100th Inf.Bde.
33rd Div.

WAR DIARY

1st BATTN. THE QUEEN'S (ROYAL WEST SURREY REGIMENT).

J U L Y

1 9 1 6

Attached:

Appendices XXIX,
XXIXa, XXX & XXXI.

WAR DIARY
or
INTELLIGENCE SUMMARY

Army Form C. 2118

1st Queen's Regt. July 1916.

Place	Date	Hour	Summary of Events and Information	Remarks and references to Appendices
CUINCHY LEFT.	1.		Some T.M. & rifle grenade activity, otherwise quiet. Aeroplane on both sides very active; one of ours brought down in flames. Casualties, 1 killed, 1 wounded. Our offensive started on the Somme today.	
	2.		Heavy rifle grenade, T.M. & artillery bombardment by us 12.15 a.m. – 1.15 a.m; 2nd Worcester and 16th K.R.R. carried out raid on CUINCHY front; Worcester very successful, killing many, & bringing in about a dozen prisoners. K.R.R. got enfiladed by M.G. fire & suffered heavily. Our trenches somewhat knocked about by enemy retaliation. Repair & damage all day; some T.M. activity. Casualties, 1 killed, 1 wounded.	
	3.		A quiet morning. "Minnie" very active in right & left company frontages in afternoon & evening. Casualties, 4 killed, 2 wounded. At 10.30 p.m. were relieved by 1st Middlesex, & proceeded to billets in LE QUESNOY.	
LE QUESNOY	4.		General cleaning up & rest, after 20 days continuous in trenches. In evening had company commanders conference. A wet day.	

Army Form C. 2118

WAR DIARY
or
INTELLIGENCE SUMMARY
(Erase heading not required.)

1st Queen's Regt.   July 1916

Instructions regarding War Diaries and Intelligence Summaries are contained in F.S. Regs., Part II. and the Staff Manual respectively. Title Pages will be prepared in manuscript.

Place	Date	Hour	Summary of Events and Information	Remarks and references to Appendices
LE QUESNOY.	5.		Working parties of 510 men during day & night. Very few parades in consequence.	
	6		Baths at BEUVRY all day; ordinary company parades. At 3.0 p.m. we received sudden orders to be ready to move tonight. Between 11.0 & 12.0 p.m. were relieved by a battalion of Hampshire Regt. (138th Brigade) & formed up outside billets. Draft of 6 other ranks arrived today.	
BUSNETTES.	7.		After some delay while waiting for transport, moved off at 1.0 a.m. & marched via BETHUNE & CHOQUES to BUSNETTES, arriving 4.40 a.m. Distance, 9 miles. Were billeted here in quite good billets; troops rested all day. In evening, got orders to be ready to move at 1 hours notice next morning.	
LILLERS	8.		Orders for move received in morning; troops rested. Transport moved off at 2.35 p.m.; rest of battalion at 5.50 p.m. Marched to LILLERS, and entrained there. The Drums accompanied & played for the troops. The transport was loaded in 45 minutes; trucks for the troops very dirty. Train started 7.50 p.m., destination SALEUX. The 33rd Division is being relieved from BETHUNE area, & is moving down by train & to the SOMME in support to our offensive there	

Army Form C. 2118

WAR DIARY
or
INTELLIGENCE SUMMARY
(Erase heading not required.)

1st Queen's Regt.

July 1916.

Place	Date	Hour	Summary of Events and Information	Remarks and references to Appendices
LILLERS.	8 (continued)		Later we learnt we were relieving 31st. Division, who had been cut up. There we left XI Corps, & joined III Corps in the IV Army. The Battalion having been in the Trenches since June 1915 but in the BETHUNE AREA since Xmas 1914 –	
SALEUX	9.		At 3.30 p.m. arrived at SALEUX. Transport unloaded by 4.40 p.m. (2 ramps in use; actual time of unloading 1 hour.) Moved off at 5.0 p.m.; marched for 1 hour; then stopped for 40 minutes for men's breakfasts; marched via DREUIL and ARGOEUVRES to SAINT SAVEUR, arriving & getting into billets at 8.50 a.m. Men rested till the division. At 2.0 p.m. got sudden orders to move at 2.30 h.	
SAINT SAVEUR			marched to via AMIENS to DAOURS. Men very tired, as none had started marching without having had dinners; quite a number fell out. Got in to billets at DAOURS at 7.50 p.m.; fairly good billets for the men; bad for officers. A very hot day; distance marched 8½ miles in morning; 12½ miles in afternoon. Heat helmets were worn; this may have been cause of some men falling out. Learnt	
DAOURS			later that the arrival of the Australian Corps was the reason of our having to move from SAINT SAVEUR. The Drums played excellently throughout both marches.	

WAR DIARY or INTELLIGENCE SUMMARY

Army Form C. 2118

July 1916

Place	Date	Hour	Summary of Events and Information	Remarks and references to Appendices
DAOURS	July 10th		Remained in billets resting. Excellent bathing facilities in streams and canal and all Battalion bathed. Drums played in the evening. Special orders received from Bde H.Q. re Corps in Division leaving this Corps.	Appendix XXIX
	11th		Marched at 7.30 am to MORLANCOURT 12 miles. Town very full and no billets for Officers who slept in a loft. During afternoon the 2 Coys under command of 2/Lt Langhorne marched through the town. This evening all the mens books were collected and sent —	
MORLANCOURT	12th		Remained in billets. Hand carts for Lewis guns were drawn from motor division and guns completed to eight. Marched at 10.0 pm to BICORDEL 4½ miles where Battalion bivouacked just N.E. of the village.	
BICORDEL	13th		In afternoon C.O. & Coy commanders visited 2nd Batt Bivouac near old British front line south of MAMETZ village and 2/Lt Langhorne accompanied them. Its left edge about the BIVOUAC and pointed out our visible features — a good view obtained of CONTALMAISON - MAMETZ wood and the two BAZENTINS. This is held by the Germans. Special orders from Gen Rawlinson Comdg 4th Army received	Appendix XXIX (Q)

Army Form C. 2118

July 1916

WAR DIARY
or
INTELLIGENCE SUMMARY
(Erase heading not required.)

Instructions regarding War Diaries and Intelligence Summaries are contained in F.S. Regs., Part II. and the Staff Manual respectively. Title Pages will be prepared in manuscript.

Place	Date	Hour	Summary of Events and Information	Remarks and references to Appendices

BÉCORDEL

July 14

Battalion under orders to form in readiness to move at 3.25 am, but did not move until 10.50 am when Battalion met with a portion of assembly South of MAMETZ main road, close to FRICOURT CEMETERY & Q.A. Transport was brigaded but parted behind British Bivouac later in the day. 16th K.R.R's were assembled South of the Road with the Queens - 2nd Batt. The Warwickshire Regt. and 9th H.L.I. on north side of its Road.

Hit in Coffs Nicholson, 9th Brigade was remanded with its Transport. The following Officers were also left:- 2nd Lieut. Flynn - Fallowes Roff & Montigo with Capt. Harrison transport officer and Lieut. Walls quartermaster - 5 Subalterns and an liason officer 1st Brigade Major G.P. Parnell attempt command of the Battalion and had with him 15 following officers -

A Cay T/Capt Fisher, 2nd Lieut Brocken, Drayforth, Burnet & Lieut Thorpe.

B. T/Capt Sheets, Richard, Harland, Bottomley, Robinson.

C. T/Capt Gerry, Bennett, Foulis, Bowes, Butterworth

D. Lieut Pelham, Wrabe, Farrant, Fry, Melvin.

H.Q. Major Parnell Capt & Adjt Coolidge, Lieut Brown (Signal), 2nd Lieut Cork (Bombs), 2nd Lieut Owlette (Louis guns)

The strength of the Battalion going into action was 25 Officers 699 other ranks. Coy Sgt Major, Coy Q Master Sgt, I drummer were left with 1st Transport and reserve men formed in Villiers jun & Stokes mortars.

FRICOURT

At 6.40 pm 1st Brigade moved along the FRICOURT-MAMETZ Road to a point of assembly near FLAT IRON COPSE -

WAR DIARY or INTELLIGENCE SUMMARY

Army Form C. 2118

July 1916

Place	Date	Hour	Summary of Events and Information	Remarks and references to Appendices
[Bazentin]	14th July	10.0 pm	On night of 14–15th the Battalion moved to a position near BAZENTIN LE PETIT. A, B Coys had orders to dig in a road from cross tracks near X to cross tracks Y in sketch – C, D Coys in reserve at Z near BAZENTIN LE GRAND WOOD – The 9th H.L.I. were to dig in on our right from Y to N.W. corner of HIGH WOOD – Coys were in position by midnight. A Coy sent out patrols to get in touch with the 9th H.L.I – they failed, but the N.W. corner of HIGH WOOD but failed to find H.L.I – 2nd Lieut Rouquette afterwards went out & found the H.L.I about half way along west edge of wood, having been unable to get any further in the enemy were in position at N. end of the wood –	Ref Appendix XV X
BAZENTIN	15 July		About 3.0 am 15th it was found necessary to withdraw battn & adjacent flank on the right of A Coy owing to untenable fire from the known in HIGHWOOD down & around from the Batt were holding – for the from a bank our troops into field before we got Peronne reported positn & to Batt – About 7.0 am orders were received that the Battn was to retake the ground running west from HIGH WOOD thru a M.G. gunner switch – The H.L.I were to come up on the right our 1st the Middlesex Regt of 98 Bde were to attack our left – No very definite orders were received so company commanders order would be given much information except that the left would be 200 yards East of the cross tracks at X & that the objective would be 500 yards the direction being practically N. Orders were given for A, B & C Coys to	

Army Form C. 2118

July 1916

WAR DIARY
or
INTELLIGENCE SUMMARY
(Erase heading not required.)

Instructions regarding War Diaries and Intelligence Summaries are contained in F.S. Regs., Part II. and the Staff Manual respectively. Title Pages will be prepared in manuscript.

Place	Date	Hour	Summary of Events and Information	Remarks and references to Appendices
BAZENTIN	July 15th		to form the firing line with D Coy in support — The front companies were to advance in two waves of 2 platoons each, with 2 waves at original distances Companies were in position by 8.0 a.m — Bombardment was to start at 8.30 a.m. and to last for half an hour. At 8.55 a.m. the front wave was to advance 15 distance. Two front lines about 400 yards. While companies were getting into position, the enemy opened heavy rifle fire with rifle M.G.'s & shrapnel causing several casualties. Capt Gunner being wounded — Right company commander asked for bombardment of NW corner of HIGH WOOD, but few shells were sent. Front wave started as ordered at new zero under heavy fire from both flanks and the front at 2nd Lieut Richard & many men were hit. Second wave came under similar conditions, but 2nd Lieut Richard & many men were hit. Fire position two within about 200 yards of the German trenches, men were being rather in the process gave and started to work back at this stage while the men were being rallied in this process to lead came up in the left with Capt & got forward on with and gallant man. its steady, but was almost immediately hit. He was killed & Cpl Gunliffe was afterwards known to have been killed — Cpl Gunliffe also —	
			The remaining line fell & broke up by the situation was so desperate & only from it up in the Wood. The busy of reinforcing company was sent forward to dig in & hasten forward the support company was sent forward to dig in. the push had the line left.	
WEST OF HIGH WOOD		9·25	At 9.25 a.m. the A Coy 2nd South Staffords arrived. Until his orders & front situation was from many point (this had worked out of H.L.I.) had not come up. Bombay didnot reach the support line.	

1875 Wt. W593/826 1,000,000 4/15 J.B.C. & A. A.D.S.S./Forms/C. 2118.

Army Form C. 2118
July 1916

WAR DIARY
or
INTELLIGENCE SUMMARY
(Erase heading not required.)

Instructions regarding War Diaries and Intelligence Summaries are contained in F.S. Regs., Part II. and the Staff Manual respectively. Title Pages will be prepared in manuscript.

Place	Date	Hour	Summary of Events and Information	Remarks and references to Appendices
[illegible]	July 15th	10.5am	Lieut Stump in C/O sent back list of [illegible] up by wire & ordered for bombardment to commence at five am. Owing to the O.C. & bombardier started after 12 noon but no shells were sent. Enemy getting behind our own line.	
		10.30am	No reinforcements coming up. Other than [illegible] have empties out & decided to withdraw. Orders was considered dangerous to withdraw being cut off from its rept. Retirement commenced in small parties to original position & [illegible]. The position was much shelled during the remainder of the afternoon & evening and during the night of 15th-16th — being the night floor's patch was sent out to get in wounded & bring in 15 wounded. The casualties this day were 5 officers killed, 11 officers wounded, 28 killed, 52 missing, 209 wounded. Other ranks Officers killed - Major Parnell, Capt Slater, 2nd Lt Buckle, Ronquette & Bower. Wounded: Capt Gurney, 2nd Lts Richards, Burrard, Harding, Bottomley, Robinson, Fancock, Faville, Foley, Capt & Adjt Custance. Missing Lieut Brown (reported killed).	
WEST 38 HIGH WOOD			The casualties amongst N.C.O's have been 20 Sergeants and 58 other N.C.O's having [illegible] the casualties.	

1875 Wt. W593/826 1,000,000 4/15 J.B.C. & A. A.D.S.S./Forms/C. 2118.

Army Form C. 2118

WAR DIARY
or
INTELLIGENCE SUMMARY
(Erase heading not required.)

July 1916

Place	Date	Hour	Summary of Events and Information	Remarks and references to Appendices
BAZENTIN	16th		At about 4.0 a.m. the Battalion was relieved by 1/5 6th SWB & Rifle 19th Brigade and went back to some pits in the open ground E of MAMETZ WOOD, when Battalion rested and made up ammunition &c — Enemy was quiet till about 11.0 p.m. when enemy started sending over gas shells & 2nd Lieut Burch who was asleep was gassed. Shelling went on till about 2.30 a.m. Casualties other ranks 1 killed 10 wounded.	
MAMETZ WOOD	17th		Battalion remained in Bivouac near MAMETZ WOOD — Quiet day and till 6.0 pm when orders were received to withdraw to bivouacs with 6/S.W.L. — At 10.0 p.m. orders received to prepare to move and relieve 13th North Fus. 13/Rifle in MAMETZ WOOD — Battalion moved about 11.0 p.m. and took up position with 3 coys inside N W edge of the wood and one company in West edge — Battn HQ in wood's ground near Track running N & S through it — Relief completed by 3.0 am 18th. Casualties 3 O.R. wounded.	

Army Form C. 2118

July 1916

WAR DIARY
or
INTELLIGENCE SUMMARY
(Erase heading not required.)

Instructions regarding War Diaries and Intelligence Summaries are contained in F.S. Regs., Part II. and the Staff Manual respectively. Title Pages will be prepared in manuscript.

Place	Date	Hour	Summary of Events and Information	Remarks and references to Appendices
MAMETZ WOOD	July 18th		At about 10.0 am enemy commenced shelling wood with gas shells for about an hour. No casualties. Afternoon held by Brigade in Bois de Fne in afternoon — Battalion relieved 16 men into NORD RESERVE TRENCH in West of MAMETZ WOOD — 9 officers & 6 [men] to man in defence of the Wood and Battalion left in reserve trench at Nord relief. The rest in support in reserve at Bivouac — Relief complete at 6.0 pm — on a mobile scheme to support in relieve of Brigade. Relief complete at 6.0 pm — moved up to North edge of wood with remainder. Carrying parties of B.M. & A.D. men.	
"	19th		Quiet mnt. No casualties. Quiet day — men resting, improving trenches — at 9.0 pm ordered to relieve 2 Warwicks in N edge of wood — Relief complete by 10.0 pm at 10.30 pm. Orders received that 15/14 Bde with 2 Warwicks were to attack HIGH WOOD and SWITCH TRENCH next morning & our 100th Bde were in reserve and the ready to move at short notice after 4.0 am.	
			Casualties other ranks wounded 5. Telegram received from G.H.Q. that Capt S. M. Reid has been awarded Military Cross.	
"	20th		Attack of HIGH WOOD by 15/14 Bde & 2 Warwicks commenced at 3.25 am — At 10.0 am attack reported to be progressing favourably.	

WAR DIARY
or
INTELLIGENCE SUMMARY
(Erase heading not required.)

Army Form C. 2118

July 1916

Place	Date	Hour	Summary of Events and Information	Remarks and references to Appendices
MAMETZ WOOD	20th	about 6.0 pm	orders were issued for the immediate move — in from of C.O. held by B.HQ. Guides 1/16th KRR's were sent up to HIGH WOOD later with the relief of 1st Brigade. Battalion moved off at 9.0 pm to N.E. East corner of MAMETZ WOOD, where Capt Foster met Battn & held a conference with Co. Commanders — Capt Foster and Lt Cope were [illegible] to HIGH WOOD led by guides of S/Staffs Rifles. [illegible] known, he left one about four officers & scouts who was wounded. Shortly before midnight 2 guides were out [illegible] report at 2.0 am RE [illegible] at dawn and in of BAZENTIN LEGRAND WOOD — in the army [illegible]	
HIGH WOOD	21st		a report was made by scouts that [illegible] troops had been registered by enemy — further reports [illegible] at 7.0 a.m. a large [illegible] to open [illegible]. At about 12 midnight [illegible] reserved this worn on & still in our hands and 1st Capt Foster was wounded. At 5.0 a.m. relief [illegible] came in & 17th [illegible] arriving about 8.0 a.m. — 5.0 a.m. I went in to look over [illegible] to Queens & 1/6/KN R.R's battn command by Capt. & Lt Wenham 16th KRR's [illegible] KRR's held East edge of wood & HFB — A.& C. held tr. West Keel & St Serpentine. A & D [illegible] held by Dt of Queens. FkE. by C Coy. F tr G. A tr. by 5th K.R.B. — at E ten a strong point [illegible] [illegible] constructed by R.E. — Trenches are [illegible] not been plotted there was some detailed body scratches of these the [illegible] being [illegible] withdrew. It was considered that if Bosche should break through [much [illegible]] one section was no [illegible] counter batteries & in the [illegible] and however about [illegible] the firm an appearance that holding the trenches & N.E. corner & did not appear to be holding the Wood West terms in any strength.	appendix XXXI

1875   Wt. W593/826   1,000,000   4/15   J.B.C. & A.   A.D.S.S./Forms/C. 2118.

WAR DIARY
INTELLIGENCE SUMMARY

July 1916

Place	Date	Hour	Summary of Events and Information	Remarks and references to Appendices
HIGH WOOD	21st	11.0 p.m	Soon after dawn the Germans were heard shouting and a few were seen moving about. Snipers(?) active. Rapid fire was opened and enemy retired but was frequently seen afterwards in front enemy. This appeared to be Battn. works & 2/Lieut Butterworth was killed and 2/Lieut Crosse & Faulkner wounded. Flies in 2nd Midn[?] battle & patrol of 20 men and manning the wood.	
		3.0 p.m	About 3.0 p.m. the same Officer took out a patrol of 5 men in rear of our trenches. to join hands with AUSTRIANS in the right. Several of them were wounded. 2/Lt. Midner went out again to find them & was not seen again — a search party tried to discover him.	
		5.0 p	About 5.0 p.m. 2 patrols of enemy were seen to come out & machine gun in a position on the left flank about 600 yds away - Lewis gun & rifle fire dispersed them. After dark endeavour was made to connect the trenches in the front line but the strong points on right & left.	
		11.30 p	Battalion was relieved by the 1/1st London — previous to this heavy rifle fire had broken out in DELVILLE WOOD and the Germans brought up heavy reinforcements of HIGHWOOD and Battn in relief had to go through the Barrage of hostile Curtailed drift to - Battalion marched back along valley west of MAMETZ WOOD where tea and	

Army Form C. 2118

July 1916

WAR DIARY or INTELLIGENCE SUMMARY

(Erase heading not required.)

Place	Date	Hour	Summary of Events and Information	Remarks and references to Appendices

BICORDEL	22nd	3.20am	Gas shells were encountered but not company marched 1.5 bivouac half mile East of BICORDEL at 3.20am. The bivouac Establishes A & B has moved to this bivouac. It's previous evening & has to be from ready for 1st Battalion. Casualties 20th–21st. 1 officer 2/Lt Bruckwelth killed & 1/6 2/Lt Richer missing. 3 officers Capt Foster, 2/Lt Faulkner & Crofts wounded. other ranks 6 killed 39 wounded 12 missing — Total casualties for period 15th to 21st July 1916
			
			          Officers O.R.
			 Killed 6 35
			 Wounded 15 262
			 Missing 1 65
			          22 362	

BICORDEL			Remainder of day spent in resting & cleaning up. Capt Bruckwelth returned from Army School.	

Army Form C. 2118

July 1916.

WAR DIARY
or
INTELLIGENCE SUMMARY
(Erase heading not required.)

Instructions regarding War Diaries and Intelligence Summaries are contained in F.S. Regs., Part II. and the Staff Manual respectively. Title Pages will be prepared in manuscript.

Place	Date	Hour	Summary of Events and Information	Remarks and references to Appendices
BILLON DEL	July 23	9am	Battalion struck bivouac and marched X via MEAULTE and VIVIER MILL to fresh bivouac just west of DERNACOURT – ALBERT Railway and 1 mile from ALBERT. Bivouac pitched behind a 2' wall in a grass field – surrounded by cornfields – Afternoon no company worked in rain ½ mile off – Draft of 108 other ranks East Surrey, Buffs & Queens arrived – This was without warning & camp put up.	
New ALBERT	24th		The Battalion carried on inspection parades and Bayonet-fighting classes in the morning. A draft of 36 other ranks arrived about midday – Royal Sussex and Royal West Kents composed the draft. The afternoon the men rested and in the evening 40 newly promoted NCO's were instructed under Company arrangements. Two NCO's per Battalion commenced attending a B.E.F. Bayonet fighting course in the morning at 9 am course to last 4 days. 2 Lt E d'A Collings joined from the Base for duty	
New ALBERT				

Army Form C. 2118

July 1916

WAR DIARY
or
INTELLIGENCE SUMMARY

(Erase heading not required.)

Instructions regarding War Diaries and Intelligence Summaries are contained in F.S. Regs., Part II and the Staff Manual respectively. Title Pages will be prepared in manuscript.

Place	Date	Hour	Summary of Events and Information	Remarks and references to Appendices
near ALBERT	25th		Train under Company arrangements. Bayonet fighting and take on Army Gymnastic Instructs in attendance. Troops rested during the afternoon and NCO's classes were carried on took under Company arrangements after tea.	
"	26th		Bayonet fighting between 9 am and 11 am aut devoted to Company training. Afternoon aut Commander of Horse Training of foot NCOs.	

1875 Wt. W593/826 1,000,000 4/15 J.B.C. & A. A.D.S.S./Forms/C. 2118.

Army Form C. 2118

July 1916

WAR DIARY
or
INTELLIGENCE SUMMARY
(Erase heading not required.)

Place	Date	Hour	Summary of Events and Information	Remarks and references to Appendices
near ALBERT	27th		Ordinary Routine - Bayonet fighting included - Draft to other ranks arrived Mid day 1st Bn & 2nd Bn Queens - & 7th Bn Queens. 5 O.R. found Medically unfit and sent to Divisional Coy - at BUIRE-SUR-ANCRE. NCO's Bn Bayonet fighting course ends -	
"	28th		Battalion Route March starting 8.45 am, took towards ALBERT and back towards BUIRE SUR ANCRE. Back in Camp by 11.15 am. C.O lectured all Officers & effective NCO's in afternoon on points to be observed in Open warfare. Company having of the tea Draft 23 O/R (nco) Ranks - 6th, 7th & 10th Batt Queens. Fresh NCOS & Bayonet fighting Class commenced	

Army Form C. 2118

July 1916

WAR DIARY
or
INTELLIGENCE SUMMARY
(Erase heading not required.)

Place	Date	Hour	Summary of Events and Information	Remarks and references to Appendices
Near ALBERT	29th		Training under Company arrangements. Two men Sent on a day's course on Pigeons at Trevor. At about 11.30 a.m. a fatal Bomb-up accident occurred while 2/Lt A Mundy was training a Class of Bombers. They were throwing live Mills Bombs when one sent off prematurely after immediately after leaving Pte Chatfield's hand, who was being instructed. The bursting bomb mortally wounded 2/Lt A Mundy & 929 Sgt West & and 7220 Pte Chatfield 65. These three died from their wounds within half an hour of the accident. 8719 Sgt Erler who was also in the Bombing Sap was wounded in the left forearm, he was taken to the Field Ambulance. The Bodies of the three who were killed were carried to the Mortuary Tent at the 13th Field Ambulance preparatory to being buried the following day. At about 5 pm 8585 Sgt Tupper T and 9298 Sgt Hood S. were practising Bayonet fighting when an accident occurred and hit Sgt Tupper has wounded in the Right thigh in several nicks. Sgt Tupper sent to hospital. The Bayonet gone	Casualties ——— 3 killed 2 wounded

Army Form C. 2118

July 1916

WAR DIARY
or
INTELLIGENCE SUMMARY
(Erase heading not required.)

Place	Date	Hour	Summary of Events and Information	Remarks and references to Appendices
Near ALBERT	29th		Under authority granted by His Majesty the King the Corps Commander granted Military Medals to the undermentioned NCO's and men, for gallantry and devotion to duty during the operations of the 1st - 15th July 21st — 10143 Sgt. Hammond J. (O. Room Clerk) 4073 Pte. Pelham A 1011 L/Cpl. Hope T. Soanes P. 9813 Sgt. Bater P. 6811 Pte. Kinegar C. 8758 L/Cpl. Jones B. 2505 Pte. Daniels W. 9211 Pte. Cook T. (4th R. Fusiliers att'd)	

Army Form C. 2118

July 17/16

WAR DIARY
or
INTELLIGENCE SUMMARY
(Erase heading not required.)

Instructions regarding War Diaries and Intelligence Summaries are contained in F.S. Regs., Part II. and the Staff Manual respectively. Title Pages will be prepared in manuscript.

Place	Date	Hour	Summary of Events and Information	Remarks and references to Appendices
Near ALBERT.	30=		Coys carried out attractive attack from 8.30 A.M. till 10 a.m. The Battalion paraded for Church Service which was held in Camp at 11:30 am. At 2.30 pm the Divisional Commander, Major General Landon, presented Medal Ribbons to those who had been granted the Military Medal in the 100= Bat. The Whole Brigade was present at the function. At 3.pm the Remains of 2/Lt. Mundy E, Sgt. Went & Pte Chatfield were buried at the Cemetery on the Main road between DERNANCOURT and BUIRE Sur ANCRE. 1 Platoon of C. Coy (2nd Mundy's Coy) and 1 Section respectively from B & D Coys attended the funeral. The party marched direct the remains from the Stationary Tent at 135 FA ambulance to the Cemetery accompanied by the Drums. The Rev. Captain EWBANK took the Burial Service. A Draft consisting of 40 other Ranks arrived consisting of Royal Fusiliers men.	

Army Form C. 2118

July 1916

WAR DIARY
or
INTELLIGENCE SUMMARY

Place	Date	Hour	Summary of Events and Information	Remarks and references to Appendices
Near Pibret	31st		The Battalion practised The Attack on some ground near to Camp, which was admirably suited for this operation. The attack took place in the Morning, and many useful points were learnt from it. A draft of 30 other Ranks consisting of various Battns of the Queen's arrived — (1st Battn, 2nd, 6th, 7th, 8th & 11th Battns of the Queen's) In the evening a Concert was given to the Brigade in Camp by the Divisional Troupe (The Shrapnels)	

J M Cull Ill[?]
Cmdg 1/RWK Th Queens

A P P E N D I C E S

XXIX
XXIXa
XXX
XXXI

CONFIDENTIAL.

A.11.
33rd Div.

G.O.C.,
  33rd Division.

XI Corps.R.H.S.1137.

    I wish you to convey to all ranks in your Division my great appreciation of the successful operations they have carried out during the time they have been in the Corps, operations which have received frequently the approbation of the General Officer Commanding the First Army, and of the Commander-in-Chief.

    The many raids that have been undertaken by the 33rd Division have furnished models for other Divisions, newly arrived from England to join the Corps, and the two recently carried out by the GLASGOW HIGHLANDERS and the ROYAL WELSH FUSILIERS, respectively, have shown a brilliance in design and gallantry in execution which could not be surpassed.

    I have to thank all ranks for the ready response that they have made whenever I have called upon them to undertake any offensive operations. I have found a fine fighting spirit throughout the Division at all times, and it is with the greatest regret that I have to say "Good-bye".

    I have seen and spoken to nearly all the officers, and to many of the N.C.Os. and men of the Division, and I shall regret your departure more than that of any of the sixteen Divisions that have been in my Corps since it was formed, because you are all such fine fighting soldiers.

    I wish you 'God speed and victory', and I hope before the end of the war that I may again have the high honour of including the 33rd Division in the XIth Corps under my Command.

                            (Sd) R. HAKING, Lieut.General.
8th July 1916.   Commanding XIth Corps.

- 2 -

ALL UNITS, 33rd Division.

    It gives the G.O.C. great pleasure to forward to you, for communication to all ranks, the above copy of a letter received from Lieut.General Sir H.HAKING, Commanding XIth Corps.

Hemmings

10th July 1916.

Lieut.Colonel,
A.A. & Q.M.G.
33rd Division.

Appendix XXIA (a)

FOURTH ARMY.

SPECIAL ORDER OF THE DAY.

The Commander-in-Chief desires that the following may be made known at once to all the troops:—

"The Russians are attacking in great force and with success on many parts of their front and have captured many thousands of prisoners and much war material in the last few days.

The Italians have pressed the Austrians back a considerable distance and are following up their advantage vigorously.

The French troops on our right have already gained brilliant successes and captured a large number of prisoners, guns, etc. They are pressing on steadily; their left flank co-operating closely with our right.

On the main front of attack our troops have broken, on a front of 12,000 yards, right through systems of defence which the enemy has done his utmost for nearly two years to render impregnable. We have inflicted heavy loss on him, capturing 8,000 prisoners and many guns, mortars, machine guns and other war material.

The enemy has already used up most of his reserves and has very few now available.

The defences which remain to be broken through are not nearly so deep, so strong, or so well prepared as those already captured, and the enemy's troops, exhausted and demoralized, are far less capable of defending them than they were ten days ago.

The battle is, in fact, already more than half won. What remains to be done is easier than what has been done already and is well within our power.

Let every attack be pushed home to its allotted objective with the same bravery and resolution as on the 1st July.

Let all objectives gained be held against all comers as British soldiers have alway known how to hold them.

There is no room for doubt that steady, determined, united, and unrelenting effort for a few days more will definitely turn the scale in our favour and open up the road to further successes which will bring final and complete victory within sight."

Headquarters, Fourth Army.   **H. Rawlinson,** General,
12th July, 1916.   Commanding Fourth Army.

1st Printing Co., R.E. 4th Army Section. 458

Army Form C. 2118

July 1916

Appendix XXX

WAR DIARY
or
INTELLIGENCE SUMMARY
(Erase heading not required.)

Summary of Events and Information

Instructions regarding War Diaries and Intelligence Summaries are contained in F. S. Regs., Part II. and the Staff Manual respectively. Title Pages will be prepared in manuscript.

Place	Date	Hour		Remarks and references to Appendices

Map showing High Wood, Martinpuich, Bazentin le Petit Wood, Bazentin le Grand Wood, Mametz Wood, German Switch, Cemetery, 2nd Line

Wt. W593/826 1,000,000 4/15 J.B.C. & A. A.D.S.S./Forms/C. 2118.

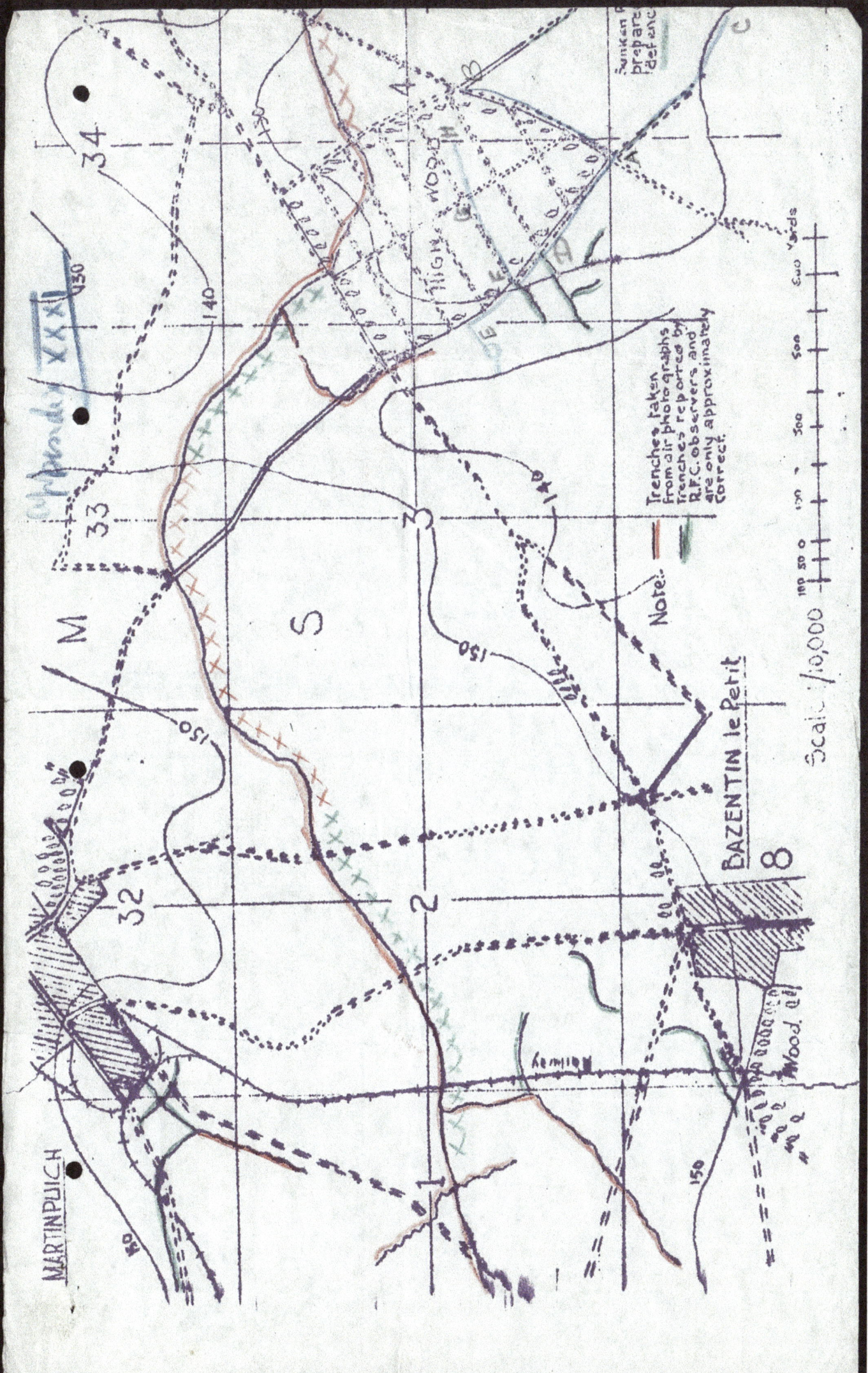

100th Brigade.
33rd Division

1st BATTALION

THE QUEEN'S ROYAL WEST SURREY REGIMENT

AUGUST 1916

1/13th The Queen's

Army Form C. 2118

August 1916

100/33

VOR 22

8 1/RWS

WAR DIARY
or
INTELLIGENCE SUMMARY
(Erase heading not required.)

Place	Date	Hour	Summary of Events and Information	Remarks and references to Appendices
Near ALBERT	1st Aug.		Training to be carried out under Company arrangements.	
Near ALBERT	2nd Aug.		Owing to heat of the day - work started earlier - Reveille 6 am + first Parade 6.45 am - till 7.45 am - work ceased at 11.30 am in the morning, and resumed after teas at 5 pm. Fresh class of Bayonet fighting for NCO's commenced -	Summer Hours -

Army Form C. 2118

August 15th

WAR DIARY
or
INTELLIGENCE SUMMARY

(Erase heading not required.)

Place	Date	Hour	Summary of Events and Information	Remarks and references to Appendices
Near ALBERT	3rd Aug		All officers attended a lecture on Communications between Infantry and Aeroplanes during attack – at H.Q. 2/10th Bn. – Training was carried out as usual – 2 Companies (C & B Coys) did night-operations from 9 P.M. till about 10.30 P.M.	
Near ALBERT	4th Aug		Reveille 5.45 am Breakfast at 6.30 am Battalion marched off on Route March 7.30 am getting back to camp about 10.15 A.M. Commanding officer & OC B & C Coys went up to reconnoitre the line held by the Forward Brigade of the 51st Divs at 3 PM. returning at 8 PM. A & D Coys did night operations – at about 9.45 P.M. orders were received that the Bn would relieve a Bn of the 51st Divs in the line on the night of 6th/7th. Capt Gatsford rejoined from training centre ETAPLES and took over 2nd in Command –	

Army Form C. 2118

WAR DIARY
or
INTELLIGENCE SUMMARY
(Erase heading not required.)

August 1916

Place	Date	Hour	Summary of Events and Information	Remarks and references to Appendices
Near ALBERT	5th Aug.		Capt Godfrey & O.C. A & D Coys went up to BAZENTIN LE GRAND to reconnoitre the line — Weapon work and training — On completion of this, gave over roll of officers who have served in 1st Bn The Queen's in France attached	Appendix XXXII
"	6th		Sunday — Troops rested & got ready to move up the line —	
"	7th		Rouse 2.0 am — Battalion marched off at 2.10 am with advanced billets companies. Thence passed through into act. From FRICOURT moved in single file to support trenches in rear of HIGH WOOD — no casualties going up the Valley — Battalion relieved 5th Seaforths 51st Division — Relief completed by 7.30 am — Batt HQ in pit East of Bazentin Le Grand village — Transport moved in Brigade at 5.0 am and bivouaced at F.20.0.2 half mile West of FRICOURT. Lieut Wilson & Sinnix field Coys remained with its transport	

Army Form C. 2118

August 1916

WAR DIARY
or
INTELLIGENCE SUMMARY
(Erase heading not required.)

Instructions regarding War Diaries and Intelligence Summaries are contained in F.S. Regs., Part II. and the Staff Manual respectively. Title Pages will be prepared in manuscript.

Place	Date	Hour	Summary of Events and Information	Remarks and references to Appendices
BAZENTIN LE GRAND	August 7th		Capt Golffin took over command of the Battalion in the lines – Day passed quietly – at 5.30 pm our artillery bombarded enemy position between HIGH WOOD & DELVILLE WOOD for ½ hour – slight enemy retaliation – night very quiet – on visit been shelling on both sides chiefly round HIGH WOOD – Casualties 1 O.R. wounded –	
do	8th 11 am		Our artillery guns bombarded enemy lines till 6.0 am – 2 Officers visited R.E. camp & Galifira to HIGH WOOD at 7.0 am and again at 9.0 pm enemy shelled enemy line West of HIGH WOOD during afternoon – enemy fair chiefly directed on Valley in rear of HIGH WOOD – night fairly quiet – enemy parties provided for R.E.	
do HIGH WOOD	9th		Capt Golffin to ey commanders conference was held by 4th M.E.I. in HIGH WOOD – Reliefs started by platoons at 8.30 pm and completed at 8.10 pm as follows: C Cy R.W.F. front – D Cy centre & sups. B Cy left front & sups with A Cy in support along S. edge of wood. Battn H.Q at junction of HIGH ALLEY and T3 LACKWATER TRENCH. Nothing happened	

Army Form C. 2118

WAR DIARY
or
INTELLIGENCE SUMMARY
(Erase heading not required.)

August 1916

Instructions regarding War Diaries and Intelligence Summaries are contained in F. S. Regs., Part II. and the Staff Manual respectively. Title Pages will be prepared in manuscript.

Place	Date	Hour	Summary of Events and Information	Remarks and references to Appendices
	August		Except continuous shelling chiefly around Batt HQrs —	
HIGH WOOD	10th		Intermittent shelling of TRAMWAY TRENCH and guns in rear of wood — Enemy's continual improvement of trenches was stopped — Stand patrols sent out after dusk to engage any enemy patrols — Sharp fight between enemy patrols and our own; a heavy Barrage of Artillery fire was placed on the man edge of HIGH WOOD and the enemy also opened rapid rifle & machine gun fire. The situation however quietened down by 1.35 am & everything became normal again — The remainder of the night passed more peacefully, there was however intermittent rifle Machine gun and artillery fire —	

Army Form C. 2118

August 1916

WAR DIARY
or
INTELLIGENCE SUMMARY
(Erase heading not required.)

Place	Date	Hour	Summary of Events and Information	Remarks and references to Appendices
HIGH WOOD	11th		The day passed more quietly. Work on Saps and Spare RE Construction were carried on with. At about 8.40 PM the enemy suddenly opened a terrific Artillery Barrage on the Rear edge of the Wood and also in the Valley beyond it. This went on for about one hour, when the Situation became more or less normal again. At about 1 am the enemy sent out a bombing party and bombed our front line and Saps heavily. Little damage however resulted to his own trenches again, our artillery was called up and asked for Support. They opened fire with very little delay and continued to do so for about 15 minutes. When the Situation had again quietened down. At about 3.30 am the enemy again shelled the rear edge of Wood heavily. This continued for just about one hour, after which the Situation became normal again.	
	Night of 11th/12th			

Army Form C. 2118

August 1916

WAR DIARY
or
INTELLIGENCE SUMMARY

Place	Date	Hour	Summary of Events and Information	Remarks and references to Appendices
HIGH WOOD	12th		The day passed normally with the exception of intermittent shelling of the valley behind the wood & of the communication trenches leading from the wood to BAZENTIN le GRAND position. Work was in progress all day in the shape of deepening & improving the existing trenches and Saps. Orders for our relief by the 98th Inf Bde were received. The night passed more peacefully than might have been expected. We were warned to expect an attack so dispositions for the defence of the front line were strengthened and a party of Bombers in readiness for counter attack were also placed in a covered position. Strong fighting patrols went out to cover our front and stayed out most of the night.	

Army Form C. 2118

August 1916

WAR DIARY
or
INTELLIGENCE SUMMARY
(Erase heading not required.)

Instructions regarding War Diaries and Intelligence Summaries are contained in F. S. Regs., Part II. and the Staff Manual respectively. Title Pages will be prepared in manuscript.

Place	Date	Hour	Summary of Events and Information	Remarks and references to Appendices
HIGH WOOD-	13.		The relieving regiment began to arrive by 5. AM and by 7. am the Battalion was completely relieved and had got clear of BAZENTIN LEGRAND Wood without mishap or casualties -	
Bivouacs between			The Battalion has now went into Divisional Reserve + is in Bivouacs between BECORDEL + MEAULTE Villages and as some grass had to be west of the road going from the two places - the Companies arrived in independently and were all in by 9.30 am -	
BECORDEL + MEAULTE			The rest of the day was spent in cleaning up and the afternoon is rest - Constructing their Bivouacs from the 6th inst- till 9.30 am Bn lost were as follows -	
			Our Total Casualties from the 6th inst- till 9.30 am Bn lost were as follows :-	
			Killed - 7 officers 38 " Total . 96 Wounded - 38 " Missing - 1 "	

Army Form C. 2118

August 1916

WAR DIARY
or
INTELLIGENCE SUMMARY
(Erase heading not required.)

Place	Date	Hour	Summary of Events and Information	Remarks and references to Appendices
BIVOUACS BÉCORDEL	14th		Companies carried out inspection of Rifles and Gas and Gas on left training under their own arrangements. The detachment from 1st Army H.Q. AIRE rejoined us — 1 Officer and 43 O—Ranks — Also 2 Lt Elkam joined the Battalion for duty from the Base.	
"	15th		The Battalion supplied a working party for 222nd Field Coy R.E. of 300 O.Ranks and 6 officers — to work on communication trenches up near BAZENTIN LE GRAND — There were no casualties —	

Army Form C. 2118

August 1916

WAR DIARY
or
INTELLIGENCE SUMMARY
(Erase heading not required.)

Place	Date	Hour	Summary of Events and Information	Remarks and references to Appendices
Bivouacs. BECORDEL	16th		Another working party consisting of 50 O.Ranks and 1 Officer went up to the Somme area as yesterday and did work under the supervision of 222nd Field Coy R.E. There was 1 O.Rank wounded. The remainder of Battalion carried on Training under Company arrangements. The 2nd Batt.s were found the quite close to us in fact in the old the camp we had at ALBERT,	
	17.		The Battalion found a working party of 7 Officers and 350 other ranks to go up to 222nd Field Coy R.E. for work on trenches — there were no casualties. Brigade sports were	

Army Form C. 2118

WAR DIARY
or
INTELLIGENCE SUMMARY

(Erase heading not required.)

August 1916

Place	Date	Hour	Summary of Events and Information	Remarks and references to Appendices
Bivouacs M¹⁵			held. The Battalion were successful in bus 2ⁿᵈ in the Tug of war, both for officers and O Ranks. The 9ᵗʰ H.L.I. were 1ˢᵗ in the Boot throwing competition with the best throw by C.S.M. Elderkin of 64 yards. Our teams the Battalion gained 2ⁿᵈ Place for all events. The 9ᵗʰ H.L.I. gave first and the 2ⁿᵈ Worcestr's 3ʳᵈ place. 2/Lt W.J. Howell joined the Batt⁰.	
BECORDEL	18ᵗʰ		Corps carried out training under their own arrangements.	

WAR DIARY or INTELLIGENCE SUMMARY

Army Form C. 2118

August 1916

Place	Date	Hour	Summary of Events and Information	Remarks and references to Appendices
BIVOUACS BÉCORDEL	19th		The Battalion received orders to move into reserve trenches near MAMETZ WOOD at about 10 a.m. The line was reconnoitred by an officer in the morning. Lt. Col. L. M. Crofts went up with the Battalion Staff and were at about 4.30 p.m. and were in position in the reserve trenches by 7 p.m. Carrying parties were found by the Battalion for the 9/H.L.I. and 2nd Worcesters who went to line, the Brigade retained 41st Bde in the line between DELVILLE WOOD and HIGH WOOD.	
POMIER Trucks nr MAMETZ VILLAGE	20th		The Battalion still in the same place. Carrying up and fatigue parties furnished for front line regiments.	

Army Form C. 2118

August 1916

WAR DIARY
or
INTELLIGENCE SUMMARY
(Erase heading not required.)

Place	Date	Hour	Summary of Events and Information	Remarks and references to Appendices
POTTIER Trenches	21		The Battalion still remained in the Same Reserve trenches until moved up into Support to an attack by the 9/H.L.I and 2nd WORCESTERS on the new German position on the West of DELVILLE WOOD, at about 10.45 p.m. The Battalion were not required and moved back again to POTTIERS Trenches at about 1 a.m. 22nd inst.	
"	22"		The Battalion received orders to move up to relieve the 9/H.L.I now in the front line trenches the West of DELVILLE WOOD in the evening. The Battalion moved by Companies at about 5 p.m. the relief being completed by about 11 p.m. No casualties were incurred.	

Army Form C. 2118

August 1916

WAR DIARY or INTELLIGENCE SUMMARY

(Erase heading not required.)

Place	Date	Hour	Summary of Events and Information	Remarks and references to Appendices
TRENCHES west of DEVILLE WOOD	23		The Battalion had one Company in the front line & 2 in Support and one in reserve. The enemy shelled our front and support line continuously throughout the day and night. Operation orders were issued by the 100th Inf Bde for an assault on the Hun German position to be made by the 2/KRRs, 2nd Worcesters & 1st Queens Regt in the afternoon of the 24th inst. Killed – 2 Lt Colling – E d'A —— 5 O.Ranks. Wounded —— 11 O.Ranks ——	
"	24.		The morning passed more quietly than before. Operation orders were issued to Companies and everything explained to all Company by Lt Col L.M. Smith – D & C Coys were the two assaulting Companies, B were to be in immediate support and A in reserve. Companies were all allotted to their assembly places and were to be in position by 3. p.m.	

Army Form C. 2118

August 1916

WAR DIARY
or
INTELLIGENCE SUMMARY
(Erase heading not required.)

Place	Date	Hour	Summary of Events and Information	Remarks and references to Appendices
TRENCHES near A DEVILLE Wood.	24		Objective. The two assaulting companies were to capture and hold the two German positions. Their two points were the two German and that WOOD LANE on a front going East of 300X. A Bombing post was to be established as far up WOOD LANE in a Northerly direction as possible, this task was allotted to 2/Lt Carpenter. 16 Regimental Bombers under 2/Lt Carpenter. Zero hour was at 5.45 pm. at 65 minutes after that hour our assaulting Coys. launched their attack, with the 1st 19/KRRC and the 2/Gordons cooperant on our right. There was a preliminary Artillery Bombardment of 2 hours and a final barrage of intensive 30 minutes before the assault was launched, the Barrage lifting as the front troops drew up to it. The objective was reported as taken and the work of consolidation in progress at 8.30 pm — and reinforcements were asked for —	

Army Form C. 2118

August 1916

WAR DIARY
or
INTELLIGENCE SUMMARY
(Erase heading not required.)

Place	Date	Hour	Summary of Events and Information	Remarks and references to Appendices
TRENCHES near DELVILLE WOOD	24.		2 Companies of the 9/H.L.I. were sent up in Support — Messages were received from the front line to say that the Battalion had suffered very heavy Officer Casualties, both due to Shell fire prior to the assault. At about 12 midnight It. Col Croft's Orderlies and It. Col Darling of the 9/H.L.I. were sent up to ascertain the Situation. It. was agreed to let the relief of the Battalion by the 9/H.L.I. It. Col Croft was wounded before reaching the front line, leaving Capt. Broadhurst H.L.I. in command of the Battalion. Col Darling continued on his way and arranged for the relief of the Battalion by the 9/H.L.I. It. Capt. Broadhurst H.L.I.	
	25.		The Battalion was relieved by the 9/H.L.I. and came back to the Support Reserve line at about 5 am on the 25th inst. The Battalion were successful in taking their objective and the Bombers advanced about 100 yards up WOOD LANE Trench and captured a German Block, established their own about 10 yards in advance of it, the Signal for Their	

Army Form C. 2118.

August 1916

WAR DIARY
INTELLIGENCE SUMMARY.
(Erase heading not required.)

Hour, Date, Place	Summary of Events and Information	Remarks and References to Appendices
TRENCHES near DELVILLE WOOD. 25th	but the position was to Very lights first seen upon a platoon of the 2nd Royal Fusiliers came up and took over the post. Captured by the Battalion and proceeded to Corbiedalk Jt. Casualties were as follows for the action 1st to 24th inst. O'Ranks Killed 19 – wounded 76. Officers Killed 4 wounded 6. Total 95. OFFICERS KILLED (names) OFFICERS (wounded) (names) 2/Lt Pope. J.A. Lt Col L.H. Crofts 2/Lt Bennett. L.E. Capn. O.S. Flenico 2/Lt Long. A.W.E. Capn. Martyn. S.E. (sickshock returned duty 26th inst.) 2/Lt Campbell. A.M. 2/Lt Bennett. L.A. (relieved duty 26th inst) 2/Lt Howell. W.T. 2/Lt Carpenter. T.W.	

Army Form C. 2118.

August 1916

WAR DIARY
or
INTELLIGENCE SUMMARY.
(Erase heading not required.)

Instructions regarding War Diaries and Intelligence Summaries are contained in F. S. Regs., Part II. and the Staff Manual respectively. Title pages will be prepared in manuscript.

Hour, Date, Place	Summary of Events and Information	Remarks and References to Appendices
TRENCHES near DELVILLE WOOD 25th	The Battalion remained in the Reserve trenches until orders were received for the relief at about 2.pm. by the 98th Inf Bde. The relieving Regt arrived but the relief was completed without mishap. the Battalion moved into Trenches in FRICOURT WOOD and were settled in by 8 pm. The Battalion were relieved in the DELVILLE WOOD trenches by the 2nd Argylls & S. Hrs. There were no casualties.	
FRICOURT WOOD 26th	The Battalion remained in Brigade reserve and spent the day which was a very wet one in resting.	

Army Form C. 2118.

August 1916

WAR DIARY
or
INTELLIGENCE SUMMARY
(Erase heading not required.)

Place	Date	Hour	Summary of Events and Information	Remarks and references to Appendices
FRICOURT WOOD	27		The Battalion still in Brigade reserve in the wood. The weather was very inclement. Orders were received for the relief of the Battalion by the 2nd R.W.Fus 19th Bde. and the relay was completed by 10 pM the Battalion marching into Bivouacs with the rest of the 100th Inf. Bde. at BECORDEL in the same place as on the 13th not arriving in Bivouacs at about 11 pM. The following Officers were reinforcements joined the Batt. viz. Lieut. A.C. Allen – 2Lt. H.D. Taylor. 2Lt. N.B. Avery – 2Lt. D.G.H. Millard	
BIVOUACS. BECORDEL	28.		The Battalion rested and cleaned up. Companies were worked at the discretion of their Commanders and men were allowed to wash their clothes etc.	

Army Form C. 2118.

AUGUST 1916

WAR DIARY
or
INTELLIGENCE SUMMARY

(Erase heading not required.)

Place	Date	Hour	Summary of Events and Information	Remarks and references to Appendices
BIVOUACS BECORDEL	29th		The Battalion still in same place in Divisional reserve – Companies carried on their own programmes of Training – Bayonet fighting etc. Draft of 38 other Ranks joined the Battalion.	
Becordel Mon b RIBEMONT.	30.		The Battalion moved by Brigade route march to RIBEMONT being BECORDEL at 7.30 am – Route via MEAULTE – DERNANCOURT – BUIRE – Billets in RIBEMONT. Passed the 8th Battalion en route for Trench MEAULTE, they were going up into the line. The Battalion reached RIBEMONT at about 10.30 am and were billeted. Trained all day from early morning to late evening. etc. N.T. Coy fired ¼ Battn and 2 other ranks	

Army Form C. 2118.

WAR DIARY
or
INTELLIGENCE SUMMARY
(Erase heading not required.)

AUGUST 1916

Place	Date	Hour	Summary of Events and Information	Remarks and references to Appendices
Billets RIBEMONT. Move to MIRVAUX.	31.		The Battalion moved into Billets in MIRVAUX via Main ALBERT – AMIENS road – LA HOUSSOYE – QUERRIEU – S¹ GRATIEN – MOLLIENS to Billets by Bde Route march passed Started point at 8AM. It was a lovely day and the march was the hottest of thirteen miles passing through Fourth Army Head Quarters which were at QUERRIEU where we turned off the Main ALBERT- AMIENS road in a Northern direction to S¹ GRATIEN. The Battalion completed the march in good order and arrived in very good Billets at MIRVAUX at about 2 PM. The Major General LANDON visited the Battalion at about 6 PM and addressed the men praising them in warm tones on their conduct throughout their operations in the parts from which he had just come and	

Army Form C. 2118.

WAR DIARY
or
INTELLIGENCE SUMMARY
(Erase heading not required.)

AUGUST 1916

Place	Date	Hour	Summary of Events and Information	Remarks and references to Appendices
BERTE- MIRVAUX	31		Their conduct under the most trying circumstances during what must be part of the great offensive on the SOMME. He wished them all the best of luck and expressed his confidence in them to carry on in the future as they had done in the past — upholding their fame as examples of Englands best troops — The Battalion received orders for a move by Route March to BRUCK in TALMAS about 5½ miles distant on the 1st September to moving off at 8 a.m.	

9. 1/R.W.S. AUGUST 1916 Appendix XXXII

List of Officers in 1st Battalion The Queen's Regt
from commencement of hostilities 1914 up to 11th August 1916

Lt. Col. D. Warren — K	Lieut. R.H. Schunck K	Lieut. J.B. Close W	2/Lieut R.E.L. Harland W
Lt. Col. H.B. Pillean K	Capt. E.L. Barton P	B.W. Johnson K	to Strangers
Capt. C.E. Wilson K	J.P.M. Thorneycroft M	F.S. Ball S	J.G.S. Morrison W
B. Major E.B. Matthew Lannowe W	C.B.M. Hodgson S	Capt. L. Harrison	C.W. Farwell W
Major M.G. Heath K	Lieut. T. Tanqueray W	T. Breeding W	C.W. Roff
B. Major C.F. Watson D.S.O. Tr	L.H.C. Knatt S	Lieut. H.P. Foster W	A. Mundaye K
Capt. A.E. Macnamara W	W.F.C. Green P	to F. Clenshaw S	R.C. Slatter K
R.F. Creek M	J.M. Peat-Irons P	F.G. Plant K	Capt. J. Clausen R.A.M.C.
R.A. Hunter W	P.R.O. Trench Tr	C.D.M. Fowler K	2/Lieut A. Fairlie W
Lt. B.M. Kenny W	Capt. Loames P	R.C. Joyson-Hicks W	R. Foley W
F.W.H. Benton W	Capt. Wood W	A.M. Allen S	D.A. Brown W
R.B. Pringle K	Lt. W.B. Williams M	Major J.H.L. Bunbury W	J.C. Rouquette K
J.D. Boyd Tr	Capt. R.B.M. Kirkham Tr	Lieut. R. Stutfield Tr	P. Gurney W
C.E. Ironmonger W	G.B. Parnell K	J.R. Drew W	A.D.G. Bottomley W
B. Hayes W	Lt. Col. H.S.C. Wilkins Tr	A.C. Armitage K	Capt. R. Brockhurst-Bell
R.F.D. Henriques K	Lieut. H.E. Chandler W	H.S. Goldberg R	2/Lieut G.R. Bower R
E.B. Drew W	Capt. H.W.H. Pain W	H.C. Williams K	W.C. Butterworth K
L. Bustell W	H.W. Stenhouse Tr	B.McGrey Tr	W.A.J. Robinson W
R.N. Buchan W	Lieut. C.B. Brook W	Lt. Col. L.M. Croft	C.D.G. Thrupp
M. Eastwood K	N.J.B. Howell K	Capt. F.B. Storey S	J.A. Cook W
H.B. Strong K	A.W.A. Bradshaw K	J. Walpole Tr	H.J. Buist W
Capt. M.V. Soy K	Capt. R.F.B. Heath K	F. Godfrey	C. de A. Collinge
Lt. W.E. Phillips S	Lieut. B.H. Pickering S	Lieut. A.B. Abercrombie Tr	J.S. Milnes W
P. Thompson W	W.J.K. Nichols W	W.B. Carslake W	Lieut. G.B. Pillean
Capt. F.C. Longbourne W	H.E.A. Hodgson Tr	R. Faulkner W	
G.H. Payer S	G.P. Thomson S	W.E. Symons S	
R.G. Clarke S	S. Walsh Tr	S.S. Skeate Tr	
F/Lt A.G.H. Wallis	F.J. Vison Tr	J. Buchner Tr	
Capt. A.H. Rose P	Capt. P.C. Esdaile Tr	G.E. Wheeler	
Lt. Col. B.T. Pell K	Lieut. J. Burrell W	A.J. Crichton K	
Lt. A. Burton W K	A. Tweedie-Smith M	O.S. Flynn	
J.B. Hayes S	B. Eltham W	J.S. Bennett	
M. Pound K	L. Hayes S	H.K. Richards W	
		M. Luskin	

1/R.W.Surrey

"A" Form. Army Form C. 2121.
MESSAGES AND SIGNALS.

Prefix....Code....m.	Words	Charge	This message is on a/c of:	Recd. at....m.
Office of Origin and Service Instructions.				Date
CONFIDENTIAL	Sent At....m.		....Service.	From
	To			By
	By		(Signature of "Franking Officer.")	

TO 100th Inty Bde HQ

| Sender's Number. | Day of Month | In reply to Number | **A A A** |
| UA 230 | 1st | | |

Herewith War Diary for Month Ending 30th SEPTEMBER also attach append en XXX ii for the month of AUGUST omitted in error, which is much regretted.

From 1st Queens
Place
Time

The above may be forwarded as now corrected.

(Z) Gaitiean Lieut adjt

Censor. Signature of Addressor or person authorised to telegraph in his name.
* This line should be erased if not required.

for OC 1st Queens

Army Form C. 2118.

10/6

SEPTEMBER

WAR DIARY
or
INTELLIGENCE SUMMARY
(Erase heading not required.)

Date	Hour	Summary of Events and Information	Remarks and references to Appendices
1st		Battalion moved by Route March to TALMAS starting at 8 am and arrived at that Place in Buses at about 11. am.	
2nd HEUZECOURT		The Battalion moved by Route March from TALMAS to HEUZECOURT about 24 kilometres - Busses were parked on the line of march just near BERNAVILLE. The Battalion arrived in billets about 5. PM.	

Army Form C. 2118.

September 1916

WAR DIARY
or
INTELLIGENCE SUMMARY

(Erase heading not required.)

Place	Date	Hour	Summary of Events and Information	Remarks and references to Appendices
HENZECOURT	3rd		The Battalion remained in Billets resting - 15 Officers Reinforcements joined from 60 Bde as follows - 2Lt. Cowan - T.R.G. 2Lt. Barnard J. " Perkins - L. " Langhorne E.H. " Walker R.S. " Norman K.Y. " Eade K.M. " Boxer F.J. " Lloyd R.C. " Stevenson G. " Self B.E. " Protis A. McN. " Hobbs P.R. " Holliday J. " Burghope.	

Army Form C. 2118.

WAR DIARY
or
INTELLIGENCE SUMMARY

(Erase heading not required.)

September 1916

Place	Date	Hour	Summary of Events and Information	Remarks and references to Appendices
BURBERS SUR CANCHE	4th		The Battalion moved by Route March from HEUZECOURT to BOUBERS-SUR-CANCHE at 8.15 am — to having arrived in this billet at about 2. pm	
SIRACOURT	5th		The Battalion moved by RouteMarch to SIRACOURT from BOUBERS-SUR-CANCHE arriving in their Billets at about 12 noon	

Army Form C. 2118.

September 1916

WAR DIARY
or
INTELLIGENCE SUMMARY
(Erase heading not required.)

Place	Date	Hour	Summary of Events and Information	Remarks and references to Appendices
AVERDOINGT	6.		The Battalion moved by Route March to AVERDOINGT from SIRACOURT. Arrived + went into Billets soon after noon.	
AVERDOINGT	7.		The Battalion rested. Companies spent the time in cleaning up and refitting. A Short Route March by Companies was carried out in the morning. The Drums played in the village square in the afternoon.	

Army Form C. 2118.

September 1916

WAR DIARY
or
INTELLIGENCE SUMMARY
(Erase heading not required.)

Instructions regarding War Diaries and Intelligence Summaries are contained in F.S. Regs., Part II. and the Staff Manual respectively. Title Pages will be prepared in manuscript.

Place	Date	Hour	Summary of Events and Information	Remarks and references to Appendices
HALLOY HALLOY.	8th		The Battalion moved by Route march to TERNAS where the whole Brigade got into Motor Busses and were transported via FREVANT and DOULENS to HALLOYS where the Battalion de-Bussed and were billeted, settled into Billets by 11.30 am. The Division is now transferred to the VII F Corps.	
HALLOY.	9th		The Battalion remained at Halloy in Billets rested. Companies carried out training under their own arrangement. The Drums played out in the evening in the Square. C.O. and Company Commanders went by Motor Bus to reconnoitre the line at GOMMECOURT where the 100th Bde is to go to relieve the 59th Bde in the line, probably on the 12th inst.	

Army Form C. 2118.

WAR DIARY
or
INTELLIGENCE SUMMARY
(Erase heading not required.)

September 1916

Place	Date	Hour	Summary of Events and Information	Remarks and references to Appendices
SOUASTRE	10th		The Battalion moved by Route March to SOUASTRE from HALLOY about 8 kilometres — arriving — Billets at about 11.30 am.	
SOUASTRE	11th		The Battalion remained at SOUASTRE and training of the men was carried out — under Company Commanders arrangements. Officers and N.C.O's Battalion went to Corps Rest Camp near BOLOGNE for one week.	

Army Form C. 2118.

WAR DIARY
or
INTELLIGENCE SUMMARY
(Erase heading not required.)

September 1916

Place	Date	Hour	Summary of Events and Information	Remarks and references to Appendices
SOUASTRE	12th		The Battalion spent the day cleaning up Billets and fitting up prior to moving into the trenches at FONQUEVILLERS to relieve the 52nd Bttn. The first Company left SOUASTRE at 8 pm and went into the FRONT LINE trenches in front of GOMMECOURT relieving the 10 Royal Lancashire Fus., the remaining Companies followed at intervals. the Battalion completed the relief by about 11. pm into wood 9/12/N/3A. Without any incident. Distribution of Companies as follows. A + B FIRING LINE - C + D Coy Support.	

Army Form C. 2118.

September 1916

WAR DIARY
or
INTELLIGENCE SUMMARY
(Erase heading not required.)

Instructions regarding War Diaries and Intelligence Summaries are contained in F. S. Regs., Part II. and the Staff Manual respectively. Title Pages will be prepared in manuscript.

Place	Date	Hour	Summary of Events and Information	Remarks and references to Appendices
FRONT TRENCHES (LEFT BN$^\text{s}$) in front of GOMMECOURT.	13$^\text{th}$		The day passed quietly, the Companies employed the men in cleaning and improving the trenches. The enemy kept very quiet. Our T.M's and his artillery & T.M's were unusually inactive. Strong reconnoitering patrols went out during the night for instructional purposes	
"	14$^\text{th}$		The day passed quietly. — The same as the day before. — Two men were accidentally wounded by a rifle grenade. Two patrols went out by night for the purpose of instruction as all was reported quiet on the enemy's lines	
"	15$^\text{th}$		Enemy inactive, same as day before. Patrols the same.	

Army Form C. 2118.

WAR DIARY
or
INTELLIGENCE SUMMARY

(Erase heading not required.)

September 1916

Place	Date	Hour	Summary of Events and Information	Remarks and references to Appendices
FRONT TRENCHES BOMMECOURT?	16th		The day passed quietly as usual — with the exception of a few enemy Trench Mortars which bombed two huts obliterating same as the day before. By night there was an intercompany relief — C Coy relieving A Coy in the front line & D Coy relieving B. No relief was completed without incident. Patrols kept out all night as usual. Draft of 68 O'Ranks arrived from England.	
" "	17th		The day passed quietly — work carried on as usual. Patrols as usual. Draft of 43. O'Ranks arrived from England.	

Army Form C. 2118.

September 1916

WAR DIARY
or
INTELLIGENCE SUMMARY
(Erase heading not required.)

Place	Date	Hour	Summary of Events and Information	Remarks and references to Appendices
TRENCHES BOMMECOURT	18th		The day passed quietly, with the exception of slight shelling by the enemy's artillery of some gun positions immediately in rear of Batt. HQ dug out the Shrine in FONQUEVILLERS village. 11 o'clock Reinforcements arrived, both wounded men + men from Hospital. 35 Men + 1 Officer. 1 Lewis Gun instructor returned from 3rd Army Post Camp. 9. O Ranks rest.	
" "	19		The day passed quietly, as before, working in positions on the trenches. Major H.N.A. Steele joined the Battalion and assumed Command from that date. Patrols went out as usual by night for instruction	

2449 Wt. W14957/M90 750,000 1/16 J.B.C. & A. Forms/C.2118/12.

Army Form C. 2118.

WAR DIARY
or
INTELLIGENCE SUMMARY

(Erase heading not required.)

September 1916

Instructions regarding War Diaries and Intelligence Summaries are contained in F. S. Regs., Part II. and the Staff Manual respectively. Title Pages will be prepared in manuscript.

Place	Date	Hour	Summary of Events and Information	Remarks and references to Appendices
TRENCHES GOMMECOURT.	20		The day passed quietly, enemy his been quiet. The Battalion were relieved by the 2nd Worcesters on the night of the 20th/21st Bays & 4th Oxon & Bucks Coming back into the village defences of FONQUEVILLERS and D Coy going to CHATEAU de la HAIE. The relief was completed by 11. pm and no incident of importance occurred.	
FONQUEVILL-ERS.	21		Permanent Tunnelling fatigues of 100 men & 2 Officers were found. The first party of 1 Officer + 50 men worked in the morning and 1 Officer + 50 men in the afternoon. This fatigue is permanent with the Battalion in FONQUEVILLERS. The remainder of the men were employed cleaning up billets and enforcements.	

Army Form C. 2118.

September 1916

WAR DIARY
INTELLIGENCE SUMMARY
(Erase heading not required.)

Place	Date	Hour	Summary of Events and Information	Remarks and references to Appendices
PONCQUEVILLERS	22nd		Working parties & Fatigues the same as previous day. The CO. went through with the Conditions That Wire defences should be improved both to R.E. company put the hut into repair	
FONCQUEVILLER	23		Working Parties & Fatigues the same as Previous day. The men had hot baths.	
"	24		Working Parties & Fatigues the same as Previous day. Thereunder finished their hut baths	

WAR DIARY

Army Form C. 2118.

September 1916

Place	Date	Hour	Summary of Events and Information	Remarks and references to Appendices
PONQUEVILLERS	25th		The same as previous day. A few Trench Mortar shells fell in the vicinity of B Coy Billets in the village. No man slightly wounded. Divl R.O. Major Gen Landon handed over command of the 33rd Divn to Assume command of the 35th! Divn Major Gen. Pinney. assumed Command of 33rd Divn.	
	26th		The same as previous day. The t Divl General paid a visit to the C.O. in the afternoon. The Battalion relieved by the A & S.H., K.O.Y.L.I., 1/4 8th KOR and went to Billets at HUMBERCAMP	

Army Form C. 2118.

September 1916

WAR DIARY
or
INTELLIGENCE SUMMARY
(Erase heading not required.)

Place	Date	Hour	Summary of Events and Information	Remarks and references to Appendices
HUMBERCAMP	27th		Battalion in Billets. The day was devoted to cleaning up Billets and Company inspections. Training was carried out under Company arrangements. Draft of 28 O.Ranks joined the Battalion.	
WARLUZEL	28th		The Battalion moved by Route March to WARLUZEL arriving here by about 11.30 a.m.	

Army Form C. 2118.

WAR DIARY
or
INTELLIGENCE SUMMARY
(Erase heading not required.)

September 1916

Place	Date	Hour	Summary of Events and Information	Remarks and references to Appendices
SUS St LEGER	29th		The Battalion moved by Route March to SUS - St LEGER. About 4 ½ miles distant. In the afternoon a battalion Parade was held, but had to be dismissed early owing to inclement weather.	
BREUILLERS			The Battalion moved by Route march to BREUILLERS. arrived in Billets at about 10.30 am. The afternoon was spent in cleaning up billets and inspection by Companies. Draft- 9 12 O Ranks Joined the Battalion	

J.N.McInnes
Major. Comm'd'g Battalion

Army Form C. 2118.

WAR DIARY
or
INTELLIGENCE SUMMARY

(Erase heading not required.)

1st Bn. The QUEENS (ORIGINAL)

10 1/R.W.S.

Place	Date	Hour	Summary of Events and Information	Remarks and references to Appendices
	OCTOBER			
BRENNERS	1st		Training carried out under Company arrangements.	
"	2nd		Battalion in Rest Billets. Training carried out under Company arrangements.	
"	3rd		Training parade.	
"	4th		do.	
"	5th		do.	
"	6th		do.	
"	7th		do.	
"	8th		do.	
"	9th		do.	
"	10th		do.	

Army Form C. 2118.

WAR DIARY
or
INTELLIGENCE SUMMARY.
(Erase heading not required.)

Instructions regarding War Diaries and Intelligence Summaries are contained in F. S. Regs., Part II. and the Staff Manual respectively. Title Pages will be prepared in manuscript.

Place	Date	Hour	Summary of Events and Information	Remarks and references to Appendices
BREVILLERS	11th		Training Period. Training carried out under Coy. arrangements.	
	12th		do.	
	13th		do.	
	14th		do.	
	15th		do.	
	16th		do.	
	17th		Lieut. Col. S.T. Watson D.S.O. joined the Battalion and assumed command from that date. Major H.M.A. Hovels transferred to Appx. 4th Div. 4th Div. Concert Party arrived & performed to Battalion on parade.	

WAR DIARY or INTELLIGENCE SUMMARY

Army Form C. 2118.

(Erase heading not required.)

Place	Date	Hour	Summary of Events and Information	Remarks and references to Appendices
Bresillons	18th		Training carried out under Coy. Arrangements.	
Bresillons	19th		Training carried out under Coy. arrangements. Battalion Transport moved by Road to Talmas. The Battalion moved by Route March to Boves & thence entraining for Corbie, detraining at Corbie & marching to Billets at Merricourt arriving in Billets about 8 p.m. Battalion Transport left Talmas at 3.30 p.m. for Merricourt arriving about 12.00 midnight.	
Merricourt	20th		Battalion in Billets at Merricourt. Training carried out under Coy. Arrangements.	
Meaulte	21st		The Battalion moved by Route March to Meaulte arriving in Billets at about 12 o. midday. The afternoon was spent in cleaning up billets & inspections by companies.	

WAR DIARY
or
INTELLIGENCE SUMMARY

Army Form C. 2118.

Place	Date	Hour	Summary of Events and Information	Remarks and references to Appendices
Mansel Camp	22nd		The Battalion moved by Route March to Mansel Camp arriving in Camp about 1 p.m.	
"	23rd		The Battalion under cover in Mansel Camp - The CO and Company Commanders went forward to reconnoitre the line near LES BOEUFS	
"	24th		Still at MANSEL Camp. Parades under Company arrangements, the Battalion was under orders to move but they were cancelled -	

Army Form C. 2118.

WAR DIARY
or
INTELLIGENCE SUMMARY
(Erase heading not required.)

Place	Date	Hour	Summary of Events and Information	Remarks and references to Appendices
BERNAFAY WOOD	25th		The Battalion moved into Bivouacs between BERNAFAY Wood and TRONES Wood leaving MANSEL Camp at 11am and marched across country with 200+ internal between companies. The Battalion here settled into their Bivouacs by 2.0 pM	
	26		In the same place as before in Bivouacs. The weather has been most inclement, rain all day but a strong S.W. wind. The men worked on improving their shelters. The 19th & 99th I. Bdes are in the line	

2449 Wt. W14957/M90 750,000 1/16 J.B.C. & A. Forms/C.2118/12.

Place	Date	Hour	Summary of Events and Information	Remarks and references to Appendices
BERNAFAY WOOD	26		and the 100th J. Bde. are in reserve.	
"	27th		Still in Bivouacs, the CO and all officers went forward to reconnoitre the routes to the FLERS LINE, which would be the position to be taken up by the Battalion in case of hostile attack. The weather continues bad.	
"	28		Large working Parties were provided for the R.E. for the purpose of laying a path of Trench boards from	

WAR DIARY or INTELLIGENCE SUMMARY

Army Form C. 2118.

Place	Date	Hour	Summary of Events and Information	Remarks and references to Appendices
BERNAFAY WOOD	28th		GINCHY to LES BOEUFS owing to the state of the Country due to the bad weather. C.S.M. Butler and 10 O.R. rejoined the Battalion from the Base as reinforcements.	
	29th		Working Parties provided for R.E. and men worked on improvements to the Bivouacs.	

Army Form C. 2118.

WAR DIARY
or
INTELLIGENCE SUMMARY
(Erase heading not required.)

Place	Date	Hour	Summary of Events and Information	Remarks and references to Appendices
BERNAFAY WOOD	30th		Orders were received that the Bde would go into the Front line — 2nd Border in & 9th H.L.I. to go into the Front line — 1st Queen's to Guillemont and 16th K.R.R. to the Hog's Back — but the former in Reserve and the latter in Support. The Battalion moved into its new position in GUILLEMONT by Companies at 20 minutes interval Starting at 2. p.m.	
GUILLEMONT	31st		Remained in bivouac. Captain F. GODFREY joined the Divisional School as assistant commandant. Lieut. G.A. PILLEAU ordered to report to Divisional Head Quarters for duty.	Scrdon, Lt.Col. Comg. 1/Queen's

Army Form C. 2118.

160/33.

1st Bn. THE QUEENS

WAR DIARY for NOV. 1916.
or
INTELLIGENCE SUMMARY
(Erase heading not required.)

Place	Date	Hour	Summary of Events and Information	Remarks and references to Appendices
GUILLEMONT	Nov 1st		Remained in Bivouacs. Two Companies (A & B) were moved forward to OX TRENCH to be in close support during an attack on BARITSKA TRENCH by the 9th H.L.I. These Companies were lost wet during the operations. The weather continued bad. The bivouacs chiefly consisted of shell holes the greater part of which were half full of water. Material for building shelters was not to be had. A & B Coys had 7 casualties amongst other ranks.	
	2nd		Orders were received that the Bⁿ would relieve the 9th H.L.I. on the right front then becoming the right battalion of the British line and joining with the 66th (French) Infantry Regt. During the morning verbal instructions were received to the effect that the Battalion would attack BARITSKA TRENCH at a time to be fixed by the CO on 3rd. The Bⁿ left GUILLEMONT at 4.15 p.m. and met guides at GUINCHY CORNER and arrived at Bⁿ H.Q. of the 9th H.L.I. at about 8 p.m. The Brigade had been asked to provide a working party to continue the trench partly dug parallel to BORITSKA and about half way between that trench and ANTELOPE TRENCH. This was done owing to the digging party missing the guides. That portion of the trench already dug was known locally as NEW TRENCH. Companies were ordered to occupy the following positions. "B" Coy NEW TRENCH. A Coy ANTELOPE TRENCH, D Coy GERMAN TRENCH & C Coy MUGGY TRENCH. Bⁿ H.Q. was in the Sunken road S.W. of LESBOEUFS. vide attached sketch marked A. B Coy was no less than nine hours getting into position from the time they left Bⁿ H.Q. The trenches were in a dreadful state and were were standing to in mud and water up to well above the knee. Some found it impossible to move and had to be dug out after remaining in the mud for some hours.	

WAR DIARY / INTELLIGENCE SUMMARY

Army Form C. 2118.

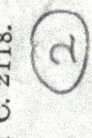

Place	Date	Hour	Summary of Events and Information	Remarks and references to Appendices
LESBOEUFS	3rd		The orders for the attack on BARITSKA and MIRAGE are attached and marked B.1, B.2, B.3. The field artillery barrage was carried out by the French. From information obtained by means of observation it was seen that the barrage was not effective. The N.W. end of the trenches was not touched and the shooting on the remainder of the trench was mostly short. The barrage lifted at 3.50 instead of 4 p.m. At 4 p.m. the Battalion left the trenches and head-forward in splendid style in spite of the adverse condition of the trenches and weather. Artillery observing officers spoke very highly of the manner in which they have advanced. After getting about half way to the first objective the advance was held up by heavy rifle and machine gun fire from the left front. Most of the officers became casualties and the casualties in other ranks was heavy. When it was found that no further headway could be made the three companies withdrew and occupied their original positions. The following are the casualties amongst officers — Killed, 2nd Lts L. PERKINS, W.H.B. GROSS, R.C. LLOYD. Wounded and missing Lt C.W. ELTHAM. Wounded 2nd Lts R.V. NORMAN, W. STRANGER, A. McN. AUSTIN, E.H. LANGHORN. The casualties amongst other ranks is difficult to fix the exact numbers as the Bn remained in action until 6th. The total casualties between 3rd and 6th were — killed 41. Wounded 131. missing 54. Of these latter 18 have been traced. It is not believed that any were taken prisoner. During the night orders were received for the three front companies to be withdrawn to the high level head of BARITSKA TRENCH. C. Coy. was also ordered to withdraw to the Sunken road at Bn. HQ in order to be left as fresh as possible for further operations on 5th.	B.1, B.2, B.3

Army Form C. 2118.

(3)

WAR DIARY
or
INTELLIGENCE SUMMARY
(Erase heading not required.)

Instructions regarding War Diaries and Intelligence Summaries are contained in F.S. Regs., Part II. and the Staff Manual respectively. Title Pages will be prepared in manuscript.

Place	Date	Hour	Summary of Events and Information	Remarks and references to Appendices
LESBOEUFS	4th		All reports received from Company spoke of the exhausted condition of the men owing to the state of the weather and the ground. Companies remained in the positions as for the night of 3rd–4th. The hostile fire was heavy during the day. BARITSKA TRENCH was bombarded by our artillery. Orders were received for the attack on that trench to take place at 11.10 a.m. on 5th. This time the whole Brigade was to take part in the attack instead of only one Battalion as on 3rd. The attack was to take place on the front by the 1st QUEENS on the right and 16th KRRC on the left while the 2nd WORCESTERS and 9th H.L.I. were to attack the right flank through the French lines. This was subsequently altered and the 9th H.L.I. were told in Brigade Reserve. Two Coys 9th H.L.I. were attached to 1st B" THE QUEENS. Only one Company (C) 1st QUEENS was to take part in the attack. The Brigade operation order for the attack are attached and marked "D". The B" operation order for the attack are attached and marked "C CI-CII. NEW TRENCH. C Coy was ordered to occupy the front line trench known as NEW TRENCH. Before leaving Bn HQ. OC "C" Coy had the scheme explained to him. Unfortunately conditional verbal instructions were given to him not to advance until and unless he saw the attack of the WORCESTER Regt developing on his right and unless he had sufficient men to attack with. It was considered that the main attack was to be made by the WORCESTERS seeing that a whole battalion was being employed and that the artillery barrage was lifting yards to their immediate front. "C" Coy arrived in position in ANTELOPE TRENCH about 5 a.m. only about 70 strong the remainder having lost the bayoneting to the darkness and bad state of the ground. They failed to find NEW TRENCH before daylight.	

Army Form C. 2118.

WAR DIARY
or
INTELLIGENCE SUMMARY
(Erase heading not required.)

Instructions regarding War Diaries and Intelligence Summaries are contained in F.S. Regs., Part II. and the Staff Manual respectively. Title Pages will be prepared in manuscript.

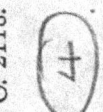

Place	Date Nov.	Hour	Summary of Events and Information	Remarks and references to Appendices
LESBOEUFS.	5th.		Two companies 9th H.L.I. having reported B Coy was ordered to occupy ANTELOPE TRENCH in close support of C Coy QUEENS and "C" Coy was held at Bn HQ for the purpose of finding carrying parties. At 11.10 am the attack started. Infantry were seen to be advancing in good formation. Acting on the verbal order C. Coy QUEENS did not advance. This was not known until 3pm. The WORCESTERS and 16 KRRC gained their objective and pushed on to the line T.5.b.0.8. — T.5.b.8.5. without much opposition and without many casualties. At 1.10pm. B Coy 9th H.L.I. was ordered to move two platoons to consolidate the line paying special attention to our junction with the French at T.5.b.8.6. At this time a report was received from the French that they had captured a part of MOON TRENCH some distance on our right. At 3.15pm an order was sent to C Coy QUEENS to advance at once and assist in the consolidation of the line gained. This was done and they turned to the left of the 16th KRRC to prolong the line to the left and join with the West Brigade. At 4.10pm it was however that the whole Brigade would be relieved. A B & D Coys were relieved about 10pm by 5th SCOTTISH RIFLES and occupied OX TRENCH about 800ft in rear of LESBOEUFS. The guide for C Coy lost their way and this company was not relieved until the following night. During the whole time the Battalion was in the front line trenches the question of getting rations and water to them was most difficult. Fortunately each man went into the line with two days rations. Ration and water parties frequently lost their way. On the first night in the trenches hot soup was sent up & carried in hot food containers. This party left Bn H.Q. about 8pm and returned at	

Forms/C.2118/12.

Army Form C. 2118.

WAR DIARY
or
INTELLIGENCE SUMMARY

(Erase heading not required.)

Instructions regarding War Diaries and Intelligence Summaries are contained in F. S. Regs., Part II. and the Staff Manual respectively. Title Pages will be prepared in manuscript.

Place	Date	Hour	Summary of Events and Information	Remarks and references to Appendices
OX TRENCH	6th		About 5 a.m. the following morning enemy having found our movement Bn H.Q. moved back to Ox TRENCH at about 7am. The neighbourhood of this trench was fairly heavily shelled during the morning but the Bn suffered no casualties. At 3 p.m. the Battalion was relieved by the 2nd NOTTS & DERBY'S and marched to huts at CARNOY. Hot soup of most excellent quality was provided at Brigade H.Q. as the Bn marched through GUILLEMONT at about 6 p.m. All companies and H.Q. arrived except C Coy arrived at the huts CARNOY about 9 p.m. The Bn was very exhausted owing to the very bad weather conditions and the bad state of the road. C Company was relieved in the front line trenches and arrived at CARNOY at 8 am on 7th. A point well worth noting was the fact that only 37 men of the battalion had been evacuated sick by the Medical Officers since the Bn had arrived in the SOMME area on 21st October. The following telegraph message was received from Major Gen. PINNEY on 4th:— The Corps Commander wishes me to convey to you and your troops his high appreciation of your splendid effort yesterday which though not successful was none the less glorious. These efforts which have it not always successful have the desired effect of keeping Germans on this front instead of allowing them to reinforce ROUMANIA. We must also support by their attack. (Signed) R. J. PINNEY M.G. (Lt. French to their attack) (Signed) R. J. PINNEY M.G.	

Army Form C. 2118.

WAR DIARY
or
INTELLIGENCE SUMMARY
(Erase heading not required.)

Place	Date	Hour	Summary of Events and Information	Remarks and references to Appendices
CARNOY	7th		The Bn moved at 2.30 pm to the CITADEL and occupied tents.	
CITADEL	8th		Remained in Camp.	
"	9th		Orders received to move near ABBEVILLE. The transport left by road the remainder of the Bn ordered to move by train the following day. A draft of 155 other ranks arrived nearly all these were from the 4th & 5th (Territorial) Bns.	
"	10th		Marched at 7.30 am to entrain at BUIRE a distance of about 7 miles. Entrained at noon. Detrained at AIRAINES at 4 pm and marched to LIERCOURT - DONCQ a distance of about 6 miles. Occupied billets.	
LIERCOURT	11th		Remained in billets and started cleaning up. It had been impossible to touch in this line before owing to the state of the country. The transport arrived about 6 pm. Only two horses had been evacuated sick during the time the Bn was in the SOMME area.	
"	12th		Church parade at 7.30 am.	
"	13th		Draft of 26 other ranks arrived. No 11247 Sergt A. McCABE granted a regular commission. Training was started; this included musketry drill open warfare.	
"	14th		Remained in billets. Company training continued.	
"	15th		" " " " "	
"	16th		" " " " " Draft of 18 other ranks received	

Army Form C. 2118.

WAR DIARY
or
INTELLIGENCE SUMMARY
(Erase heading not required.)

Place	Date	Hour	Summary of Events and Information	Remarks and references to Appendices
LIERCOURT	17th		Remained in billets. Company training continued.	
"	18th		" " " " "	
"	19th		" " Church Parade.	
"	20th		" " Company training continued. Draft of 100 other ranks received.	
"	21		" " " " "	
"	22		" " " " Draft of 8 other ranks received.	
"	23rd		" " " " No 4537 Regt. Sergt/Major NEVINS granted a regular commission.	
"	24th		Remained in billets. Company training continued. Tempy. Lt. H. BATTISCOMBE returned to duty from 33rd Division H.Q.	
"	25		Remained in billets. Company training continued.	
"	26		" " " Church Parade.	
"	27		" " " Company training continued. Warning orders received that the Brigade would probably move forward to the front area on 5th Dec. and transport moves forward by road on 5th Dec.	
"	28th		Remained in billets. Company training continued.	
"	29th		" " " notification received that the following had been awarded the MILITARY MEDAL - No 10053 Pte H.J. SPIERS, No 1999 Pte H. MEARS + No 2057 Pte(L/C) J. HACKETT R.A.M.C. attached to the Bn.	

Sgd Salmons Lt-Col.
Comdg. 1st Bn. The Queens

S E C R E T.   Copy 1.

                                        Headquarters,
                                            100th Infantry Brigade.

                                        3rd November 1916.
            100th INFANTRY BRIGADE ORDER No:154.

1. The French have reached the line N.36.8.0- T.6.b.8.4.; it is
   essential that they should not be left unsupported by the 33rd
   Division.

2. The 100th Infantry Brigade will therefore attack BORITSKA Trench
   from T.5.d.3.8. to D.5.b.0.3. this evening and push forward
   promptly to the line T.5.b.9.4.mT.5.a.9.3.

3. There will be no preliminary bombardment by heavy artillery
   of HAZY and BORITSKA Trenches, but only of objectives further
   in rear.

4. FROSTY Trench and T.head of SNOW, within 100 yards of HAZY
   must be cleared by the 16th K.R.R.C. by Zero minus 1 hour
   at the latest.

5. The attack will be carried out by the 1st Queen's.
   2nd Worcesters will hold one Company in readiness to provide
   carrying parties for the 1st Queen's and will move on receipt
   of orders from O.C. 1st Queen's.
   16th K.R.R.C. will open an intense fire at zero with rifles
   and Lewis Guns upon HAZY Trench to their immediate front.

6. The attack will be carried out as follows :-
   (a) At zero minus one hour, there will be a field artillery
       barrage on BORITSKA, MIRAGE and HAZY Trenches.
   (b) At zero the infantry will their trenches and advance to
       the assault.
   (c) The barrage will lift from BORITSKA Trench at zero plus
       5 minutes, and from MIRAGE at zero plus 10 minutes.
   (d) A barrage will be formed at zero on the line N.35.d.9.0.
       - T.5.b.0.5. and will remain on it to cover consolidation.

7. (1) Once BORITSKA Trench is captured the attacking troops will
       conform to our barrage and gain touch with the French at T.5.
       b.9.4.; the right of the attack will therefore have to swing
       round through MIRAGE Trench, the final line to be taken up
       being as shewn on the attached map.
   (11) O.C., 11th Field Coy, R.E. will arrange to establish and
        garrison strong points as follows :-
         (a) T.5.b.9.4. at junction with French.
         (b) T.5.b.6.3.
         (c) T.5.b.0.3. at junction of BORITSKA and HAZT Trenches.
        1st Queen's will attach 1 Lewis Gun team to each R.E. section
        in these posts
   (111) O.C. 100th Machine Gun Coy will be prepared to send
         forward 1 Machine Gun to each of the strong points as soon
         as the position is consolidated.
     (1v) It is of extreme importance that the whole of the ob-
         -jective laid down should be gained and all ground gained must
   X. be held at all costs.

8. Zero hour at present arranged will be 4.0 pm.
   This will be confirmed by wire in Code A.

9. A Communication Trench will be dug as soon as possible after
   BORITSKA is captured from point of junction of BORITSKA and
   HAZY back to present front line.

B2

10. Owing to the extreme difficulty in getting back information it is of the greatest importance that a system of runners at short intervals from front to rear should be established and every effort must be made to send back information of the situation (particularly as regards getting in touch with the French) while it is still daylight. The importance of this is to be particularly impressed upon all Officers.

11.
(a) Flares will be lit as soon as the objective is gained, and when called for by contact aeroplanes; a plentiful supply of flares must therefore be carried.
(b) Signalling flags will be carried and will be waved to shew the Artillery the positions of the Infantry.
These flags will on no account be stuck in the ground.

12. Prisoners will be sent to the cage at T.8. where they will be taken over by the A.P.M.
It is of the greatest importance that the regiment of prisoner and place where captured should be wired to Brigade H.Q. as soon as possible.

13. Stragglers' Posts E. of LES BOEUFS will be established under arrangements to be made by the O.C. 2nd Worcesters.

14. A watch with synchronised time will be sent to 1st Queen's H.Q's. before 1.0 pm.

15. Advanced Brigade H.Q. will be established at the Brigade Test Point about T.8.d.9.0. by one hour before zero.
Liaison Officers from
          1st Queen's
          16th K.R.R.C.
          100th M.G.Company.
will report to advanced Brigade Headquarters half an hour before Zero.

                    (Sd)   O.C.DOWNES.
                              Captain,
                              Brigade Major.

Issued through Signals at 1.0 am.

Copy No:
1 1st Queen's
2 2nd Worcesters
3 16th K.R.R.C.
4 9th H.L.I.
5 100th M.G.Company.
6 100th T.M.Battery.
7 Staff Captain.
8 Bde Signal Officer.
9 Bde Bombing Officer.
10 11th Field Coy R.E.
11 101st Field Ambulance.
12 19th Infantry Brigade.
13 98th Infantry Brigade.
14 4th Div: Artillery.
15 8th Div: Artillery.
16 33rd Division "G"
17 33rd Division "Q"
18 66th French Infantry Regiment.
19 File.

S E C R E T.   OPERATION ORDER NO:
by
Lieut: Colonel S.T.WATSON, D.S.O.
Commanding 1st Battalion "The Queen's" Regt:

COPY NO:

1. The French have reached the line N.36.c.8.0. - T.6.b.8.4. It is essential that they should not be left unsupported by the 33rd Division.

2. There will be no preliminary bombardment by heavy artillery of HAZY and BORITSKA trenches but only objectives further in rear.

3. FROSTY trench and T.head of SNOW within a 100 yards of HAZY must be cleared by Zero minus one hour at the latest.

4. The enemy are reported to have been working in considerable numbers on BARITSKA trench at 8.0 pm last night.

5. The attack will be carried out as follows :-
   (a) At Zero minus one hour there will be a field artillery barrage
   (b) At Zero "B"Coy will leave our trenches and assault BARITSKA trench and "A"Coy will leave their trench and pass through "B"Coy and assualt MIRAGE. "D"Coy will move under cover to ANTELOPE Trench and hold that line.
   "C"Coy will remain in its present position.
   (c) At Zero plus five minutes the barrage will lift from BORITSKA ; and at Zero plus ten minutes from MIRAGE.
   (d) A barrage will be formed at Zero on the line N.35.d.9.0. - T.5.b.0.5.

6. When MIRAGE has been captured a line of strong points will be established on the line T.5.b.9.4.(joining the French) - T.5.b.6.3. - T.5.b.0.3. These points will be constructed and manned by troops detailed by O.C.11th Field Coy R.E.
Two Lewis Guns of "C"Coy and one from H.Q, will be detailed to form part of the garrison of these strong points. The hour these guns are to report to O.C.11th Field Coy R.E. will be notified later.
"A"Coy will assist in the consolidation of this line by pushing men forward on the line of strong points and maintain touch between them.

7. It is of extreme importance that the whole of the objectives laid down should be gained and all ground gained must be held at all costs.

8. Zero hour as at present arranged will be 4.0. pm.

9. O.C."C"Coy will detail one platoon to dig a communication trench as soon as BORITSKA is captured between that trench and our present front line.

10. Owing to the difficulty of getting back information runners will take messages from their present Coy H.Q. to the nearest one in rear and so on.
Information is of the utmost importance.

11. Flares will be lit as soon as each objective is gained and when asked for by Contact Aeroplanes. A plentiful supply of flares must therefore be carried.

12. The position of Battalion Headquarters will not change.

13. ACKNOWLEDGE.

(Sd) H.J. CARPENTER 2/Lieut: & A/Adjt,
1st Battalion "The Queen's" Regiment.

Copy No: 1 "A"Coy.   Copy No:2 "B"Coy.
"   "   3. "C"Coy.   "   "   4   "D"Coy.
"   "   5. L.G.Officer. "   "   6. 11th Field Coy R.E.
"   "   7. 100th Inf:Bde: "   "   8. O.C.16th K.R.R.C.
"   "   9. O.C.2nd Worcesters
"   "   10. 125th French Infantry Regiment.

S E C R E T.   Copy 1.

                                         Headquarters
                                          100th Infantry Brigade.

                                         4th November 1916.

                    WARNING   ORDER.
                    ----

1. There will be a general attack on November the 5th by the French 6th Army, and our 4th and 5th Armies.

2. The French on our right are attacking BUKOVINA Trench and ROCQUINY.

3. 33rd Division will attack BORITSKA, MIRAGE, and HAZY Trenches.

4. BORITSKA and HAZY Trenches will be attacked from the front by the 1st Queen's and 16th K.R.R.C. respectively, and from the flank by the 2nd Worcesters and 9th H.L.I. who will be moved into the French area this evening for this purpose.

5. Two Battalions of 19th Infantry Brigade will be in Divisional Reserve and will occupy this evening SUNKEN ROAD by 1st Queen's Headquarters. One Battalion 19th Infantry Brigade will be advancing along the ridge in N.35.c. to join up with our left.

6. Zero hour will probably be at 11.0 am.

7. Further details will be issued later.

                                         (Sd) O. DOWNES.
                                               Captain
                                               Brigade Major.

Issued through Signals at 1.30 pm.

Copy No: 1   1st Queen's
          2   2nd Worcesters
          3   16th K.R.R.C.
          4   9th H.L.I.
          5   100th M.G. Company
          6   100th T.M. Battery
          7   Staff Captain
          8   Bde Signal Officer
          9   11th Field Coy R.E.
         10   101st Field Ambulance
         11   19th Inf:Brigade.
         12   98th Inf:Brigade.
         13   4th Divisional Artillery
         14   8th Divisional Artillery
         15   33rd Division "G"
         16   33rd Division "Q"
         17   66th French Infantry Regiment.
         18.   File.

SECRET.   Copy 1.

Headquarters
100th Infantry Brigade

4th November, 1916.

100TH INFANTRY BRIGADE ORDER NO:155.
o-o-o-o-o-o-o-o-o-o-o-o-o-o-o-o-o-o-o

1. The Division will attack tomorrow as follows :-
    (a) 100th Inf:Bde:
            Objective :- BORITSKA, MIRAGE, and HAZY Trenches.
        To advance in the morning from present front and from
        French area E. of the objective.
    (b) 19th Infantry Bde.
            Objective :- The line from HAZY to ORION as detailed
        below. To advance after dark from present front.
    (c) Two Bns. 19th Inf:Bde: in Divl: Reserve.

2. 100th Infantry Brigade will attack in accordance with verbal
    instructions given to Officers Commanding 1st Queen's, 2nd
    Worcesters and 16th K.R.R.C. by Brigadier General this afternoon.
    Dispositions of Units are shewn on attached sketch map.
    9th H.L.I. will place two companies at disposal of O.C.,1st Queen's
    9th H.L.I. less two companies will be in Brigade Reserve in SUNKEN
    ROAD. in T.10.A.
    The attack from the flank by 2nd Worcesters must be carried out
    across the open as well as along the trenches, the bayonet being
    resorted to as much as possible.
    1st Queen's and 16th K.R.R.C. will advance by platoons in succession
    from the right of 1st Queen's as the barrage lifts. The barrage
    must, therefore, be very carefully watched.

3. 11th Field Company R.E. as soon as the objectives are gained will
    send forward parties to establish strong points to join up with
    the French left as shown on the attached map.
    9th H.L.I. will detail four parties each of 1 Officer and 25 men
    to be at disposal of O.C., 11th Field Coy R.E. for carrying
    purposes. This party will await orders in SUNKEN ROAD by Hd:Qrs:of
    1st Queen's.

4. O.C. 100th M.G.Company will arrange for indirect M.G. fire to be
    brought to bear upon all approaches from LE TRANSLOY, particularly
    upon the Cemetery with 8 guns from positions already selected by
    him.
    He will also hold 4 guns in readiness to push up into the strong
    points directly the position is consolidated.

5. During the morning up to Zero, there will be bombardment by heavy
    artillery of all localities in rear and of field artillery of
    BORITSKA, MIRAGE, and HAZY Trenches.

6. At Zero an intense barrage will be placed on BORITSKA, MIRAGE, and
    HAZY Trenches, and along the line N.35.A.2.5.-N.35.A.7.0.-N.35.c.
    7.6.- N.35.c. 9.2.

7. (a) At Zero plus 3 minutes the barrage in front of the flank attack
    of the 100th Inf:Bde: will commence to lift, and will move along
    BORITSKA and HAZY at the rate of 25 yards a minute.
    (b) The barrage along the rest of the Divisional front will commence
    to creep at Zero 25 yards per minute for 45 minutes and then at 50
    yards a minute as far as the Cemetery.

8. Flares will be lit by the 100th Inf:Bde: on reaching their objective,
    at 1.10 pm and at 3.30 pm.

9. Zero hour will be at 11.10 am

10. Watches with synchronised time will be sent to Headquarters, 1st Queen's, 2nd Worcesters, 16th K.R.R.C. and 9th H.L.I. during the night 4/5th November.

11. Brigade Headquarters will open at Brigade Test Point at T.8. at 10.15 am on 5th instant.
The following will detail Liaison Officers :-
      1st Queen's
      16th K.R.R.C.
      100th M.G.Company.

          (Sd) O.DOWNES.
          Captain
          Brigade Major.

Issued through Signals at 10:15 pm.

Copy No: 1 1st Queen's
    2 2nd Worcesters
    3 16th K.R.R.C.
    4 9th H.L.I.
    5 100th M.G.Company
    6 100th T.M.Battery.
    7 Staff Captain
    8 Brigade Signal Officer
    9 11th Field Coy R.E
    10 Advanced Dressing Station
    11 19th Inf:Brigade.
    12 98th Inf:Brigade.
    13 4th Divisional Artillery.
    14 8th Divisional Artillery.
    15 33rd Division "G"
    16 33rd Division "Q"
    17 66th French Infantry Regiment.
    18. File.

S E C R E T.   Operation Order No: Copy No: D
                        by
            Lieut:Col: S.T.WATSON D.S.O.
            Commdg: 1st Batt:"The Queen's"Regt.

1. There will be a general attack on Nov:5th by the French 6th Army and our 4th and 5th Armies.

2. The French on our right are attacking BUKOVINA (our MOON) Trench and ROCQUINY.

3. 33rd Division will attack BORITSKA, MIRAGE, and HAZY Trenches.

4. BORITSKA and HAZY Trenches will be attacked from the front by 1st Queen's and 16th K.R.R.C. respectively and from the flank by the 2nd Worcesters and 9th H.L.I. who will be moved into the French area for that purpose this evening.

5. Two Battns. 19th Infantry Brigade will be in Divisional Reserve and will occupy the Sunken Road near 1st Queen's Headquarters, tonight.

6. The probable hour of Zero will be 11.10 am.

7. The attack by 1st Queen's will be carried out by "C"Coy "A","B", and "D" Coys will remain in their present positions "D"Coy must however be prepared to form close support to "C"Coy should the attack fail.

8. "C"Coy will occupy NEW Trench (the short trench between BARITSKA and ANTELOPE Trench) tonight in preparation for the attack.

9. The artillery barrage will creep at 25 yards interval in a north westerly direction, that is in the direction which the 2nd Worcesters are attacking. At the time of the first lift the right platoon of "C"Coy will advance in a north easterly direction in conjunction with the advance of the 2nd Worcesters. On the next lift of barrage the right centre platoon of "C"Coy will advance and so on. The 16th K.R.R.C. on our left will probably act in a similar manner.
The hour at which the first barrage lifts and the interval between subsequent lifts will be notified as soon as known.

10. The line to be eventually established will be HAZY Trench -T.5.b.8.3. "C"Coy will assist in establishing this line. Should it be found to be held in sufficient strength by the three other Battalions of the Brigade "C"Coy will reform in BARITSKA Trench thus forming a support to the new front line.

11. The position of Battalion Headquarters will not change.

12. Acknowledge.

                (Sd) H.J.CARPENTER, 2/Lieut: & A/Adjt:
                        1st Battn:"The Queen's" Regt:

Copy No:1.   "A"Coy.
        2.   "B"Coy.
        3.   "C"Coy.
        4.   "D"Coy.
        5.   100th Inf: Brigade (for information)
        6.   2nd Worcesters   "   "
        7.   16th K.R.R.C.   "   "
        8.   66th French Inf:Regiment.   "
        9.   Spare.

AFTER ORDERS.   Two Companies 9th H.L.I. are attached to the 1st Queen's for tomorrow's operations. No:Coy will occupy ANTELOPE Trench in close support of "C"Coy 1st Queen's but but will not advance unless "C"Coy meets with considerable difficulty. No: Coy will remain in Sunken Road at Bn:H.Q. and provide carrying parties as required.

Secret 1/1/ 100/33 Army Form C. 2118. (1)

WAR DIARY for Dec 1916.
or
INTELLIGENCE SUMMARY 1st/B" THE QUEENS
(Erase heading not required.)

Instructions regarding War Diaries and Intelligence Summaries are contained in F. S. Regs, Part II. and the Staff Manual respectively. Title Pages will be prepared in manuscript.

Place	Date	Hour	Summary of Events and Information	Remarks and references to Appendices
		DEC		
LIERCOURT	1st		The Battalion took part in a route march Combined with advance guard Scheme. Warning orders received that the "B" would probably move forward on 4th half battn of 6th.	S.W.
"	2nd		Company training continued.	S.W.
"	3rd		Church parade. The GOC 33rd Division presented medal ribbons to the following NCOs and men who had been awarded the military medal. No 5613 a/RSM W. BUTLER 9517 a/CQMS BIRMINGHAM, No 4256 L/C J. CORNFIELD, No 6925 CQMS. OWEN 8091 Sergt F. CHURCH.	S.W.
"	4th		The Battalion marched at 5.50am and marched to PONT REMY Station and entrained for MERICOURT. This place was reached at 11.40am and the Battalion marched to VAUX arriving at 1.15pm. The transport which had left LIERCOURT by road on 3rd arrived at 6pm.	S.W.
VAUX	5th		Officers proceeded to view the line to be taken over from the French. On arrival at the French Brigade Headquarters it was found that it was not possible to go further than the Regimental Headquarters by daylight. The Battalion moved unexpectedly to MORLANCOURT parading at 3pm. and arriving at about 5pm.	S.W.
MORLANCOURT.	6th		Marched to Camp 111 on the BRAY-ALBERT road and occupied huts.	S.W.
CAMP 111.	7th		Marched to Camp 107 S.W. of MARICOURT at 2.40pm arriving at 4.30pm.	S.W.
CAMP 107	8th		Marched to MAUREPAS RAVINE at 3.40pm. and occupied tents	S.W.
MAUREPAS.	9th		Marched to LE PRIEZ farm and there met guides from the 37th French Infantry. 1st Battalion at 5pm. The line taken over extended from about V26.a.3.5 to @C 2a 5.7 (ALBERT map) between RANCOURT and ST PIERRE VAAST WOOD	S.W. 1/6/ews

Army Form C. 2118.

WAR DIARY
or
INTELLIGENCE SUMMARY
(Erase heading not required.)

Place	Date	Hour	Summary of Events and Information	Remarks and references to Appendices
RANCOURT	10th		D Company was on the right front Company, C Coy the left front. A Coy in support and B Coy in reserve. The relief was complete by 10 p.m. It rained the whole day and the trenches were in a dreadful condition and falling in in many places. In many places the men were standing in water almost up to their knees without any gum boots. The trench had done plenty of work on the trenches but the heavy rain had undone it. Remained in the front line trenches. Raised the greater part of the day. The enemy shelled the ground near the Reserve Company and Battalion Headquarters at intervals throughout the day.	S.S.
RANCOURT	11th		Relieved by the HOUSEHOLD BATTALION. The relief was very slow, owing to the bad state of the trenches, and was not complete until 5 a.m. Many men stuck in the mud and had to be dug out. It rained the greater part of the day. The total casualties during the two days were two men wounded and one man killed by a shelter falling in on him. After relief the Battalion moved to shelters in MAUREPAS RAVINE. Two drafts total two officers and 85 joined the Battalion and remained with the Quartermasters Stores. The two officers were 2nd Lieuts H. J. BUIST and L. P. SMITH. 11 casuals rejoined the Battalion.	S.S.
MAUREPAS	12th		The wounds from the front line trenches to MAUREPAS RAVINE was very slow owing to the state of the men's feet owing to the water in the trenches and the absence of gum boots.	S.S.
	13th		Remained in bivouacs. Rained nearly all day. The men had very little shelter from the weather. 65 men sent to hospital suffering in the most cases, from trench feet. Remained in bivouacs. 64 men sent to hospital with trench feet.	S.S.

WAR DIARY
INTELLIGENCE SUMMARY
(Erase heading not required.)

Army Form C. 2118.

Place	Date	Hour	Summary of Events and Information	Remarks and references to Appendices
MAUREPAS	14th		30 men were sent to hospital with trench feet. The Battalion was relieved by 2nd Bn WELSH FUSILIERS and marched to Camp III arriving about 6 p.m. and occupied huts. Rained at intervals during the day.	See
CAMP III.	15th		Major R.M. GRIGG 8th Bn THE HAMPSHIRE Regt joined as 2nd in command. Rained again at intervals during the day.	See
	16th		Remained in huts – weather continued inclement.	
	17th		Ditto – Officers proceeded to view the line to be taken over by the Battalion. 2nd Lt. WATSON A.S.O. to Hospital. Returned from same.	
	18th		Entrained at 1pm. two Coys the Battalion was conveyed to MAUREPAS where guides of 17th Bn Middlesex Regt. were met. The line taken over from the Bn. N.E. of BOUCHAVESNES (C.9 and 15 – ALBERT map). A Coy RIGHT front, where RIGHT rested on the French. LEFT, B.Coy. LEFT front. D. Coy SUPPORT. D.Coy RESERVE. Movement in front of Support line had to be carried out in the open owing to bad condition of trenches. Relief was completed at 2.30 am.	
	19th		Remained in front line trenches. Snow fell late in the day and frost set in at night. Lieut C.A.KEMP. G.P.S.JACOB. C.H.PLOWMAN-BROWN joined from 3rd Battalion. Lieut RHNGVINS rejoined from leave and took over the duties of Adjutant. Frost continued.	

Army Form C. 2118.

WAR DIARY
or
INTELLIGENCE SUMMARY
(Erase heading not required.)

Place	Date	Hour	Summary of Events and Information	Remarks and references to Appendices
	20th		Remained in Front Line Trenches. Inter Coy relief were carried out after dark. 'D' relieving 'A', 'C' relieving 'B'.	
	21st		Remained in Front Line Trenches which again fell in bad condition and much wire put in owing to new orders. SUPPORT line shelled between 1 and 2 pm. 1 Killed. Undiminished rain. C.O. and Coy. Comdrs. of relieving Battn visited the line.	
	22nd		Remained in Front Line Trenches, which are now in a poor condition notwithstanding continued work on them. Battalion relieved by 16th K.R.R's relief commenced 5 pm and completed 11.40 pm Battalion marched back by Platoons on relief to Camp 17 (A.23.d.) where it reoccupied Dugouts & tents. Troops much tired on emergence of the Town in Front line in consequence of wear weather- heavy rain fell during march from Trenches.	
Camp 17	23rd		Cleaning up inspections - weather continued inclement.	
	24th		Ditto	
	25th		Ditto	
	26th		Battalion relieved by 1st K.O.R. Lancs. R. which was completed at 8pm. Marched to Camp 110-117 (L.13.c.Central - about 1 mile W. of BRAY) when it was accommodated in huts. Rain continued throughout.	

Army Form C. 2118.

WAR DIARY
or
INTELLIGENCE SUMMARY
(Erase heading not required.)

5.

Place	Date	Hour	Summary of Events and Information	Remarks and references to Appendices
Camp 119	27th		Remained in Huts. Physical Training - cleaning up - Inspection. Cold at night.	
	28th	10 a.m.	Marched to EDGEHILL and entrained at 1 p.m. for REST AREA. Detrained at LONGPRÉ at 6 p.m. and 7 p.m. marched to BUSSUS-BUSSUEL where it arrived at 11 p.m. occupying billets. Rained at night.	
BUSSUS-BUSSUEL	29th		Rested. Weather inclement. 1 Officer and 130 O.R. proceeded to Musketry School for 5 days course.	
"	30th		Physical Training - refitting. Weather inclement.	
"	31st		Refitting continued. Weather inclement.	

R. M. Knipe, Major.
Comdg. 1st Bn. "The Queen's" Regt.

Army Form C. 2118.

WAR DIARY
or
INTELLIGENCE SUMMARY

for JANUARY 1917

1/8 THE QUEEN'S REGT.

Vol 21

Place	Date	Hour	Summary of Events and Information	Remarks and references to Appendices
BÉTHUNE – BUSNES.	1st		HOLIDAY. 10 O.R. joined from Base.	
	2nd		Ordinary Routine – Company Training.	
	3rd		" – Ditto	
	4th		" – Ditto	
	5th		" – Ditto	
	6th		" – Ditto	
	7th		Church Parade in Billet of No.2 (B) Coy. Lieut R. FAULKNER and Lieut T. TRACEY joined from England (3rd Battalion) to Lieut O.R. Moncks and 30 O.R. proceded to 10th Works Batt.	
	8th		Company Training continued. 9 O.R. joined from Base.	2/Lt H.J. CARPENTER took the command for half hr
	9th		Company Training continued. Lieut FAULKNER took the command of No.2 (B) Coy.	
	10th		Company Training continued	
	11th			
	12th		Company Training continued. Battalion paraded at 2pm formed up in hollow square. The Divisional Commander attended & presented military medals to the following N.C.O'mens: 8535 A/C.S.M. T. TIPPER, 9685 Sergt. C. BRUCE, 2051 L/Cpl. T. HACKETT (R.A.M.C. attached). 6694 Pte WOODARD.	
	13th			

Army Form C. 2118.

WAR DIARY FOR JANUARY 1917

INTELLIGENCE SUMMARY

(Erase heading not required.)

1st Battn. "The Queen's" Regt.

Place	Date	Hour	Summary of Events and Information	Remarks and references to Appendices
BUSSUS-BUSSUEL	14th		On instructions from G.H.Q. Major R.M. GRIGG 2/8 Hants Regt. ordered to report at War Office. Left for England this day. 7 other ranks joined from Base.	
	15th		Training continued. Major T. WEEDING joined and assumed command of Battalion.	
	16th		Training continued. 2/Lieut (a/Cpt) SELWYN to Hospital. Capt. F. SEWELL joined and took over command of "B" Company.	
	17th		Battalion Route March — Instructional. 5 N.C.O.s + men wounded by a bomb exploding during a Brigade bomb & bombing attack. Orders for move to forward area received. Brigade placed by road & rail to Bivys 111 and 112 (near BRAY) on 20th.	
	18th		Training continued. Transport.	
	19th		Training continued. Orders received that Batt. would proceed to BRAY instead of Bivys.	
	20th		Battalion moved by road and rail to BRAY — Marched at 4.15 am via MUCY-LONG-LE-CATELET to LONGPRÉ which was reached at 7.15 am. Breakfast at Station. Entrained 8.30 am, arrived near BRAY 2.30 pm, where Bus. was billetted in Bivys. 77, 78 & "C" Coy in huts. "D" in the field. Lieut THOMPSON & JONES and 16 O.R. joined from 3rd Bn.	
BRAY	21st		61 O.R. joined from 3rd Battn.	
	22nd		Company re Training. Lieut B.A. SELFE proc'd to R.F.C. H'Qrs re "Shurwat". Struck photograph.	
	23rd		Battalion marched to Camp 19 (E.16.b) accommodated in huts. Part of Divisional Reserve. "A" Coy. C.F. WATSON, C.M.G., M.C.O. Lieut Col. Commd. Command'g 1st Bn. Battalion.	

2449 Wt. W14957/M90 750,000 1/16 J.B.C. & A. Forms/C.2118/12.

Army Form C. 2118.

WAR DIARY

For January 1917

INTELLIGENCE SUMMARY

1st Bn. "THE QUEEN'S" Regt.

(Erase heading not required.)

Place	Date	Hour	Summary of Events and Information	Remarks and references to Appendices
Bray 19	24th		Training is continued.	
	25th		Training is continued. 2nd Lieuts H. RISTON-COOKE & CHWATT joined from 3rd Battalion. Received	
	26th		Training is continued. Baln. in Rotation move into the line in relief of 1st KING'S Regt on night 27/28th. Lieut C. H. WYATT to hospital. 2nd Lieut SELWYN from Hospital & immediately to join R.F. Corps H.Q.	
	27th		Battalion paraded at 4.15pm marched to CURLU where guides were met at 6 pm. The line taken over extended from O.26.A.9.6 to I.2.A.4.6 (ALBERT Contour Sheet) N.E. of CLERY and S. of BOUCHAVESNES. Relief was completed at 2 am. Companies were situated - "A" RIGHT FRONT. "B" CENTRE. "D" LEFT FRONT. "C" SUPPORT. Night passed quietly - Weather FROST. There were no casualties.	4th Kings Regt
N.E. CLERY	28th		Battalion remained in trenches - Nothing unusual occurred - No casualties. FROST.	
	29th		Battalion remained in trenches - Intermittent shelling with H.E. & Rifle Grenades. 1 O.R wounded. FROST.	
	30th		Battalion remained in trenches - Enemy Active with T.M's & Rifle Grenades on RIGHT & LEFT FRONT Coys. 1 O.R Killed. 5 wounded. FROST.	
	31st		Battalion remained in Trenches. Enemy active with T.M's Aerial Torpedoes & Rifle Grenades fire & not part against LEFT FRONT Company. 3 O.R wounded. Relief by 16th K.R.R's commenced 6 p.m. completed 9.45 p.m. on completion of relief Battalion in SUPPORT occupying dugouts &c in vicinity of ROAD WOOD (C.25.A) FROST.	

A.B. Field Lieut Colonel
Comdg. 1st Bn. The Queen's Regt.
2.2.17

WAR DIARY or INTELLIGENCE SUMMARY

Army Form C. 2118.

FEBRUARY 1917
1st Batn. "The Queen's" Regt.

Vol 28

Place	Date	Hour	Summary of Events and Information	Remarks and references to Appendices
ROAD WOOD	1st		Working Parties furnished for improvement of Comn. Trenches ACCARIES AV. under R.E.	FROST
"	2nd		" " " " " " " "	"
"	3rd		" " " " " " " "	"
"	4th		" " " " " " " "	"
"	5th		Enemy shelled us heavily, mainly in retaliation for a bombardment carried out by us during the day. Casualties 1 O.R. Killed & 1 O.R. wounded. Battalion relieved 16th K.R.R's in FRONT LINE Trenches C 26 A 96 & I.2.A.u.6. (ALBERT combined chart). Coys: were situated as follows "A"RIGHT FRONT. "C" CENTRE. "D" LEFT. "B" SUPPORT. Relief commenced 6 p.m. completed 9.45 p.m.	FROST
N.E. CLERY.	6th		Remained in Trenches — nothing unusual occurred. Lieut. BOTTON and 88 O.R. joined from 3rd Battalion — remained with "B" Echelon.	FROST
"	7th		Remained in Trenches — A wire on the Enemy's line was carried out by the Rattr. on our LEFT (9th H.L.I.) Battalion covered by Lewis Gun, Rifle & Private fire.	FROST
"	8th		Battalion was relieved by 20th Royal Fusiliers — Specialists during daylight — to remainder under cover of darkness — Relief was completed at 11.30 p.m. FROST on Casualties 2 O.R. killed 1 O.R. wounded during morning "Stand to":—	FROST
Camp 19	9th		Relief Battalion marched by Motors to H.9. Cross Roads where lorries were in waiting which conveyed the Battalion to Camp 19 (B 16 b). Move was completed at 2 a.m.	FROST
"	10th		Remained in Camp 19 — Baths all Bn — cleaning up generally.	FROST

13 1/P.W.

WAR DIARY or INTELLIGENCE SUMMARY

Army Form C. 2118.

FEBRUARY 1917

1st BATTN. "THE QUEEN'S REGT"

Place	Date	Hour	Summary of Events and Information	Remarks and references to Appendices
Camp 19	11th		Battalion attended Divine Service. Afternoon Specially Training of the Platoon as a fighting unit" explained to all Officers. Platoon Commanders followed by a demonstration on the ground "Platoon in Attack". FROST.	
"	12th		Training – including 2 hours "Platoon in Attack". FROST.	
"	13th		Training – including 2 hours "Company in Attack." FROST.	
"	14th		Training – including 2 hours "Company in Attack. FROST. Draft of 35 O.R. joined from 2nd Battn.	
"	15th		Training – B.G.C. Lt Col Faulkner CMG. DSO inspected the Battalion. Lt Col Faulkner carried out a demonstration of the Company in Attack" before the Divisional Brigade Commanders + Coy Commanders of the units in the Brigade and to 98th Bde. following which Coy + Pl. Commanders continued demonstrations by running Platoons in Brigade.	
"	16th		Training till 11am. Brigade moving forward in relief of 98th Bde. Battalion to H.Q. OMMIECOURT Defences #12 (ALBERT Gp.) & Coy HOWITZER WOOD H.Q. A C and D Coys Battn. H.Q. at FRISE BEND G.R.B. More Gunners & pers Completed 8 & 5 from in Brigade Reserve relieving 2nd R.I. Fusrs. disposed as follows - D Coy Coy MARRIERS WOOD @ 19 Training.	
FRISE BEND	17th		Training. Working parties. 2 officers 100 O.R. in Gun Pits in MARRIERS WOOD @ 19 Training.	
	18th		Training. Working parties. 2 officers 100 O.R. on Gun Pits in MARRIERS WOOD @ 19 Siguam. Lieut CARNFORD returned from Rest "C" Coy for duty.	

Army Form C. 2118.

WAR DIARY
or
INTELLIGENCE SUMMARY
(Erase heading not required.)

1st Batt. "THE QUEEN'S" REGT

FEBRUARY 1917

Place	Date	Hour	Summary of Events and Information	Remarks and references to Appendices
FRISE BEND	19th		Training – Working Party, 2 Officers, 50 O.R. on Gun Pits in MARRIERS WOOD Coy. Orders received Battalion will relieve 16th K.R.R's in Front Line on night 20/21st	
"	20th		Battalion relieved 16th K.R.R's in Front Line trenches. 1,2 a 3.6 & I.7.b 3.6 (ALBERT Contoured Sheet) Coys were allotted as under LEFT FRONT 'A' CENTRE 'B' RIGHT 'C' SUPPORT 'D'. Relief commenced 6 p.m. completed 1.30 a.m.	
N.E. CLERY	21st		Remained in Trenches. Normal – no casualties. M. of Battn	
	22nd		Remained in Trenches. Normal – 1 O.R. wounded. 2/Lt ACEY 14th O.R. joined from 3rd Battn	
	23rd		Remained in Trenches – Normal – 1 O.R. wounded. 69 O.R. joins from 3rd Battn.	
	24th		Battalion was relieved by 16th K.R.R's in Front Line and became Battalion in R.E. Reserve. Coys allotted as follows on completion of relief :- A Coy to OMMIECOURT DEFENCES – 'C' HOWITZER WOOD. B & D – Batt H.Q. FRISE BEND. – Normal.	
FRISE BEND	25		Routine cleaning up. Working Party 2 officers 100 O.R. C. Coy at MARRIERS WOOD. 2/Lt D.V. BERNARD and 5 O.R. joins from Base. 4061 C.S.M. WEBB M.C. took over duties of R.S.M.	
	26		TRAINING. Working Party as per yesterday	

Army Form C. 2118.

WAR DIARY or INTELLIGENCE SUMMARY

FOR FEBRUARY 1917
1st Batt "The Queen's"

(Erase heading not required.)

Place	Date	Hour	Summary of Events and Information	Remarks and references to Appendices
FRISE BEND	27th		Training – Working Parts on Tramway. Orders received for Batt. to relieve 16 K.R.R. in FRONT LINE on night 28th Feby / 1st March. The following Officers struck off strength (invalided to England) Lt. Col. S.T. WATSON D.S.O. 16.2.17. Lieut A.M. ALLAN 2.1.17. Lieut P.R. HOPE 15.2.17. Lieut A.W.E. MEMBE 20.17.	
	28		Battalion relieved 16th K.R.R's in FRONT LINE Trenches 1 & 2, 3.6 & 1.7 & 3.6 (ALBERT Combined Sheet) Coys were allotted as under LEFT FRONT "D" CENTRE "B" RIGHT FRONT "C". SUPPORT "A". Relief commenced 6 pm and was completed 9.15 pm. During relief the CENTRE & RIGHT FRONT Coys were heavily shelled from about 8.10 to 8.30 pm. 1 O.R. killed & Eight O.R. joined from Base.	

J. Weeding Major
Comdg. 1st Batt "The Queens" Regt.

1/3/17.

Army Form C. 2118.

WAR DIARY

INTELLIGENCE SUMMARY

(Erase heading not required.)

1st Batt": "The Queen's" Reg.

MARCH 1917.

14 1/RWS

Place	Date	Hour	Summary of Events and Information	Remarks and references to Appendices
NECLERN	1st		Remained in Trenches. No Casualties - Normal.	
	2nd		Remained in Trenches. 2 O.R. wounded. Normal.	
	3rd		Remained in Trenches - No Casualties - Normal. 2nd Lieut H.J. BUIST to R.E. Corps.	
	4th		Division on left attacked - Demonstration on Battalion front with Rockets - 5.18 a.m. to 5.36 a.m. Considerable hostile shelling - Casualties 2nd Lieut H.H.S. JONES Killed. 2 O.R. Killed & O.R. wounded. Released by 2nd Bn. R.W. Fusiliers. Relief commenced 6 p.m. completed 7.45 p.m. Battalion went into SUPPORT. A and C and 1/2 B Coy Batt. H.Q. MAUD AVENUE 1/2 B Coy CLERY CHATEAU (H.12.b.) D Coy 2 B.L. 2+8 (H.10.6 and d).	
	5th	7.45pm	Battalion was relieved by 1st Connaughts. Relief commenced 6pm completed 7.45pm and proceeded to Camp. 19 (G.16.6.) Casualties 1 O.R. wounded. Draft of 44 O.R. from Base.	
Camp. 19	6th		Battalion marched to CORBIE from arriving 4 p.m. occupied billets in town. Lieut Q.F. ASHPITEL joins from 2nd Batt.	
CORBIE	7th		GENERAL ROUTINE - cleaning up re-	
"	8th		Training and general routine.	

Army Form C. 2118.

WAR DIARY
INTELLIGENCE SUMMARY

(Erase heading not required.)

1st Battn. "The Queen's" Regt.

MARCH 1917

Place	Date	Hour	Summary of Events and Information	Remarks and references to Appendices
CORBIE	9th		Battalion Route March and General Routine.	
"	10th		Training and general routine - 10 other ranks joined from Base - Captain R BRODHURST - HILL. 2/Lieut C.R. KEMP and 75 other ranks rejoined from Divil Works Battalion.	
"	11th		Church Parade - Conference (Company and Battalion) held. Captain R BRODHURST - HILL took over charge of "D" Company. Lieut C.G.D. THRUPP relinquished the acting rank of Captain.	
"	12th		Training and general routine.	
"	13th		Battalion Route March and general Routine.	
"	14th		Training and general routine - 2nd Lieut N.J. FOWLER joined from 3rd Battn.	
"	15th		Training and general routine.	
"	16th		Training and general routine. Draft of 30 O.R. joined from Base.	
"	17th		Battalion Route March and general routine.	
"	18th		Church Parade.	
"	19th		Training and general Routine - A Kit Inspection was held in the afternoon attended by all officers and two N.C.O's per platoon. Notified by 5th Corps MA.C 15101/2 War Office had approved the award of Italian Decoration "Bronze medal for military Valour" to 5641 Sgt F. MULCARE.	
"	20th		Training and general Routine.	
"	21st		Battalion Route march and general Routine.	
"	22nd		Training and general routine. 2nd Lieut K.A. FRAZER joined from 3rd Battalion	

A 5834. Wt. W4973/M687 750,000 8/16 D.D.&L. Ltd. Forms/C.2118/13.

Army Form C. 2118.

WAR DIARY
INTELLIGENCE SUMMARY.

1st BATTALION "THE QUEEN'S" Regt.

(3)

(Erase heading not required.)

Place	Date	Hour	Summary of Events and Information	Remarks and references to Appendices
OURBIE	23rd		Training and general routine.	
"	24th		Training including musketry on field range and general routine. Battalion furnished two companies (made up of two platoons from each Company) for Corps Ceremonial Parade at which Medal ribbons (Military Medal) were presented to the following 9567 Sgt L BROOKS. 9367 Sergt W. STREETER. 8596 Sergt. G. SMITH. 3710 Cpl W.HARRIS. 10036 Pte H. SPIERS. 12 O.R. joined from Base.	
"	25th		Church Parade and general routine.	
"	26th		Training and general routine. 2nd Lieut J.S. MILNER joined from 3rd Batn.	
"	27th		Training and general routine.	
"	28th		Training and general routine. 2nd Lieut C.H. WYATT rejoined from Hospital.	
"	29th		Training and general routine.	
"	30th		Training and general routine.	
"	31st		Training and general routine. Orders received 33rd Divn is being transferred to the III Army and for the move of the 100th Bde. from ORBIE & VILLERS-BOCAGE area on 2nd April 1917.	

E. Walden
Lieut. Colonel.
Commdg: 1st Bn The Queens Regt

1/4/17

A.5834 Wt. W4973/M687 750,000 8/16 D. D. & L. Ltd. Forms/C.2118/13.

Army Form C. 2118.

WAR DIARY
INTELLIGENCE SUMMARY
(Erase heading not required.)

APRIL 1917

1st Battn "The Queen's Regt"

Place	Date	Hour	Summary of Events and Information	Remarks and references to Appendices
CORBIE	1st		Church Parade - General routine. Lieut J.S.MILNER to 100th T.M.B for attachment.	
"	2nd		Battalion marched to VILLERS-BOCAGE (Ref Map Sh.57d.1/10000) occupying billets. 2nd Lieut L.H.BENNETT, L.P.SMITH, K.A.FRAZER, O.H.WATT, C.H.PLOWMAN-BROWN with instructions from Divisional remained at CORBIE pending departure to 10th Divisional Depot Battalion.	
VILLERS-BOCAGE	3rd		Battalion marched to BEAUVAL occupying billets.	
BEAUVAL	4th		Battalion marched to H.Q and A Coy to NEUVILLETTE. B.C & D Coys to RANSART, occupying billets.	
NEUVILLETTE	5th		Battalion marches to GRENAS occupying billets. Captain F.GODFREY rejoined from England completing Senior Officers Course.	
GRENAS	6th		Rest. 9 O.R. proceed to 7th Divisional Depot Battalion. Training (Platoon digging) and general routine.	
"	7th		Battalion marched to SOUASTRE occupying billets.	
SOUASTRE	8th		Battalion marched to ST AMAND. Church Parade.	
ST AMAND	9th		General Routine. Training re Battalion at 6 hours notice to move - Surplus Kits, Stores, Great Coats, Haversacks, instruments (Drums & fifes &c) stored in billet No.78 BIENVILLERS and under Brigade arrangements. 7 other ranks joined from Reve.	
"	10th		Training and General Routine. Orders under 6 hours notice to move.	
"	11th		Training and General Routine. Battalion movements under 3 hours notice to move.	

15 1/RWS

Army Form C. 2118.

WAR DIARY
INTELLIGENCE SUMMARY
(Erase heading not required.)

1st Batt. The Queen's Regt.

APRIL 1917

Place	Date	Hour	Summary of Events and Information	Remarks and references to Appendices
ST AMAND	12th	10.10 am	Received orders 10.10 am to move. Battalion paraded at 11 am, and marched (H.Q.D, A, B, C) via BIENVILLERS - MONCHY au BOIS - ADINFER - BOIRY to vicinity of MERCATEL (M.34.c) branched on Bivouacs. Brigade in Divil Reserve, under 2 hours notice to move.	
MERCATEL	13th		Remained in Bivouacs - working party 2 officers + 100 O.R. furnished for work on Railway. General Routine, etc.	
"	14th		Remained in Bivouacs - working party 2 officers + 100 O.R. furnished for work on Railway. 26 O.R. under 2/Lt ASHPITEL proceeded to ACHICOURT and S.of HAKRAS for duty as water Guard. Before proceeding Brigade moved into Position N of CROISELLES known as 15th Sept. relieving 2/10th Brigade. The Battalion being in Brigade Support.	
"	15th		Battalion moved in open as follows: A + D Coys to vicinity of St LEGER T.28.a. B + C Coys in Railway line S.22 and S.28. Battn HQ at HAMLINCOURT. B Echelon at BOIRY St MARTIN.	
HAMLINCOURT	16th		Dispositions same as on 15th. Working Party 5 officers 200 O.R. furnished for various works in and about St LEGER. Party also employed improving roads, shelters, etc at HAMLINCOURT.	
"	17th		as on 16th. Officers from each Coy reconnoitred front lines.	
"	18th		as on 17th. Lieut Col L.M. CROFTS, D.S.O., proceeded from England & resumed Command of the Battalion.	
"	19th		as on 18th. Working Party at St LEGER. 2 officers 100 O.R. only.	
"	20th		Training and General Routine. Lt Col G.F. WATSON, C.M.G., D.S.O., on instructions from Division proceeded to take over Command of the 17th Battalion.	

(Cont. Turn)

Army Form C. 2118.

WAR DIARY
INTELLIGENCE SUMMARY
(Erase heading not required.)

1st Batt. "The Queen's" Regt. (3)

Instructions regarding War Diaries and Intelligence Summaries are contained in F.S. Regs., Part II. and the Staff Manual respectively. Title pages will be prepared in manuscript.

APRIL 1917

Place	Date	Hour	Summary of Events and Information	Remarks and references to Appendices
HAMLIN-COURT	20th		A and D Companies were relieved by two Companies 18th K.R.R's during the afternoon and marched from vicinity of ST. LEGER & Billets in MOYENNEVILLE there being comforts by 6 p.m. Major T. WEEDING - Captain F. GODFREY and Company Commanders reconnoitred the HINDENBURG LINE from the vicinity of CROISELLES in view of operations to take place on or about 23rd Instant. Lieut K. HALL R.G.A. given an attached for a fortnight serving as an Intelligence officer.	
"	21st		Training and general routine. Battalion practised after dark in marching to a place of assembly - position of deployment - deploying - and advancing in waves to the attack.	
"	22nd		General Ruthven gave Lieutenants to take place on 23rd instant namely, in which Battalion is detailed to take part in attack on HINDENBURG LINE immediate S. of the River SENSEE. (Details on separate sheet). The Battalion (less 10% re-inforcements) paraded in Battle Order and Brown Starting point HAMLINCOURT at 7.30 p.m. in following order. D.A.C.B. The following officers viz Lieut Col. L.M.CROFTS, D.S.O., Captain R.FAULKNER, M.C., Captain H. BATTISCOMBE, Lieut C.G.D.THRUPP, 2nd Lieuts H. RIBTON-COOKE, T.R.G. Cowan, J.N.F. BARNARD, J.T.P. HUGHES, E.G. KEMP. with 10% Re-inforcements were withdrawn from Battalion and joined "B" Echelon at BOIRY ST MARTIN.	

Army Form C. 2118.

WAR DIARY
APRIL 1917
INTELLIGENCE SUMMARY.
(Erase heading not required.) 1st Batn "THE QUEEN'S REGT:

Place	Date	Hour	Summary of Events and Information	Remarks and references to Appendices
Between FONTAINE & CROISILLE Rally-Cutting T.7.9.a.	23rd		Battalion in Attack – Separate report attached.	
"	24th		Battalion in bivouac – general routine – visited by Divnl Comdr. Major Genl. PINNEY, C.B. who personally expressed his appreciation of the Battalion's work under the fight on 23rd.	
"	25th		Battalion marched to BERLES-au-BOIS (occupying Billets) via BOIRY ST MARTIN – ADINFER – RANSART – crossroads S of BELLACOURT.	
BERLES AU-BOIS	26th		Remained in Billets – General Routine and Refitting. Draft of 4 Officers 2/Lieuts L.H. BENNETT, L.P. SMITH, K.A. FRAZER, C.WATT and 513 other-ranks joined from Divnl. Depot Battn.	
"	27th		Remained in Billets – general Routine – Refitting continued.	
"	28th		— do —	Draft of 72 other ranks joined from D.D. Battn.
"	29th		Church Parade.	
"	30th		Battalion Route-March route POMMIER – STAMAND – SOUASTRE – BIENVILLERS. Warning Order received. Brigade will probably move early tomorrow.	

J.C.B.H. Lieut Colonel
Comdg. 1st Batn. The Queen's Regt.

Copy No 10

SECRET. BATTALION ORDER NO:58
by Lieut:Colonel C.F.WATSON C.M.G. D.S.O.
Comdg: 1st Battalion "THE QUEEN'S" Regiment.
SATURDAY 31st March 1917.

REF: AMIENS & LENS SHEETS 1/100,000.

1. The Division is being transferred to the 3rd Army.
2. The Battalion will move to VILLERS-BOCAGE via QUERRIEU - ALLONVILLE - COISY., on Monday 2nd April, assembling on Main Road in the following order, with head of column resting at 101st Field Ambulance, ready to move at 9.0 am.
"B" "C" Drums "D" "A" Transport. Dress...F.S.M.O. Steel helmets on packs.
3. 2/Lieut: K.M.EAST, 1 N.C.O. per Coy,& H.Q., with bicycles will rendezvous at FORK ROADS due N. of U. in LA NEUVILLE, reporting to an officer 18th K.R.R's there at 7.0 am.
4. 1st Line Transport will follow in rear of the Battalion.
5. The strictest March Discipline is to be observed throughout the march.
6. Watches will be synchronised with Bn.H.Q. at 7.15 am.
7. The following distances are to be maintained :-
Between Coy..200yds Battalion...400yds Battns: & their Transport 300yds.
8. Blankets, fastened in rolls of ten, securely tied and labelled, will be stacked at Q.M.Stores, at 6.30am.
Officers valises to be at Q.M.Stores at 7.30 am.
Kits of officers (in excess of 35lbs) will be handed in at Q.M.Stores by 6.0pm tomorrow 1st April.
9. The following officers with their servants and kits complete under charge of 2/Lieut:L.H.BENNETT will proceed by train under orders to be issued later and report to O/C Div:Depot Bn: where they will assist in training drafts -
  2/Lieut:L.H.BENNETT. 2/Lieut: K.A.FRAZER.
  " L.P.SMITH.   " C.H.WATT.
  " J.S.MILNER.   " C.H.PLOWMAN-BROWN.
10. O's C.Coys will investigate any claims and report that they have done so by 4.0 pm tomorrow, 1st April.
11. O'sC.Coys etc., will take the necessary steps to ensure billets are left clean, they will personally inspect billets prior to moving off and report to the Adjt: on parade this has been done. Sergt:Cornfield and one sanitary man per Coy will remain behind to ensure the Battalion Area is left in a clean and sanitary condition.

        (Sgd) R.H.NEVINS 2/Lieut: & Adjt:
        1st Battalion "THE QUEEN'S" Regiment.

Copies issued to -
No:1.......C.O.
 2.......No:1 Coy.
 3....... " 2 "
 4....... " 3 "
 5....... " 4 "
 6.......Qr Mr.
 7.......T.O.
 8.......Sigl:Officer.
 9.......R.S.M.
 10......Adjt:
 11......File.

Secret

Battalion Order No: 60.
by Lt: Col: C.F. WATSON. CMG. D.S.O.
Comdg: 1st Battalion "The Queen's" Regt.
MONDAY 2nd April 1917.

Detail for tomorrow
Subaltern of the Day . . . . 2/Lt. H.M. THOMPSON.

1. The Battalion will move to BEAUVAL via TALMAS tomorrow, 3rd inst, in the following order, with head of column resting on "C" Coy's Billet, ready to move at 9.15 AM. —
   "C" "D" Drums "A" "B" Transport.   Dress. F.S.M.O. Steel Helmets on packs.

2. Lieut. K.M. EAST, 1 N.C.O per Coy & 1d. Coy with bicycles, will rendezvous at Cross Roads, ½ mile N. of VILLERS – BOCAGE at 7.0 AM. L.C. G.D. THRUPP. will collect the Billeting Parties of the Bde at same time & place.

3. Transport will follow in rear of the Battalion

4. The strictest march discipline is to be observed throughout the march.

5. The following distances will be maintained –
   Between Companies 100 yards, Battalions. 200 yds
   Battalions & Transport 100 yards.

6. Blankets in rolls of ten, securely tied & labelled, together with Officers small kits, will be stacked at Q.M Stores at 7.15 am.
   Officers valises to be at Q.M Stores at 8.0 AM.

7. 9446 L/Cpl. Johns "D" Coy reverts to Private at own request from to days date.

8. 707 Sergt. Travis A. "B" Coy is transferred from "B" to "D" Coy from to days date.

9. The Comdg: Officer has noted with great pleasure the excellent behaviour of the Battalion whilst billeted in CORBIE.

10. O's C Coys will take necessary steps to ensure billets are left clean. They will personally inspect them prior to moving off, reporting to Adjt on parade that this has been done.
    Sergt. Cornfield and one sanitary man per Coy will remain behind to ensure the Battalion Area is left clean and sanitary

11. R.297 L/C. J. Low "B" Coy and 1 Pte "A", 2 Ptes "B", 1 Pte "C" & 1 Pte "D", to be selected from those having a knowledge of Horses, will be held in readiness, to proceed on Horse Conducting Duty on evening of 3rd inst.

R.H.N Evins.
2/Lieut & Adjt:
1st Batt: "The Queen's" Regt.

Copies to:—
No: 1 C.O,   No. 2 No:1 Coy
3 No:2 Coy   4 – 3 –
5 – 4 Coy   6 Q.M.
7 T.O.   8 Sig: Off.
9 Adjt   10. R S M
11. File.

TIME TABLE OF ARTILLERY BARRAGE TO ACCOMPANY
146th INFANTRY BRIGADE ORDER 221

ZERO TO ZERO plus 1	2 Batteries artillery on front of German line from U.13.b.6.5 to U.7.a.4.0.
ZERO plus 1 to ZERO plus 5	2 Batteries artillery creep from German Wire to German Front line trench from U.7.a.3.5. to U.7.a.7.5.
ZERO to ZERO plus 8	3 Batteries artillery on German Front trench from U.7.a.0.0 to U.7.a.7.5.
At ZERO plus 8	the whole barrage lifts to a line of wire 200 yards in rear of front trench remaining there till ZERO plus 10.
At ZERO plus 10	Barrage lifts to support trenches from U.7.a.7.4 to U.7.a.1.7. remaining till ZERO plus 16.
ZERO plus 18	Barrage of 3 Batteries lifts to trenches running from U.1.B.b.1.10. to U.2.c.1.1. 350 yards in rear of the support line
ZERO plus 16 to ZERO plus 23	Barrage of 2 Batteries creeps to trench running from U.S.a.i.4. to U.2.C.4. 350 yards in rear of the support line
ZERO plus 23 to ZERO plus 90	The whole barrage will remain on trench and redoubts northwards to rail junction U.1.d.3.4.

Standing Barrage

On HINDENBURG front line from U.7.a.5.8.6 U.6.d.8.2. and on support line from U.13.b.2.7.6 U.7.d.2.2. From ZERO till creeping barrage gets standing barrage when it will conform to the latter and start altogether at ZERO plus 14. If wire is formidable, to consist of smoke shells mixed with Shrapnel.

On HINDENBURG front line from U.13.b.2.7.6 U.7.d.7.a and on support line from U.13.b.6.9.9. to U.7.d.7.a and 200 yards S.E. and down to sunken road U.S.c.m.3.

From ZERO to ZERO plus 16	
ZERO plus 16 to ZERO plus 30	ZERO plus 90.
From ZERO to ZERO plus 90	Sunken road U.S.c.m.3. to U.S.a.6.5.

SECRET.   Copy No. 9

Battalion Orders No. 61
by Lieut Col V. F. Watson CMG, DSO,
Comdg. "The Queen's"
Tuesday 3rd April 1917

Detail for tomorrow   2/Lieut H. V. LACEY.
Subaltern of the day

1. The Battalion will move tomorrow. D & A. Coys to NEUVILLETTE, H.Q. B & C Coys to RANSART- forming up in the following order with head of Column resting at [DOULLENS?]
D Coys billets ready to move at 8.55 a.m.
D. A. Drums B.C. Transport. Dress F.S.M.O.
Steel Helmets will be worn. F.S. Caps on packs.

2. 2/Lieut K. M. EAST, 1 N.C.O. per Coy. & H.Qrs & 2 Signallers, with Bicycles will parade at Bn H.Q. at 6.15 a.m.

3. A distance of 500 yards will be maintained in rear of each Battalion.

4. The strictest march discipline will be observed.

5. Blankets in rolls of ten, securely tied, & labelled, will be stacked as under, by 7 a.m. B & C Coys at B Coys' H.Q. remainders at Battn H.Q.
Officers valises & small Kits at Battn H.Q. at 7.45 a.m.
Mess Baskets to be at H.Q. Mess by 8.15 a.m.

6. Watches will be synchronised at Bn. H.Q. at 7.15 a.m.

7. The undermentioned men will parade at Bn H.Q. at 8.45 a.m. to reinforce R.A. personnel carrying 2 days rations-
A. Coy. Sergt. Tracey. Ptes Bowry & Summers. B Coy Ptes Riddell,
C Coy. Ptes Berry & Alden D. Coy. Ptes Burgess & Taplin.
H.Qrs Ptes Langshaw (A) Pte Woosfold (B).

8. The afm N.C.O & men held in readiness to proceed on Horse Conducting duty will parade at Bn. H.Q. at 8.45 a.m. tomorrow
L/Cpl. Hoy & 2 Ptes B Coy. 1 Pte A. 1 Pte C. 1 Pte D.
The Transport officer will provide each with a Bridle or a substitute.

9. The Snipers will parade with their Companies tomorrow.

10. O.C. Coys &c will take necessary steps to ensure Billets are left clean. They will personally inspect them prior to moving off & reporting to Adjt on parade this has been done.
Sergt. Benfield and one sanitary man per Coy will remain behind to ensure the Battalion area is left in a sanitary state.

R. N. Nevins Lt & Adjt
"The Queen's"

Copies to:-
No. 1. to O.C. No 2. to O.C. No 1 Coy
 "   2 " O.C. No 3 Coy " 3 " "   " 4 "
 "   5 " "   " 4 "   6 " Q.M.
 "   7 " T.O. " 8 " Signalling officer
 "   9 " Adjt " 10 " R.S.M.
 " 11 File.

Secret

Battalion Orders. No: 62.
by Lieut: Col: C.F. WATSON. C.M.G. D.S.O.
Comdg Bn "The Queen's" Regt
WEDNESDAY. 4th April 1917.

Copy No: 9

Detail for tomorrow
Subaltern for the day — — — 2/Lieut: G.S. ASHPITEL.

1. Ref Map. LENS. SHEET 1/100,000.
The Bn will march to GREVAS via DOULLENS tomorrow assembling at Hte VISEE at 11.15 am. Hd. Qrs "A" Coy Drums will move at 10.15 am, "B" "C" & "D" Coys at 10.55 am. Dress — F.S.M.O. F.S. Caps on packs.
Transport will move at 11.25 am, that of "B" "C" & "D" Coys at 12.5 am, rejoining the Bn Transport as it passes at Hte VISEE.

2. Lieut R.M. EAST. I N.C.O. per Coy & Hd Qrs, with bicycles will assemble at Hte VISEE at 8.45 am.

3. All 1st Line Transport will be brigaded and march in rear of Bde Group, under command of Lieut: SMITH 2nd WORCESTER REGT.

4. Distances as under will be maintained during the March:—
Between Battns 500 yds, Rear Battns & 1st Line Transport 600 yds, between Transport of Units 200 yds.

5. Baggage Wagons will, from tomorrow, march with No: 4 Coy Divnl: Train and will join this Unit as it passes the Starting Point at 1.0pm in order as per Bde March Table.

6. Blankets will be rolled in bundles of ten, securely tied & labelled, ready for loading at 9.0am. Hd.Qrs & "A" at Qr. Mrs Stores, "B" "C" & "D" at respective Hd.Qrs. Officers valises, Hd.Qrs & "A" Coy, at Qr. Mrs Stores, at 9.AM, "B" "C" & "D" Coys at "C" Coy H.Q. at 8.0am.
Mess baskets to be ready for loading at 9.30am.

7. Sick Parade tomorrow as under,
Hd.Qrs & A Coy 9.AM, "B" "C" & "D" Coys at RANSART at 9.45 AM.

8. Until further orders Steel Helmets are to be worn on all parades.

9. O.C. Coys, etc, will ensure that all N.C.O's and men invariablely —
(a) A length of lace or string fastened in eyelet hole of Ground Sheet in order that they are always ready to wear.
(b) Protect the muzzle & nose cap of their rifle by covering with a piece of flannel.

10. Each Coy will detail an Orderly to be in readiness for attachment to Bde H.Q. Men selected should be cyclists and if possible have been employed previously as runners with Bde H.Q.

11. The Corps Commander expressed himself as highly pleased with the appearance of the Battalion to-day.

12. Reveille tomorrow will be at 6.30 AM.

(Sgd) R.H. Nevins, 2/Lt & Adjt
Bn "The Queen's" Regt

Copies issued to
No: 1 C.O. No: 2. O.C. No: 1 Coy
3 O.C. No. 2 Coy 4. O.C No: 3
5. O.C No 4 6. Qr. Mr.
7. T.O. 8. Sig: Off.
9. Adjt. 10. R.S.M.
11. File.

Battalion Order. No: 64
by Lieut: Col: C.F. WATSON CMG. D.S.O.
Comdg Bn: "The Queen's" Regt
FRIDAY. 6th April 1917.

Detail for tomorrow
Subaltern of the day   2/Lieut: A.J. CARPENTER.

1. The Battn: will march to SOUASTRE, assembling at Bn: H.Q, in the following order ready to move off at 8.55am - "B" "C" Drums "D" "A" A Echelon.
   1st line Transport &c. L.G. Limbers, Pack animals, S.A.A. Limbers, Grenade & Tool and Mess Cart. Cookers also, will be with "A" Echelon tomorrow so........ S.S.M.O.

2. 2/Lieut: L.M. East, 1 N.C.O per Coy & F.O, billetting party will assemble at Bn: H.Q. at 6.0 am.

3. "B" Echelon, 1st line Transport will move at 10am and be Brigaded and march in rear of the Bde.

4. Distances as under will be maintained during the march. between Battn 300 yds, Rear Battn: & 1st line Transport 500 yds.
   Transport of Units 200 yds.

5. Blankets rolled in bundles of ten, securely tied & labelled will be loaded at Bn: H.Q. at 7.0 am. Valises 8.0am.

6. 2/Lt A.J. CARPENTER, Sgt. Cornfield & 1 Sanitary man per Coy will remain behind to ensure the area is left clean, obtaining a certificate to that effect from Town Major.
   O.C. Coys etc will inspect Billets prior to departure & report to the Adjt on parade, this has been done.

7. O.C. "D" Coy will detail two men for duty with a wireless set. They will parade at Bn. H.Q at 8.30am tomorrow - two days rations to be carried

8. 2/Lt D. TRUPP is appointed a Member of a F.G.C.M. ordered to assemble at Hdqrs, 9th L.L.I. at a time to be notified later.

9. 37183. L/C UpGold "A" Coy will proceed to ABBEVILLE tomorrow. To parade at Bn H.Q at 8.30 am. Two days rations to be carried.

Copies to   (Sgd) R.H. Nevins 2/Lt & Adjt
No:1 C.O.   No:2 O.C. No.1   Bn: "The Queen's" Regt
  3 O.C. No.2   4 O.C. No.3
  5 O.C. No.4   6 OM.
  7 T.O.   8 Sig. Off.
  9 Adjt   10 R.S.M.
 11 File.

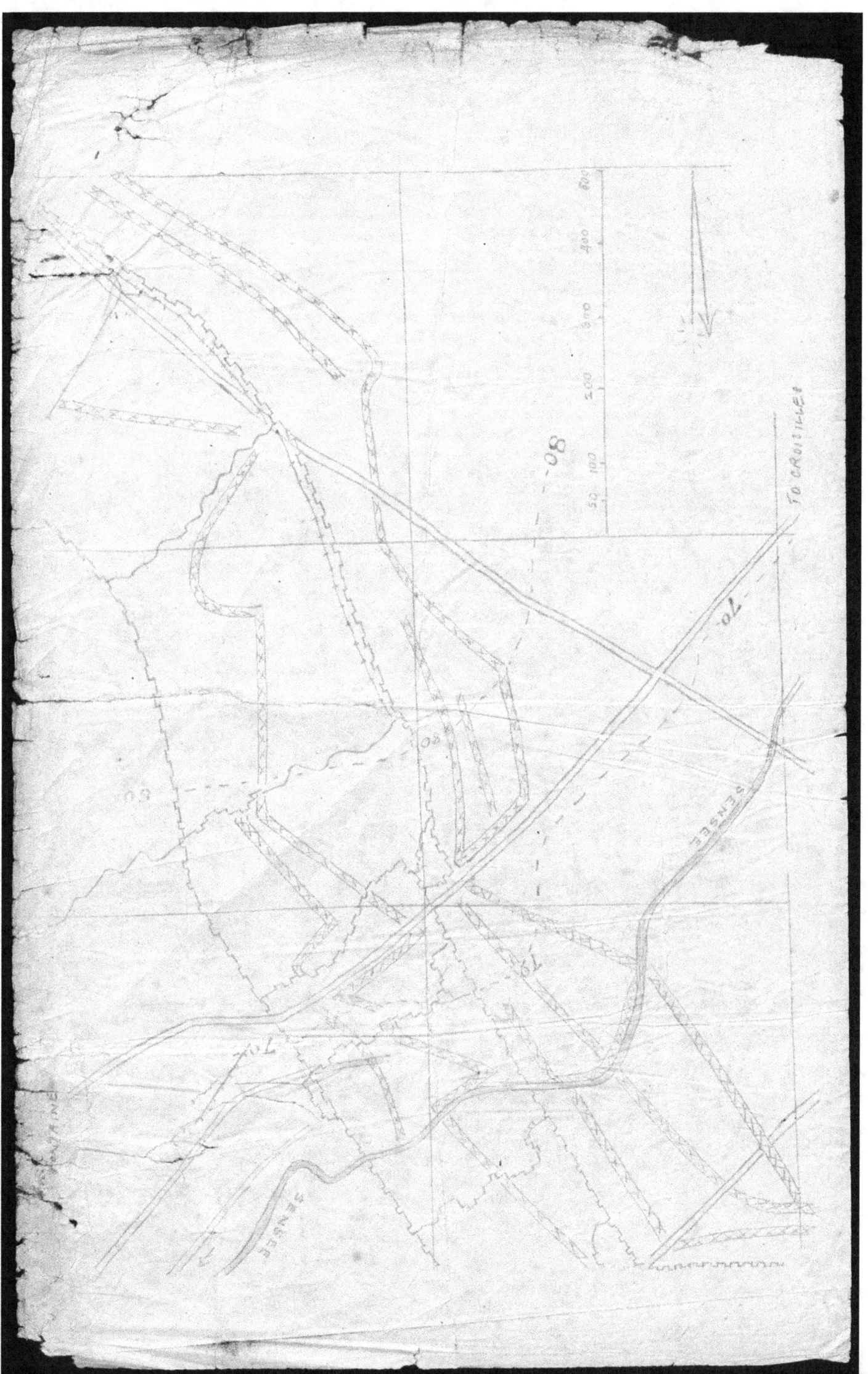

SECRET.   Operation Orders No: 1.
              by Lieut: Col: L.M. CROFTS, D.S.O.
              Comdg: Bn: The Queen's Regiment   Copy No: 12
                                                                 Sunday 22nd April 1917.

1. The Battn: will occupy and consolidate 1st & 2nd German Lines S.W. of FONTAINE, between the RIVER SENSEE and CONTOUR 80 at ZERO on 23rd inst.
2. The Battn: will be under the command of Major T. WEEDING.
3. Starting Point — CROSS ROADS by Battalion Headquarters.
4. Coys will march at 5 minutes interval in following order "D" "A" "C" "B", the leading Coy passing Battn. H.Q. at 7.30pm and march via MAISON ROUGE FARM to Cross Roads at T.27.A.1.7. where Coys will form up off the road and issue 2 bandoliers to all, except machine gun & Bombing platoons — All men will carry two bombs each.
5. From this point Coys will march with platoons at 100 yds interval to ASSEMBLY POINT at QUARRY at T.18.d.9.7.
6. Guides from 2nd Worcesters will meet Battn: at T.27.A.1.7.
7. 2 Coys of 16th K.R.Rs are attached to the Battn. and will join Battn at T.27.A.1.7. at 9.0 pm.
8. Mules will be provided to carry bags of Bombs & boxes of reserve ammunition to ASSEMBLY POINT.
9. Cocoa will be provided at ASSEMBLY POINT about 1.20am.
10. Tools will be issued at ASSEMBLY POINT.
11. At 1½ hours before ZERO, companies will move in succession to PLACE OF DEPLOYMENT on CROISSELLES – FONTAINE Road. 250 yards from Bridge at T.18.b.5.3. where tapes to mark each wave will be laid down — 150 yards on each side of road — Coys will deploy here & lie down.
12. Coys will be in two waves each at 50 yards interval, the "moppers up" of "C" & "B" following the leading waves of "D" & "A".
13. 1 Section R.E. will follow on flanks of last waves of "THE QUEEN'S".
14. 2 Coys 16th K.R.R's carrying ammunition etc, will follow the last wave of "THE QUEEN'S" at 100 yds distance. One Coy on each side of road in similar formation to "THE QUEEN'S".
15. Magazines will be charged before leaving bivouacs with NO round in chamber. Bayonets will be fixed at place of deployment.
16. At 20 minutes before ZERO, the whole will move forward marching by the road and will lie down on leading wave reaching bank running thro' V.7.d.4. which will be picketted during night by 2nd Worcesters Regt.
17. Table of Artillery Barrage attached.
18. At ZERO, waves will move forward and must be within 80 yards of Barrage at moment it lifts from front trench. i.e. 8 minutes after ZERO.
19. Objectives "D" Coy, the German Support Line, South of the Road exclusive to the junction at V.7.d.6.7. inclusive.
    "C" Coy, the Communication Trench (unfinished) from V.7.d.6.7. (exclusive) to V.7.d.0.5. (inclusive).
    "A" Coy, the German Support Line, North of the Road, (inclusive), to junction with river at V.7.b.1.7. (inclusive)
    "B" Coy, the Line of the river from V.7.b.1.7 (exclusive) to V.7.A.3.5. (inclusive)
    K.R.R.s   German Front Line.
    R.E.   Outer flank of German Support Line.
20. The line will be consolidated immediately by construction of Strong Points. Bombing parties must be pushed forward along all trenches without delay. Blocks are to be made in the trenches & tunnel blown in well beyond the points to be held.
21. The K.R.R's will form a F.O. Ammunition dump in front line.
22. Detachments of "A" & "B" Coys are to push forward North from the river to the line of the communication trench from V.7.A.7.6. to V.7.b.1.8. and consolidate this as soon as the blockhouse at V.7.A.6.7. has been reduced.
23. Two tanks will co-operate with Battn moving on right of the attack & will then turn north up the enemy's lines to the SENSEE RIVER.
    It is to be clearly understood that the assaulting infantry are on no account to await the arrival of the tanks, but carry out their assault as laid down entirely independently without them. Only signal to be used to tanks will be helmet raised on rifle indicating "TANK WANTED".
    Two other tanks will accompany the attack of 18th Bde from the North.

                        Continued on Sheet 2.

Sheet 2. of Operation Order No 1.   22.4.17

23. Battn: H.Q. will be in small pit near Bridge at T.18.b.5.3.
24. Battn. Aid Post in Quarry at T.18.d.9.7.
25. Wounded to remain in our lines until Bde on left has cleared hills to the north — Walking Wounded will proceed by bed of SENSEE RIVER
26. Prisoners when sent back must be under escort to M.P. on road between CROISSELLES & ST. LEGER.
27. A Contact Aeroplane, marked by one black band under right lower plane with streamers behind the band will be in the air during the attack Front line & Blocks will light flares when called up by aeroplane on claxton horn. Flares will also be lit at ZERO + 1½ hrs & ZERO + 1½ hours at extreme right & left of position gained.
28. Signal flags will be waved by Infantry on reaching objectives but will not be stuck in the ground.
29. Only 1/20,000, 51. B. S.W. MAPS will be carried by Officers.
30. A watch for synchronization will be sent to O.C. "The QUEEN'S" at 12 m.n. 22nd/23rd.
31. 4 Machine Guns will be pushed forward as soon as position has been captured.

R.H. Nevins.
2/Lieut: & Adjt.
Bn. The Queen's Regt.

Issued at 1.0 pm 22nd inst.
Copies to:
1. O.C. A Coy
2. O.C. B Coy
3. O.C. C Coy
4. O.C. D Coy
5. K.R.R's
6.
7. R.E.
8. Major T. WEEDING
9. Capt. F. GODFREY
10. Office
11. Spare
12 War Diary

WAR DIARY or INTELLIGENCE SUMMARY

APRIL 1917

1st Batt. "THE QUEEN'S" REGT.

REPORT ON OPERATIONS — 23rd APRIL 1917. — Ref Map 51B.S.W. 1/20000.

The Battalion had orders to attack and hold the 1st and 2nd Line of the HINDENBURG LINE for about 400 yards to the SOUTH of the SENSÉE RIVER in conjunction with an attack by the 98th Brigade from the NORTH.

Two Companies 16th K.R.R. Corps and No. 222 Field Coy. R.E. were attached to the Battalion which was under the command of Major T. WEEDING.

Two TANKS were attached to Brigade with the Battalion.

The Battalion passed HAMELINCOURT at 7.30 p.m. on 22nd, and picked up extra ammunition, tools, and Bombs at a point near JUDAS FARM and reached the Line of Assembly in the Quarry at T.17.d.9.7 at 11.3 p.m. Troops were disturbed 20 per Company and not over were known not at 2.0 a.m. 23rd Instant.

At 3.30 a.m. the Battalion moved off to the assembly point in front of Deployment — 300 yards N.E. of Ridge T.18.b.5.3 — and deployed on a front of 300 yards on tapes previously laid out 150 yards on each side of the CROISILLES — FONTAINE road.

The first two Waves were commanded of "D" Coy. was Captain R BRODHURST-HILL, the Right of the road and "A" Coy. Lieut. and Lieut. L.H.J. CARPENTER, on Left of road; forming up. "B" and "C" Coys forming a 3rd Line to first Wave Tanks

WAR DIARY or INTELLIGENCE SUMMARY

Army Form C. 2118.

APRIL 1917

1st Batt. "THE QUEEN'S" REGT.

Place	Date	Hour	Summary of Events and Information	Remarks and references to Appendices

REPORT ON OPERATIONS – 23RD APRIL 1917 – continued :–

The 3rd and 4th Waves at distance of 50 yards were composed of "C" Coy under Captain P. BALL, on Right and "B" Coy under 2nd Lieut. J. HOLLIDAY, on left with ½ Section of R.E. on each flank of 2nd Line.

The 5th and 6th Waves were composed of the Carpiquet 16th K.R.R Corps at distance of 100 yards carrying extra ammunition and bombs.

Battalion H.Qrs. were to have established at 7.15.b.8.9.

Carpiquet on German Line was under command of Captain F. GODFREY.

DESCRIPTION OF COUNTRY :–

1000 yards of open country along the Valley of the SENSEE River, which is only a slightly advancing slope with a very small glimpse of cover not commanded generally from the high ground on each side. The FRONT German Trench was protected by at least two rows of barbed wire radiating from where Trench crosses the Road, not it more thick wire between 1st and 2nd Line. The German Front Line Trench was much knocked about and for the most part not more than 4 feet deep. It was enfiladed from the NORTH.

PLAN OF ATTACK. — At 10 minutes before ZERO the Force was to advance to the line of a Sunken Road crossing the CROISILLES–FONTAINE Road at U.7.c.u.u. which had been
 Detailed

Army Form C. 2118.

WAR DIARY
or
INTELLIGENCE SUMMARY

APRIL 1917

1st Batt: "THE QUEENS" REGT:

(Erase heading not required.)

REPORT ON OPERATIONS - 23rd APRIL 1917.

Picketted during the night by 2nd Batt: WORCESTER Regt, and there lie down and wait for "Barrage" to commence. "Barrage" was timed to dwell for 8 minutes on FRONT Line, 10 minutes on 2nd. Line and continue behind the 2nd Line until 90 minutes after ZERO by which time it was expected the 98th. Brigade would have joined up. "D" and "A" Companies were to cross the German 1st Line and occupy and consolidate the 2nd Line.

"C" Company was to form Blocks on Right of 1st Line and form a Defensive Flank along Communication Trench running through Contour 85.

"B" Company to form Blocks on the Left and Defensive Flank along the SENSEE River.

The two Companies 16th K.R.R. Corps to form a central dump of Bombs &c and to occupy and consolidate German 1st Line.

R.E. were to blow up and block each end of tunnel in German 2nd. Line when captured.

The two TANKS were to follow on the Right Flank of the Attack and work down to the Enemy's Lines towards the River.

At 4.15 a.m. Battalion advanced and moved in good order to Sunken Road and lay

WAR DIARY

APRIL 1917

Army Form C. 2118.

INTELLIGENCE SUMMARY

1st Battn: "THE QUEEN'S" REGT:

(Erase heading not required.)

(4)

Place	Date	Hour	Summary of Events and Information	Remarks and references to Appendices
			REPORT ON OPERATIONS – 23rd April 1917 – Continued:–	

lay down to await ZERO – fixed for 4.45 a.m. – without being detected by the Enemy.
The Attack started punctually at 4.45 a.m. and worked up to within 50 yards of the "Barrage" entering the Front Trench with few casualties. This contained only a few Germans who were quickly disposed of.
The leading Companies pushed forward towards the German 2nd Line but was held up by very strong wire which was uncut and the "Barrage" on lifting was taken too far back and noted beyond instead of on the 2nd Line and Enemy were able to man their parapet – Our men took cover in shell holes between the two lines. A small party of "A" Coy only reached the 2nd Line.
The two TANKS which by now should have arrived never turned up having broken down before ZERO.
Two telephone lines were laid along the SENSEE River and communication to Battalion Headquarters was kept up till 5.50 a.m. when wires were cut and all attempts afterwards to repair them failed.
The Line to Brigade Headquarters went at 5.4 a.m. and communication from then onwards had to be kept up by runners.
In the German 1st Line on the Right of the Road two "Strong Points" were captured and bombing parties pushed 100 yards beyond Communication Trench at Cotout

80

WAR DIARY or INTELLIGENCE SUMMARY

Army Form C. 2118.

APRIL 1917

1st Batt. "THE QUEEN'S" REGT.

REPORT ON OPERATIONS — 23rd APRIL 1917 — continued —

So until held up by another "Strong Point" and a double block was made and Post established in Communication Trench. These blocks were maintained until 11.0 a.m. when Germans made a determined attack with Rifle Grenades and Bombs but were driven back by parties under C.S. Major ELDERKIN. In the left a block was first made at the River but on the "Box Barrage" lifting the Enemy attacked and were repulsed with Rifle Grenades and the party under Corporal Spooner following them up for 450 yards captured a concrete Block-House and Machine Gun which on Enemy again attacking was blown up with a bomb. A Block was then made 50 yards from the Blockhouse and held till the end. The First Line soon became blocked with wounded and it was difficult to pass bombs to threatened points — and bombing was incessant at quite 5 points.

At 5.8 a.m. 2nd Lieut. HOLLIDAY telephoned that 1st Line letters but 2nd strongly held by Germans and no tanks had arrived.

At 5.25 a.m. 5 prisoners of 99th Regt were brought back.

At 7.10 a.m. 2nd Lieut CARPENTER arrived at Battalion Headquarters wounded and reported the Battalion was running out of Bombs. This was confirmed by a message from Captain GODFREY, timed 6.45 a.m., reporting shortage of bombs

WAR DIARY APRIL 1917
INTELLIGENCE SUMMARY
1st Bn. "THE QUEEN'S" REGT:

Army Form C. 2118.

⑥

REPORT ON OPERATIONS - 23rd APRIL 1917 - Continued.

bombs and L.G Ammunition and that situation was critical.
Parties from the two Reserve Companies 16th K.R.R.C. in the Quarry took up nearly 1500 bombs during next few hours.
At 10.10 am Captain GODFREY reported that advance of 98th Brigade had relieved the pressure — that casualties were heavy but men cheery and confident — more L.G ammunition and bombs wanted.
At 12.20 pm Captain GODFREY reported Enemy massing with repeated bombing attacks and supply of bombs getting low.
At 1.20 pm the last carrying party of 9 men of 2nd Bn Worcester Regt. with 800 bombs went up but before they reached the line the Enemy commenced strong bombing attacks from 15 different points.
At 1.45 pm the Germans moved on the right and rushed the Works under a "barrage" of Aerial Torpedoes and Rifle Grenades. the bombs at this point having given out.
The pressure of the Enemy on the Right Flank forced a retirement and the men in the Central Communication Trenches were cut off.
Many casualties occurred during this retirement. The men were rallied at Battalion Headquarters. From 3 pm the Quarry and Valley were heavily shelled and many casualties caused.

Continued

WAR DIARY / INTELLIGENCE SUMMARY

Army Form C. 2118.

1/1th THE QUEENS' REGT.

APRIL 1917

REPORT ON OPERATIONS – 23rd APRIL 1917 – continued

At 8 p.m. orders were received to move back to Railway Cutting near JUDAS FARM. During this action the Battalion was ably assisted by the 16th K.R.R.C. who performed valuable work in bringing up bombs and ammunition across the open under heavy fire and suffered severe casualties.

The Section R.E. also had many casualties, both Officers being wounded and one partly blown up by explosion of their cartridges.

The retirement was caused by the following:–

1. Failure of the 62nd Brigade to come up.
2. Non-appearance of the Tanks.
3. The fire being incessant between our and German lines.
4. The difficulty in keeping up the supply of bombs &c.

and following casualties occurred.

Officers Killed:– 2nd Lieuts: D. E. H. MILLARD, FOWLER, BURGHOPE.
Wounded:– 2nd Lieuts: H. J. CARPENTER, F. T. BOWER.
Missing:– Captains F. GODFREY, F. S. BALL, R. BRODHURST-HILL, 2nd Lieuts O. V. BOTTON, S. HOLLIDAY, R. S. WALKER, G. F. S. JACOBS, H. M. THOMPSON. (wounded).

2nd Lieut. H. R. LACEY was the only Officer who got back unwounded from the German line.

Other Ranks – Killed 26. Wounded 101. Missing 208.

Continued

Army Form C. 2118.

WAR DIARY APRIL 1917
or
INTELLIGENCE SUMMARY.

(Erase heading not required.)

1st Batt. "THE QUEEN'S REGT:"

Place	Date	Hour	Summary of Events and Information	Remarks and references to Appendices
			REPORT ON OPERATIONS – 23rd APRIL 1917 – CONTINUED:-	
			The following Messages "received and "sent" are appended.	
			From Brigade – Messages 1st B.M. 4. 5 and 6.	
			From Captain F. GODFREY – Messages Timed. 6.45 am 10.10 am 12.20 pm. 12.23 pm	
			SENT:-	
			N 63. 64. 65. 65A. 66. 68. 69. 70. 71. 72. 72A. 73. 74.	
			Also Maps enlarged from Air Photographs.	
			[signature] Lieut Colonel	
			Comdg: 1st Battn "THE QUEEN'S" Regt	
	30.4.17.			

"A" Form.
MESSAGES AND SIGNALS.

Army Form C.2121 (in pads of 100).

TO — FRUGAL

Sender's Number.	Day of Month.	In reply to Number.	
N 74	23.		A A A

Your BM 6 received aaa Everything possible is being done aaa Enemy firing harder especially the last two arriving bunched together badly sustaining casualties aaa. Gaffey reports Enemy pressing with repeated Bombing attacks which have been successfully repulsed aaa Carrying party just arrived has been sent up aaa.

From Place — FURNACE

Time —

"A" Form.
MESSAGES AND SIGNALS.

Army Form C.2121
(in pads of 100).
No. of Message _____

Prefix .... Code .... m.	Words	Charge	This message is on a/c of:	Recd. at .... m.
Office of Origin and Service Instructions.				Date ....
	Sent		.... Service.	From ....
	At .... m.			
	To			
	By		(Signature of "Franking Officer.")	By ....

TO — FROGAL

| Sender's Number. | Day of Month. | In reply to Number. | AAA |
| N 68 | 23 | | |

The attack started well the first line being captured with few casualties. Several German dead in first line.
The Barrage was not properly on 2nd line but beyond it — the Enemy were consequently manning the parapet, the situation is obscure as to whether we have penetrated Support line at any point.
Six prisoners have been sent back.
Supply of Bombs is being rapidly used up as a continual bombing fight is being fought, consequently unless get your hands soon it will be necessary to eg send up Bombs.
One of the Reserve Coys of GALLIC has been used to carry up Bombs.

Continued

From
Place
Time

The above may be forwarded as now corrected. (Z)

Censor. Signature of Addressor or person authorised to telegraph in his name.
* This line should be erased if not required.

"A" Form.
MESSAGES AND SIGNALS.

Army Form C.2121 (in pads of 100).

Prefix .... Code .... m.	Words	Charge	This message is on a/c of:	Recd. at .... m.
Office of Origin and Service Instructions.	Sent		.... Service.	Date ....
	At .... m.			From ....
	To			
	By		(Signature of "Franking Officer.")	By ....

TO

Sender's Number.	Day of Month.	In reply to Number.	
68	Continued		A A A

I would suggest that an Artillery Box Barrage be arranged should the second Reserve Coy of Hedge C have to be again sent up with Bombs. aaa Later reports confirm that we have no one in German Front line and heavy Barrage required at once aaa.

From
Place: FURNACE
Time:

The above may be forwarded as now corrected. (Z)

"A" Form.
MESSAGES AND SIGNALS.
Army Form C.2121 (in pads of 100).

Prefix ...... Code ...... m.	Words	Charge	This message is on a/c of:	Recd. at ...... m.
Office of Origin and Service Instructions.	Sent		.... Service.	Date ....
	At ...... m.			From ....
	To		(Signature of "Franking Officer.")	By ....
	By			

TO { FURNACE

Sender's Number.	Day of Month.	In reply to Number.	
* BM.5	23rd		AAA

Message for Brigadier begins If you can ascertain definitely second line is still untaken by us I will order crushing barrage to be put on it for ten minutes starting at 4.30 a.m. when it must be rushed aaa Try and remind Infantry to use white VERY LIGHTS to indicate lengthen range aaa Barrage will not be put on at 4.30 a.m. unless I hear from you aaa ends

R.A. Newton

From
Place
Time

"A" Form. Army Form C.2121
MESSAGES AND SIGNALS.

TO: Captain Godfrey

Sender's Number: N 69
Day of Month: 23rd
AAA

Reference attached Message (BM 5) from Brigadier — The Barrage will be put on at 4.30 a.m. after which you will rush the second line and should any of your men be in second line they are to be withdrawn in time to escape Barrage as

From Place Time: 4. 10 a.m.

"A" Form.
MESSAGES AND SIGNALS.

Army Form C.2121 (in pads of 100).

TO: Captain Godfrey

Sender's Number: N70
Day of Month: 23rd

AAA

Message from Bde begins Situation of Left Brigade as follows aaa 12th Suffolks Regt Battalion 9th Bde are within 200x of SENSEE river in the HINDENBURG SUPPORT LINE aaa Que. A & B Coys and 1/ Middlesex have gained objectives and TANK is proceeding down Southwards above Hindenburg Line towards SENSEE RIVER aaa

From: G. Staff

"A" Form.
MESSAGES AND SIGNALS.

Army Form C.2121 (in pads of 100). No. of Message ....

Prefix .... Code .... m.	Words	Charge	This message is on a/c of:	Recd. at .... m.
Office of Origin and Service Instructions.	Sent		.... Service.	Date ....
....	At .... m.			From ....
....	To			
....	By	(Signature of "Franking Officer.")	By ....

TO — FRUGAL.

Sender's Number.	Day of Month.	In reply to Number.	
* N71	23rd	BM 5	AAA

I have told Captain Jeffrey that the Barrage will be put on at 11.30am and ordered him to rush Support line as I am told we have no men in Support Line but have instructed Jeffrey should there be any to withdraw them in time before Barrage ends

From Place — FURNACE
Time — 9.55am

(Z) RHM

The above may be forwarded as now corrected.
Censor. Signature of Addressor or person authorised to telegraph in his name.

* This line should be erased if not required.

"A" Form.
MESSAGES AND SIGNALS.

Army Form C.2121 (in pads of 100).
No. of Message ....

Prefix .... Code .... m.	Words	Charge	This message is on a/c of:	Recd. at .... m.
Office of Origin and Service Instructions.				Date ....
	Sent		.... Service.	From ....
	At .... m.			
	To			
	By		(Signature of "Franking Officer.")	By ....

TO: Capt Godfrey

Sender's Number.	Day of Month.	In reply to Number.	
N 72	30		AAA

Ref Barrage at 11.30 a.m.
Divl Artillery also contemplates
a Bombardment. Suit if you
from 11.0 to 12 noon as it will
interfere with the other arrangements. Will
let you know later

From
Place: 11 Bar.
Time: 11.30 a.m.

Nevill

The above may be forwarded as now corrected. (Z)
Censor. Signature of Addresser or person authorised to telegraph in his name.
* This line should be erased if not required.

"A" Form.
MESSAGES AND SIGNALS.
Army Form C.2121 (in pads of 100).

TO: FRUGAL

Sender's Number: N72A.
Day of Month: 23

AAA

Situation in the line continues very grave. The 98th Bde do not appear to be in touch with us yet. Bomb fighting is incessant and Bombs are expended at a greater rate than we can send up.

An officer i/c carrying party just returned reported enemy attacking from both sides and that the bombs had been practically finished when he arrived. I think that continuous Artillery Support is absolutely necessary and probably another Battalion for carrying parties.

Place: FURNACE
Time: 10.35 pm

(Z) R.S. N___

"A" Form.
MESSAGES AND SIGNALS.

Army Form C.2121 (in pads of 100).

TO — ~~Frost~~ Godfrey

Sender's Number: N 73
Day of Month: 23rd

Practically no men left for carrying parties. Can you spare any aaa they should move along N side of FONTAINE - CROISILLES Road aaa moving in very small parties aaa

Time: 12.42pm

From: R.J. ...

"A" Form.
MESSAGES AND SIGNALS.
Army Form C. 2121 (in pads of 100).

SECRET

TO FURNACE

Sender's Number: *BM 4. Day of Month: 23/4. AAA

Situation of left Bde as follows. aaa 4th Suffolks Right Batty 98th B are within 200x of SENSEE on in the HINDENBURG support line aaa 2 Kaskand 1/Hudd have gained objectives aaa BG has asked for barrage to be put on for five minutes from 17 d 8 1 - FONTAINE - CROISILLES road aaa on enemy's support line aaa The remaining coy GANNIC is at your disposal aaa Please inform OC Gallic aaa Please report what action if any is taken aaa Tank is proceeding down Southwards above Hindenburg line towards SENSEE River aaa

From
Place Frugal
Time 8.40am

"A" Form.
MESSAGES AND SIGNALS.

Army Form C. 2121 (in pads of 100)

SECRET

TO: FURNACE

Sender's Number	Day of Month	In reply to Number	
BM 5	23/4		A A A

If you can ascertain definitely second line is still untaken by us. I will order intense barrage to be put on it for ten minutes starting at 11.30 a.m. when it must be rushed aaa Try and remind infantry to use white Very lights to indicate eighteen range. aaa Barrage will not be put on 11.30 a.m. unless I hear from you aaa

From Place:
Time: 9.0 am

Frugal

H. White Paul Capt

"A" Form.
MESSAGES AND SIGNALS.

Army Form C. 2121 (in pads of 100).

TO Furnace

Sender's Number: * BM 6.
Day of Month: 23/4

AAA

Use every endeavour to keep line supplied with bombs by sending forward small parties carrying them as received They should keep along N side of FONTAINE - CROISILLES road aaa Strong bombing fight appears to be going on in front line at U7c 9.8 aaa Acknowledge aaa

Ack RJM

From / Place / Time: 12.7 pm Frugal

FURNACE

No:

Situation somewhat doubtful
but reports point that
we did not get Second
Line –

Reports show shortage
of Bombs & L.G Ammn.
Enemy endevouring to
Bomb us out of our
position.
Situation Critical.

8-45 am   GODFREY

The Attack started well. The first line being captured with few casualties. Several Germans staying behind to man the Barrage was not taken on 2nd line but beyond it. The enemy were consequently manning the parapet. The situation is obscure. Supply of bombs is being rapidly used up as a continual bombing fight is being fought. Consequently unless 98th join hands soon it will be necessary again to send up bombs.

One of the Reserve Coys of C.A.L.L.C. has already been used to carry up bombs.

I would suggest that an artillery box barrage be arranged should the second Coy G.A.L.L.C. have to be sent up with bombs.

FURNACE

SITUATION 10-10 a.m.

Quieter and pressure not so great.

We are only in Enemy front-line from C trench at 80 Contour to within 100ˣ of RIVER.

The advance of 98th Bde has undoubtedly relieved pressure here.

Our Casualties are heavy I fear.

Troops quite cheery and confident.

If called upon to beat off counter attack I hope to be able to make a good show.

Ammunition for Lewis Guns ought to be replenished if possible —

Further supply of Grenades wanted.

GODFREY

FURNACE

SITUATION 12-20

Enemy are pressing with repeated Bombing attacks, which have been successfully repulsed, but our Supply of Grenades are again at a very figure.

If pressure continues it will be difficult to keep them at Bay until Evening. Send Bombs, urgent.

Can you run out a new telephone wire from your End.

GODFREY

FURNACE   12-23 pm

Reference Generals order to rush
Enemy Support line,
I regret that owing to
Circumstance it was
absolutely impossible,
I am no longer able
to carry on an offensive
action,

GODFREY

"A" Form.
MESSAGES AND SIGNALS.
Army Form C.2121
(In pads of 100).
No. of Message ....

Prefix .... Code .... m.	Words	Charge	This message is on a/c of:	Recd. at .... m.
Office of Origin and Service Instructions.	Sent			Date ....
....	At .... m.		.... Service.	From ....
....	To			By ....
....	By		(Signature of "Franking Officer.")	

TO — FRUGAL

| Sender's Number. | Day of Month. | In reply to Number. | A A A |
| * N.63 | 23 | . | |

Our Machine Guns opened half minute before ZERO

From
Place — FURNACE
Time

The above may be forwarded as now corrected. (Z)   R H Nevin /Lt

Censor.   Signature of Addressor or person authorised to telegraph in his name.

* This line should be erased if not required.

"A" Form.
Army Form C.2121
(in pads of 100).

MESSAGES AND SIGNALS.

No. of Message _____

Prefix .... Code .... m. | Words | Charge | This message is on a/c of: | Recd. at .... m.
Office of Origin and Service Instructions. | | | | Date ....
_____ | Sent | | _____ Service. | From _____
_____ | At .... m. | | |
_____ | To _____ | | (Signature of "Franking Officer.") | By _____
| By _____ | | |

TO { FRUGAL

* Sender's Number: N6w | Day of Month: 23D | In reply to Number: | AAA

At Zero plus 20 no reports received

From
Place: Furnace
Time

The above may be forwarded as now corrected. (Z)

Censor. | Signature of Addressor or person authorised to telegraph in his name.
* This line should be erased if not required.

"A" Form.
MESSAGES AND SIGNALS.
Army Form C.2121 (in pads of 100).
No. of Message ....

Prefix ...... Code ...... m.	Words	Charge	This message is on a/c of:	Recd. at ...... m.
Office of Origin and Service Instructions.	Sent		.... Service.	Date ......
	At ...... m.			From ......
	To			
	By		(Signature of "Franking Officer.")	By ......

TO — FRUGAL

Sender's Number.	Day of Month.	In reply to Number.	
N 65	23		A A A

Verbal Report received from wounded we are in first line

From
Place — 5.0am Furnace
Time

Signature of Addressor or person authorised to telegraph in his name. R.H. Kennell?

"A" Form.
MESSAGES AND SIGNALS.

Army Form C.2121
(in pads of 100).
No. of Message _____

Prefix .... Code .... m.	Words	Charge	This message is on a/c of:	Recd. at .... m.
Office of Origin and Service Instructions.	Sent		................Service.	Date ....
....	At .... m.			From ....
....	To			By ....
....	By	(Signature of "Franking Officer.")		

TO { FRUGAL

| Sender's Number. | Day of Month. | In reply to Number. | AAA |
| N65A | 23rd | | |

One Company Commander reports
front line taken but was strongly
held

From: 5.8am
Place: Frankins Lt adjt
Time:

The above may be forwarded as now corrected. (Z)

Censor. Signature of Addresser or person authorised to telegraph in his name.
* This line should be erased if not required.

"A" Form.
MESSAGES AND SIGNALS.
Army Form C.2121 (in pads of 100).
No. of Message ....

Prefix .... Code .... m.	Words	Charge	This message is on a/c of:	Recd. at .... m.
Office of Origin and Service Instructions.				Date ....
....	Sent		.... Service.	From ....
....	At .... m.			
....	To			
....	By	(Signature of "Franking Officer.")	By ....

TO { KROG R B

Sender's Number.	Day of Month.	In reply to Number.	
* N 66	23rd		A A A

First line trenches aaa wounded men report help regarding second line aaa. All lines back are disturbed aaa Report sent by pigeon to LENA aaa line also taken but it is not confirmed aaa prisoners are from 99th Regt aaa

From
Place: FURNACE
Time:

The above may be forwarded as now corrected. (Z) R.J. Nevis Capt.
Censor. Signature of Addresser or person authorised to telegraph in his name.
* This line should be erased if not required.

1. Queens R.
MAY 1917
Army Form C. 2118.
16 1/R.W.S
Vol 31

WAR DIARY
INTELLIGENCE SUMMARY.
(Erase heading not required.)

Place	Date	Hour	Summary of Events and Information	Remarks and references to Appendices
BERLES AU BOIS	1st		Battalion marched to BLAIREVILLE (accommodated in bivouacs) via RANSART. 2nd Lieuts J.E. SHIPTON and J.M. HOWCROFT and 63 other ranks joined from Divl. Depot. Battalion Officers + N.C.Os received instruction at night in marching by Compass and study of Stars. Orders received Battalion would march to BOIRY ST MARTIN about 11pm tomorrow. 2nd Lieuts J.S. MILNER and PLOWMAN BROWN and two OR. reported from attachment to 100th T.M. BATTERY.	
BLAIRE-VILLE	2nd		Specialist at Tactical work – general routine. Battalion marched at 1pm. via HENDICOURT to BOIRY ST MARTIN (occupying bivouacs). Under 1 hour notice to move.	
BOIRY ST MARTIN	3rd		Training and general routine – Battalion remained under 1 hour notice to move.	
"	4th		Training and general routine – Battalion under 4 hour notice to move. Divisional Conference held at 11am. at which all officers attended.	
"	5th		Training and general routine – remained under 4 hour notice to move.	
"	6th		Training and general routine – Church Parade – remained under 4 hour notice to move.	

Army Form C. 2118.

WAR DIARY
or
INTELLIGENCE SUMMARY.
(Erase heading not required.)

MAY 1917 (2) 1st Battn. THE QUEEN'S Regt.

Place	Date	Hour	Summary of Events and Information	Remarks and references to Appendices
BOIRY-ST MARTIN	7th		Training and general routine. Remained under 6 hours notice to move. Moved to H.HAYNES joined on appointment (commanded from ranks — 2nd Batn)	
"	8th		Training and general routine. Remained under 6 hours notice to move.	
"	9th		Training and general routine. Battalion Entertainment stood to at 5pm.	
"	10th		Training and general routine. Tactical Exercise cancelled - Batn moved fwd - Battalion will relieve 8th LEICESTERS - Brigade relieving 110th Inf. Bde on Right. Scots - 21st Divisional Front on 7th and night 11th/12th.	
"	11th		Battalion moved forward in Brigade support relieving 8th Bn. Leicestershire Regt in bivouacs in T.23.a. Relief completed 6.20 p.m.	
Near CROISILLES (T.22.a)	12th		Battalion remained in Brigade Support.	
"	13th		Battalion remained in Brigade Support, 2/Lt K.A.FRAZER & 25 O.R. & No 222 Coy R.E. (Field) /m attached during demonstration in Front line.	
"	14th		Battalion remained in Brigade Support. One platoon under 2nd Lt L.P.SMITH, at 9.45 p.m. went forward to reconnoitre Hindenburg line S. of the CROISILLES - FONTAINE Road in U.7.d. and F.K.9773.M.657. 75/7050.Pn.9141. Returned 11.5 p.m. and reported FRONT line (German)	

WAR DIARY MAY 1917

INTELLIGENCE SUMMARY of Both "THE QUEEN'S" REGT.

Army Form C. 2118.

Place	Date	Hour	Summary of Events and Information	Remarks and references to Appendices
Near CROISILLES (T.22.a)	14th (continued)		unoccupied and almost unrecognisable. Wire no obstacle. Advanced to within about 200 yds of 2nd Line which was observed to be strongly held. Many lights were sent up including Red Lights. Patrol was fired on and Enemy endeavoured to outflank it. Patrol withdrew. Casualties One O.R. slightly wounded (at duty).	
"	15th		Orders received Battalion would be relieved the afternoon by 2nd R. W. Surrey. Relief commenced 4 p.m. completed 4.45 p.m. Battalion marched to MOYENNEVILLE into bivouac.	
MOYENNEVILLE	16th		Orders received Battalion to take over found Posts of 1st Cameronians in T.19 and 18 and furnish carrying parties to a strength of 6 officers 120 O.R. in view of operations to take place on 17th. At 6 p.m. Orders received stating operations were postponed until 20th Inst. Troops will remain in present area. 2/Lieut K A FRAZER wounded whilst employed with 222 Field Coy R.E.	
"	17th		Training and general routine. Visited by Corps Commander Lt Gen Sir T. D'O SNOW K.C.B, K.C.M.G.	
"	18		Training and general Routine. at 1.15 p.m Battalion formed into two Companies paraded (continued)	

Army Form C. 2118.

WAR DIARY
INTELLIGENCE SUMMARY.
(Erase heading not required.)

1st Bn "THE QUEEN'S" Regt.

MAY 1917

Place	Date	Hour	Summary of Events and Information	Remarks and references to Appendices
MOYENNE- VILLE	18th Continued		and marched to high ground ½ mile W. of village where Brigade formed up in Hollow Square where Medal Ribbons were presented to NCOs and men by the Corps Commander as follows. 3710 Pte S. HAZZARD. 5400 Pte A.E. RAY. 189 Pte F. WARE. 9558 Sergt G. FIELDER. 5408 L/Cpl J. CLEGG. 5203 " C. BARNES. 1006 L/Sgt P. TERRY. 8825 Sergt R. WALKER. 18850 Pte G. GILLESBY. 11039 Pte J. DEADMAN. BAR to MILITARY MEDAL:- 10683 Sergt A. SPOONER. 3710 L/Sergt W. HARRIS. After the inspection the Corps Commander addressed the men - Speech delivered by Lieut Gen. T.D'O. SNOW K.C.B., K.C.M.G. was approximately as follows:- "I don't think you will hear me very much as I would say much. I always " needs to meet brave men and to present " on such, to be noticed for their gallantry. You are all brave men but everyone has not the chance " have won the V.C. Now a days we give the military medal to men of stamp " singled out amongst you for doing things which in former days would " the V.C. would have been given not many years ago. These men in " years to come can show their children and their children's " children, the medals they won in the great war and they will be " proud to hear the story of what their fathers did for their Country. Continued.	" " " " " " " " " " " " " " " "

Army Form C. 2118.

WAR DIARY MAY 1917
INTELLIGENCE SUMMARY
of 1st Batt. "THE QUEEN'S" Regt.

(Erase heading not required.)

Place	Date	Hour	Summary of Events and Information	Remarks and references to Appendices
			"In a few days, on Sunday or Monday, you are going over the parapet to attack the Hindenburg Line — you — the 100th Bde., the 1st Queens, and 16 resistors 1st K.R.R. and Surgeon Highlanders. The rest of the Army is waiting to see what to be taken before they can get on. I hope I am sure that it will be all "won" for the Army. Commander that the 100th Bde has taken the Hindenburg Line and not only taken but held it. As long as you put "you nerve into it and consolidate at once and use your rifles "to shoot straight as sure as I am sitting on this horse no "darned German will come near you. "You have guts and grit on your side and are fighting "for liberty and freedom the German has nothing to fight for but his "damned self. "When you go over the parapet let your cry be 'FOR GOD — MY "COUNTRY and MY KING'"	
MINNERVILLE		9.R.	Training and general Routine. Orders received Battalion to move forward the evening in view of operations taking place tomorrow.	

WAR DIARY / INTELLIGENCE SUMMARY

Army Form C. 2118.

MAY 1917 (6)

1st Battn. "THE QUEEN'S" REGt

Place	Date	Hour	Summary of Events and Information	Remarks and references to Appendices
MOYENNEVILLE	19th (contd)		Move forward commenced at 7.30 p.m. and was disposed as follows. No. 2 Coy (B & D) & forward Pcts in 718(a) and (b). Coy H.Qrs 718.c.3.6. No. 7 Coy. (A and C) Reserve Pcts T.18.C.8.3. Three Carrying Partie were furnished to Battalions attacking on D.A. vy Nos to ASHPITEL and BAYNES and 40 o.R. 2/Lts. SCHOFIELD. 2/Lts. to BARNARD and HOWCROFT & 9th H.L.I. and 2nd Lts to KEMP and WATT and 40 o.R. to 16th K.R.R. Both N.B. at 7.23 A.S.W. in relief of 2nd R.N.F. Relief was completed at 12 a.m. and carrying parties with attacking Battalions H.Q. 7/8 by 2 a.m. Operation Orders received to the effect the Brigade is attacking MINDENBURG LINE at 5 a.m. between CROISILLE - FONTAINE Road and CROISILLE - HENDECOURT Road. 9th WORCESTERS, 9th H.L.I. and 16th K.R.R.C. Right to left in order namely a Battalion 19th Left Bde on Right of 9th WORCESTERS and the 93rd Bde Brigade attacking down MINDENBURG LINE from the North.	
CROISILLES vicinity of	20th		Attack commenced at 5 a.m. a small party (carrying) accompanied 9 WORCESTERS, & the parties went forward at intervals in small batches continuously until afternoon 2nd Carrying parts to 9th H.L.I. were sent up in two batches of 20 under an officer. (2/Lts. J.N.F. BARNARD and S.M. HOWCROFT) and half the men were wounded on their journey no journey was made. The part with 16th K.R.R.C. carried continuously in small parties of 2 or 3 until afternoon of 20th. The Stores taken to FRONT Line by these carrying parties included 55 Boxes S.A.A. 140 Boxes Bombs. 900 Sandbags. 100 Petrol Tins filled with water. 12 2ro gallons. 40 picks and Shovels, and 4 Boxes VERY Lights. The Casualties of Carrying parties were 2 officers (above mentioned) and 10 o.R. ranks. Continued	

Army Form C. 2118.

WAR DIARY
MAY 1917 (7)

INTELLIGENCE SUMMARY. 1st Bat: "THE QUEEN'S" Regt.
(Erase heading not required.)

Place	Date	Hour	Summary of Events and Information	Remarks and references to Appendices
CROISILLES vicinity	21		About 9 am Captain H.E. HARRISON brought up 5 hundred bombs, under with S.A.A. and bombs, at a gallop along the HENDICOURT Road and again about 12 noon & further, the latter journey necessitated passing through a heavy Enemy barrage – the horse he rode was the only casualty being slightly wounded. Captain R. BATTISCOMBE who wounded about noon. During afternoon Lieut to carrying parties and garrisons of forward posts were with most heroic work. Captain Headquarters trenches and Companies were reorganised – orders having been received that the Battalion was to take over that portion of the HINDENBURG LINE taken by 9th H.L.I. Relief commenced at 10 pm. No 2 Company (Captain R. FAULKNER) occupied line from BLOCKHOUSE at PLUM TRENCH to 2/RWF near NELLY LANE. No 1 Coy (2nd Lieut J. SMITHER) from PLUM TRENCH to just beyond BLOCKHOUSE at 07.05-55. Where 1st K.R.R.C. joined up, a front of about 170 yards. Relief was completed about 2.45 am. 22nd. Posts were pushed forward and a block established in PLUM TRENCH about 20 yards from the front. Consolidation went on apace covered by patrols etc.	
TRENCHES	22nd and 23rd		Rain fell during the early morning greatly hindering work on trenches. About midday work was continued and trenches were deepened & greatly improved. SAA sandbags &c were sent up across the open without detection by the Enemy. Orders received that Battalion would be relieved tonight. Representative of 5th N.F. reconnoitered line and relief commenced about midnight but owing to intense darkness was not completed until 2.50 am. Battalion proceeded to MOEUVRES-VILLE men being completed about 6 am. 2nd Lieut C.S. MEAD was wounded (1st July) during relief. Total Casualties – during period 20th to 23rd) were officers 4 wounded (1 at July). Other ranks.	

WAR DIARY

INTELLIGENCE SUMMARY.

Army Form C. 2118.

MAY 1917 (8)

2nd Batt^n "THE QUEEN'S" Reg^t

Place	Date	Hour	Summary of Events and Information	Remarks and references to Appendices
	23rd contd		Killed 9. Died of Wounds 2. Wounded 39. Wounded at Duty 1. Missing 8. Was recommended of German SECOND LINE was carried out during 22nd by 9238 Sergt H. JONES and 2677 Corporal E. BONSEY, much useful information was gained by these N.C.O.s The latter part of the day was good cleaning up. Lieut J. BURRELL joined from England took over Command of "A" Coy.	
MONTENESCOURT 24th			Cleaning up continued — Refitting — Inspection generally — Battalion paraded in the lines at 12.30 p.m. Brig. Genl A.W.F. BAIRD, C.M.G., D.S.O., addressed the Battalion mentioning it was the first opportunity of seeing the Battalion on parade to speak to them as a body. He stated how much he appreciates the great work done on 23rd April especially when the Battalion captured the HINDENBURG FRONT LINE and though task allotted was to do so until the troops working from the north joined up, what was to have been the case within 90 minutes — held this line for 7½ hours with both flanks in the air, regretted not being able to include them in attacking line on 28th April owing to numbers, but involved allotted portion (of carrying) to end of the attacking Battalions whose Commanding Officers had informed him to notes. good work done by them concluding by congratulating all officers men on their excellent work with the Battalion which was on the top of its form, which means when "The Queen's" was on the top of its form being any further doubt unnecessary.	

WAR DIARY

INTELLIGENCE SUMMARY

1st Batt "THE QUEEN'S" Regt

MAY 1917

Place	Date	Hour	Summary of Events and Information	Remarks and references to Appendices
MOYENNEVILLE	25th		Training and general routine – 2Lieuts H.J. TRYTHALL and S.F. PRIOR and 20 other ranks joined from Depot Battalion. Orders received Battalion would move forward tomorrow evening in relief of 20th Royal Fusiliers in T.22. Information received the F.M. Crosslyn-Shaw has received the Military Cross & Captain No 8667 C.S.M. M.ELDERKIN. Bath. 1st Coy C/134.pm 1 21.5.17 H.S. DRESING R.A.M.C. attached to 1st Battalion, and "K" Distinguished Conduct Medal to	
	26"		Training and General Routine – Battalion moved forward to CROISILLES T 98.C.2.5.6 and W of ST LEGER. Divisions reconnaissance attack on TUNNEL TRENCH on 27th. Moved commencing at 10.15 pm. Move Completed 12.45 am.	
W of ST LEGER T78 C2.5)	27"		Remained in forward Training carried out in vicinity of CROISILLES.	
"	28"		Received orders Battalion to relieve 2nd Batt "The Camerons" and 1 Coy 25th R Brunks. tonight – Major Scaling and Coy Commanders reconnoitred the during afternoon – Battalion moved forward by Platoon commencing at 9.30 pm. took over his from NELLY TRENCH to LONG LANE (U7 and 8) – Completed 1.15 am. 3 O.R. were wounded with the relief were carried out. Work in Trench was immediately started and continued until daybreak. Posts were established. The Dispositions were RIGHT FRONT No 2 (Band D Coys) under Capt R FAULKNER. LEFT FRONT	

Army Form C. 2118.

WAR DIARY
MAY 1917 (10)
INTELLIGENCE SUMMARY.
1st Battn. "The Queen's"

(Erase heading not required.)

Instructions regarding War Diaries and Intelligence Summaries are contained in F. S. Regs., Part II. and the Staff Manual respectively. Title pages will be prepared in manuscript.

Place	Date	Hour	Summary of Events and Information	Remarks and references to Appendices
CROISILLES vicinity of	29th		M/G. (Hauu C Coy) under Lieut J. BURRELL. Both H.Q. at CHALK Pt in V.18.C. Battalion remained in Trenches. (HINDENBURG R. Line) Trenches improved. Forward Trench and Saps to it continued. Situation normal.	
"	30th		Battalion remained in Trenches. Trench to connect forward posts and Saps to them improved. Situation normal. Draw reoccd. Battalion to be relieved by 13th Northumberland Fus on night 30th/31st	
"	31st		Battalion remained in Trenches. Saps and forward Trench proceeded wk. Two Saps sufficiently advanced that Garrisons of forward Pts to can be posted by day. Relief by 13th N. Fusrs commenced from Battn. H.Q. about 11pm. Completed 12.30 am. Battalion marched out by Platoons to Camp at MOYENNEVILLE where a hot meal was given the men as they arrived between 2am and 3am. Orders received Battalion would march to BERLES-AU-BOIS on 1st June to pass Cross Roads just W of MOYENNE-VILLE at 9.25am. During relief the Enemy shelled the left of the Battn front heavily also the tracks leading out. The following casualties occurred. — Lieut G.F. ASHPITEL Wounded (at Duty). 12 Other ranks wounded. Sd. W. Cobb, Lieut Colonel. Comdg. 1st Bn. The Queen's Regt.	

WAR DIARY
INTELLIGENCE SUMMARY

Army Form C. 2118.

JUNE 1917

1st Batt. THE QUEEN'S Regt.

Place	Date	Hour	Summary of Events and Information	Remarks and references to Appendices
MOYENNEVILLE	1st		Battalion paraded at 9.10 a.m. and marched via AYETTE – ADINFER – MONCHY-AU-BOIS to BERLES-AU-BOIS – move completed 1.15 p.m. occupied Billets in S. end of village. Anniversary "Ebrico p. June". Telegram reading out HMS Gallant.	
BERLES-AU-BOIS	2nd		Rest – Hot Baths for whole Battalion – cleaning up and refitting. The following received a mention in Sir Douglas Haig's Dispatch (for Gavrell 17-15.5.17) 2nd Lieut. R.H. NEVINS. 2nd Lieut R.S. WALKER. 9583 RQM.Sgt MARSH. 5307 C.Q.M.S. A BAYFORD. Battalion attended Church Parade – 15 other Ranks joined from Base & 2 from Battn.	
"	3rd		Training including Musketry (Range Practices) and general routine.	
"	4th		Training and general routine.	
"	5th		" " " "	
"	6th		Training and general routine.	
"	7th		Training and general routine.	
"	8th		Training including Musketry (Range Practices) and general routine.	
"	9th		Training and general routine.	
"	10th		Battalion attended Church Parade.	

Army Form C. 2118.

WAR DIARY
INTELLIGENCE SUMMARY.
(Erase heading not required.)

JUNE 1917

1st Battn "THE QUEEN'S" Regt

Place	Date	Hour	Summary of Events and Information	Remarks and references to Appendices
BERLES AU BOIS	11th		Training & general routine -	
	12th		Training & general routine -	
	13th		All companies fired on range about 1 mile from the village, distances up to 300 yards -	
	14th		Training & general routine - Lieut L.A. CROOK M.C. 2nd Lt F.D TUCKER M.S.S.O.R. joined from Division Dept Battn -	
	15th		Brigade Rout march 6.30 - 9.30 am -	
	16th		Companies carried out Field Training a.m. XII corps range near RANSART from 7.0 am to 10.0 AM.	
	17th		Brigade Rifle meeting at BIENVILLERS a 10 yard range - Battalion rifle meeting held on 7.15 corps Range and Brigade ranges near LA CAUCHIE after tea -	

Army Form C. 2118.

WAR DIARY
of
INTELLIGENCE SUMMARY. 1st Battn "THE QUEEN'S" Regt

JUNE 1917

(Erase heading not required.)

Place	Date	Hour	Summary of Events and Information	Remarks and references to Appendices
BERLES AU-BOIS	18th		Battalion rifle meeting from 6.0am to 1.0pm, and continued in the evening from 5.30 to 8.0pm — Team Competition open to the Brigade, group won won by 2/Warwick's, with Queens 2nd — 91 Division Brigade Boxing Tournament was held in this afternoon, boots won by the Queens —	
"	19th		Training & general routine when recent the Battalion will move to MOYENVILLE Area on 20th to relieve 110th & 113th Divisional Reserve. During this Battn will be at BERLES and remainder in the general Line and platoon — Teams of men for platoon and packets of men for fitting own kits and who wishing and have been told this —	
"	20th	4.30am	Battalion march to 6.20 am to MOYENVILLE via MINCHY — ADINFER — AYETTE and halts in old MOYENVILLE at 10.0am to wait for relieving troops. The du 9th Comp — Battalion march to Camp C at 12.30pm — 91st Division 1st Battn at COURCELLES hell spent 15.11st Battn afternoon the 2nd Battalion and men & players and to help number of rows, men allotted drums and men & players are telling and to help number of rows, men allotted —	

Army Form C. 2118.

WAR DIARY
or
INTELLIGENCE SUMMARY.
(Erase heading not required.)

1st Batt. The Queens Regt.   June 1917

Place	Date	Hour	Summary of Events and Information	Remarks and references to Appendices
MOYENVILLE	21/?		Training and field routine. Lieut. W.B. CARSLAKE took over Command of "C" Coy.	
"	22		Training and General Routine.	
"	23		Training and General Routine. – Warning order received that Battalion would go up into front line trenches relieving 2 Companies 20th R.F. from CHERRY LANE inclusive on the Right to SENSEE River on LEFT.	
"	24		Brigade Parade for Divine Service, immediately after which Ribbons were presented, including the following Officers N.C.O's and men of the Battalion:- MILITARY CROSS.- Captain H.E. HARRISON. BAR to MILITARY MEDAL:- 9238 Sergeant H. JONES, 4314 Corporal A. BISHOP. MILITARY MEDAL:- Lieut W.H. BAYNES. 7192 Corpl H. KING. 2677 Corporal E. BONSEY. 8778 Corpl B. TAYLOR. G.8 Privt A. CHILMAN. 10182 L/Cpl T. LAWSON. ITALIAN BRONZE MEDAL for MILITARY VALOUR. 2/41 Sergeant F. MULCARE. Orders received that Brigade will attack a portion of TUNNEL TRENCH S. of CROISILLES-FONTAINE Road on 25th instant. To be carried out by 2nd WORCESTERS on Right and 1st Q.O.R. at 7pm "THE QUEEN'S" on LEFT. The Battalion took over front line from CHERRY LANE inclusive to SENSEE River	

WAR DIARY

INTELLIGENCE SUMMARY
1st Batt: THE QUEEN'S

JUNE 1917

Army Form C. 2118.

Place	Date	Hour	Summary of Events and Information	Remarks and references to Appendices
FRONT LINE TRENCHES	25		Rect from 20th R. Fust: Coys were located as under FRONT LINE - "B" on RIGHT "A" LEFT. "C" and "D" in SUPPORT. Relief was completed at 11.45 a.m. 25th — Situation normal. Battalion remained in Trenches. Attack on TUNNEL TRENCH ordered to take place 25th cancelled. Orders received that in view of operations to take place on 27th Battalion will be relieved by two Coys 8th K.R.R.C. on night 25th/26th. Relief commenced 9.30 p.m. completed 1.15 a.m. 26th. Casualties — 5/6 O.R.s ranks wounded.	
	26		On relief Battalion marched to Camp J MOYENNEVILLE - move completed 4.30 a.m. Battalion at rest during day. Evening - Operations to be carried out on 27th were practised. Our Lieuts W.L. ATKINSON and C.W.O. CHARLES joined on appointment.	
MOYENNEVILLE	27		Training and General Routine Operations ordered for 29th cancelled. Instructions received Battalion will carry out an attack on 29th not object. to secure Enemy's Block in N. end of TUNNELL TRENCH and establish a post on high ground in TUNNEL TRENCH (during night 28/29th TRENCH to be entered) by Enemy. Strength of attacking party — one Company.	Amt. 1452

Army Form C. 2118.

WAR DIARY

JUNE 1917

INTELLIGENCE SUMMARY. 1st Batt "THE QUEENS" Regt.

(Erase heading not required.)

Place	Date	Hour	Summary of Events and Information	Remarks and references to Appendices
MOEUVRES	27th		Lieut. Col. L.M. CROFTS, D.S.O. and Capt. J. BURRELL proceeded to view the ground over which operations on 28th are to take place, when just S. of CROISILLES Captain BURRELL was wounded in the left arm by shell - after being attended at Dressing Station he returned to duty. Lieut. Col. CROFTS continued. Attacking Posn. Distribution of Troops was as follows:- O.C. Lieut. W.B. CARSLAKE, 2nd Lieut. H. RISTON-COOKE, G.E.A. SHIPTON, Trench Party "A" Coy. 73. B. 28. C. 54. D. 37. Total 6 officers & 167 O.Rs Ranks. The attack was practiced over extended ground resembling the actual position to be attacked.	Battle with No 170 and will attached Cs
	28th		Lieut W.B. CARSLAKE and Lieut H. RISTON-COOKE proceeded to Front Line and viewed the ground. The attack was again practised. The Troops taking part in the attack paraded at 9.30 pm Extra Oribar-lights flares etc were issued. Party moved off about 9pm in an unprecedented tornado of thunder and rain. At 11pm 161 K.R.R. holding LUMP LANE were relieved by men who were not actually going over the next day and remainder of the attacking force was dispost in LINCOLN Trench. The Enemy showed unusual activity in vicinity of the NEBUS during the night and attempted to bomb to posts then but was driven off with Rifle & Lewis Gun fire.	
FRONT LINE TRENCHES N.E. CROISILLES	29th		At 5.30 am Hot Tea and rum was issued to the Troops. 2 Stores parties began to move into their appointed places in LUMP LANE, 2 Bombs, 2 Bomber, S.A.A.	

WAR DIARY / INTELLIGENCE SUMMARY

JUNE 1917 (7)

1st Batn. THE QUEEN'S Regt.

Army Form C. 2118.

Place	Date	Hour	Summary of Events and Information	Remarks and references to Appendices
FRONT LINE TRENCHES	7th		S.A.A. and bombs being round on the way. The trenches were nearly knee deep in places with water and mud and from the heavy rain of the previous evening and going was very difficult. ZERO was fixed for 8.50 a.m. and at 8.15 all were in their places. The attack including garrison of JUMP LANE consisted of 1 Coy reinforced to a strength of 189 O.Rs. Ranks under command of Lieut N.E. CARSLAKE. 2nd Lieut W.H. DAVIES of Bombing Section, 2nd Lieut B. PASHIPTEL of Blocking parties, 2nd Lieut H. KIRBY-CROKE of demolishing parties, 2nd Lieut H. STRYDHOLT of carrying parties and 2nd Lieut F. SHIPTON of posts in JUMP LANE. The attack was organised as a Bombing Attack to go up TUNNEL TRENCH, to start from JUMP LANE on the places and cover the broken ground between them and Mycetoma in waves. Saps had been dug out from the NEBUS and No 5 SAP and it was intended to form those up to form a jumping off place but, owing to short time available and it was found impossible to do so and the attack had to be arranged to start from JUMP LANE and the partly dug saps at NEBUS and No Sp instead. It was hoped to effect a surprise and accordingly the barrage of Stokes Mortars Machine Guns and Field and Heavy Artillery was timed to commence at	

WAR DIARY

JUNE 1917

INTELLIGENCE SUMMARY of 1st Batt THE QUEEN'S Regt.

Place	Date	Hour	Summary of Events and Information	Remarks and references to Appendices
FRONT LINE TRENCHES	7/6	At ZERO + 5.	The ground between LUMP LANE and the Stables was very broken and being but a mass of shell holes. A Recce (marked A-D on Appendix A) at about 70 yards from the N.E. Bus and 120 yds from Junction of LUMP LANE and No 5 SAP commenced LUMP LANE. The Enemy were believed to hold KITTEN Trench and a special patrol of a Lewis Gun section and Bombers under No M.883 Sergt A. Spencer, was detailed as a Right Flank Guard. At ZERO (8.50 am) Advance commenced. The leading waves of the left party, when only about 30 yards from our trenches came under a rain of bombs and to reach Nagasaki Byl B. Brooks several men wounded, the centre Wave were met with Rifle Grenade fire and only the Right succeeded in advancing and a small party of Bombers under 2nd Lieut W.H. BAYNES reached a large shell hole ("O" on Appx A) who Sergt Spencer had got too much to the left, reported his broken's which was below the Crest with a German Post in his back right and left front of him. The Surprise had failed and it would only have entailed heavy losses to push it and even then success was doubtful as it was evident that the Enemy was in strength and had a very strong position it was decided not to continue the attack. At the time Capt/Lieut ASHPITEL in the Centre was pushing on with rifle fire	See "F"

Army Form C. 2118.

WAR DIARY
INTELLIGENCE SUMMARY. 2nd Batt. THE QUEEN'S Regt

JUNE 1917

(Erase heading not required.)

Instructions regarding War Diaries and Intelligence Summaries are contained in F. S. Regs., Part II. and the Staff Manual respectively. Title pages will be prepared in manuscript.

Place	Date	Hour	Summary of Events and Information	Remarks and references to Appendices
FRONT LINE TRENCHES			was covered by Rifle Grenade fire from the left. 2nd Lieut W.H. BAYNES and four men assisted in the SHELL hole (B1) without bombs. 2nd Lieut ASPITTEL was ordered to withdraw and assist with a raiding party of Grenadiers to the Right flank of Sap 5 to cover our Lieut BAYNES withdrawal. This party did excellent work and put a barrage of Nº 23 and 24 Grenades over the heads of the Enemy (at B and D) and under cover of this 2nd Lieut BAYNES withdrew his men without loss. LUMP LANE was closed and posts reorganised. The Enemy Artillery retaliation was light and chiefly behind our lines but from 12.15 pm to 12.45 pm he put down a Box barrage on LUMP LANE and nearly shelled all the communication trenches. About 3 pm the surprise raid on BLUE LANE was carried out in small parties to MOIENNEVILLE and conveyed there by motor lorries to BARLES an BOIS returning them at 10 pm (where the remainder of the Battalion had moved at 3 pm). Losses in the Operation were :- Nº Ranks 5 killed 11 wounded. The wire instructions received from Brigade about 3 p.m. in der command of Major T. WEDING and The altering party furnished 3 p.m. under command of Major T. WEDING and	A

Army Form C. 2118.

WAR DIARY

JUNE 1917

INTELLIGENCE SUMMARY. 2nd Battn "THE QUEEN'S" Regt

(Erase heading not required.)

Instructions regarding War Diaries and Intelligence Summaries are contained in F. S. Regs., Part II. and the Staff Manual respectively. Title pages will be prepared in manuscript.

Place	Date	Hour	Summary of Events and Information	Remarks and references to Appendices
MOYENNE-VILLE	29th		Bns moved to BEAUFS.- an- BOIS by 6.00 & relief tracks H.Y. FAYETTE - DOUCHY - ADINFER-WOOD - MONCHY - more completed by an Battalion greatly relieved.	
FRONT LINE TRENCHES	30th		Major COOKE - TRYTHALL - SHIPTON and 65 O.R's ranks returned to Battalion. LUMP LANE - Other deposits of surplus stores situation was normal except at about 10 p.m when the trench was heavily shelled for about 10 minutes - On instructions from Brigade all stores of value were removed from the NE.O.D.S which were evacuated during the night. Casualties other Ranks - 1 Killed & wounded.	
"	30"		At Stand To - between about 3am and 4am the Enemy put down a Box Barrage on LUMPLANE, though the Barrage burst in front and the trench however no no land than 5 pieces no casualties occurred. Relief by the 15th Durham L. Infy commenced at 11.45am & was completed at 12.30pm. - The men slept out in small parties to MOYENNEVILLE - move completed at 3.30 p.m.	

Jn. C. S. K.
Capt. & Adjt. The Queens Regt
Comdg. 2nd Bn The Queens Rgt

SECRET.

Headquarters,
100th Infantry Brigade.
26th June 1917.

O.C. 1st Queen's.
222 F.Co. R.E. (For Information).

The operations ordered to take place on June 29th as verbally explained by the Brigadier General have been cancelled.

Your Battalion will carry out an attack on that date with the object of securing the enemy's block in the N. end of TUNNEL TRENCH and of establishing a post on the high ground in TUNNEL TRENCH which at present commands the E. end of LUMP LANE at a distance of 60 to 70 yards.

The attacking force should not exceed the strength of one Company.

KITTEN TRENCH will also have to be cleared of the enemy as far as necessary to admit of the establishment of the post referred to above.

The attack should be carried out between 8.0 and 9.0 am on the 29th instant.

Please submit proposal for the attack which should take the form of a surprise attack, supported by Rifle Grenade and T.M.Fire.

Heavy and Field Artillery will be available to deal with enemy trenches and M.G. emplacements beyond reach of our Stokes Mortars.

A detachment of R.E. will also be available for demolitions and blocking purposes.

(Sgd) H.W.M.PAUL, Captain,
Brigade Major,
100th Infantry Brigade.

Battalion Order No 3
Lt. Col. L.A. Crofts D.S.O.
Comndg Bn The Queen's Regt
28th June 1917

1. A coy reinforced to a strength of 20 N.C.Os and 124 O.Rs from B, C & D coys will attack TUNNEL TRENCH from WURT LANE with the object of storming the enemy's block in N. end of TUNNEL TRENCH and establishing a post on high ground which at present commands the E. end of LUIT LANE for a distance of 60 to 70 yds — at about 6.30 A.M. on 29th inst.

2. Capt W.B. CARSLAKE will command the operation; 2/Lt H.H. BAYKES, the forward bombers, 2/Lt G.S. ASHFIELD, the blocking parties, 2/Lt H.R. COOKE, consolidation & command of captured trench.

3. Posts No 21 & 22 will be held by 2 Lewis Guns & Grenadiers under command of 2/Lt J.E. SHIPTON.

4. LUIT LANE will be taken over from R.W.K's by C coy on evening of 28th. Remainder of attacking party will be accommodated in LINCOLN LANE during night.

5. Coy H.Q. at W. end of LUIT LANE. Bn H.Q. at junction of PLUIT LANE and BURG TRENCH from 6. a.m. 29th instant.

6. 1 Officer & 20 men each from B & D coys will march in small parties & join up the two new trenches dug from No 5 & 6 Seps. These parties will concentrate in LINCOLN TRENCH by 10.0 pm. Dress – drill order, water bottles and waterproof sheets. They will provide their own covering parties.

7. The attack will take place as practised at rest.

8. At ZERO – 3 to ZERO the 6 pr pounder T.M's will bombard the position to be attacked with object of sending... men to ground.

9. At ZERO + 5 Stokes Mortars will barrage from 100 yds N of junction of PAPEN LIERS LANE & TUNNEL TRENCH to South.

10. At ZERO + 6 Stokes mortars barrage on junction of CHERISBURG & TUNNEL & South & east of it.

11. Heavy & Field Artillery & Machine Guns will deal with enemy trenches & M.G. emplacements beyond reach of Stokes, from ZERO + 5 onwards.

12. Progress of bombers along TUNNEL TRENCH will be shown by a Blue & white flag on a stick shown above the trench.

R.A. Nevins
Lt & Adjt
Bn The Queen's Regt

Copies to:- 1. B.O. 100 Inf Bde
2. Major ... 3. O.C. Coy ... No 2
... 6. Coy ... 7. ... ...
... ...
... ... War Diary
... ... R.N. Artillery

Army Form C. 2118.

100/33

1 8 1/R.W.S.

WAR DIARY
INTELLIGENCE SUMMARY. 1st Battn. "THE QUEEN'S" Regt

JULY 1917

Vol 33

(Erase heading not required.)

Place	Date	Hour	Summary of Events and Information	Remarks and references to Appendices
BERLES AU BOIS	1st		General clean up. Inspection of Arms Clothing and Equipment.	
"	2nd		Distinguish mules about H. RIBSTON-COOKE marched from MOYANVEYLLE via HAMELINCOURT – AYETTE – POINTER – MONCHY and arrived BERLES-AU-BOIS 2pm. General Routine – Companies carried out a short Route March.	
"	3rd		Battalion paraded at 7.25am and marched to FORCEVILLE via BIENVILLERS – SOUASTRE – COURCELLES – BERTRANCOURT. Distance approximately 17 miles. There were no casualties. Completed at 12.20pm. A very trying march owing to the heat. Quartered in Billets.	
"	4th		Battalion paraded at 4.25am and marched to MOLLIENS via HEDAUVILLE – WARLOY – CANTAY – BEAUCOURT. Distance about 17 miles. There were no casualties at 9.25am. Quartered in Billets.	
"	5th		Battalion paraded at 4.15am and marched to PICQUIGNY via RAINEVILLE – COISY – BERTANGLES. ST SAVEUR – AILLY. Distance about 14 miles. There were no casualties at 10.25am. Quartered in Billets.	
PICQUIGNY	6th		General Routine. Rearrangement of Billets.	

WAR DIARY

INTELLIGENCE SUMMARY.

JULY 1917

1st Batt'n "THE QUEEN'S" Regt.

Army Form C. 2118.

Place	Date	Hour	Summary of Events and Information	Remarks and references to Appendices
PICQUIGNY	7th		Training and general routine. Capt. A.M. ALLAN 2nd Lts. W. ELLEN, V.W. RUDKIN and R.F. HIGGS — 184 Other Ranks joined from Base.	
"	8th		Battalion Church Parade. General routine.	
"	9th		Training and general routine. Nos. 1 Coy and No. 4 Coy in Billets at work in the field. 7.30 am – 12 noon. Nos. 2 Coy. Coys. at close order drill 10 to 11 am. 11 to 12 Billets. 7.30 am – 9 am from - afternoon Platoon & Company Conferences & short Musketry – Evening classes for Young Officers & NCOs. Range being opened.	
"	10th		Ditto – 2nd Lt. K.A. BROWN joined from 3rd Battalion.	
"	11th		Battalion paraded at 8am for route march. Places: F. SMO. Bud–LA CHAUSSÉE – YZEUX – HANGEST – CROUY – ST PIERRE – a – GOUY. Returned to Billets 12.30 pm. Captain J.P. COOKSON joined from 3rd Battalion. 2 pm Company Conferences. Bombing Class under Instruction Officers young Officers and NCOs Officers 5 – 6 pm. 5.30 – 7 pm Tactical Exercise for Officers & NCOs here on ground in Vicinity of LA CHAUSSÉE.	

WAR DIARY

INTELLIGENCE SUMMARY.

Army Form C. 2118.

JULY 1917

(3)

Place	Date	Hour	Summary of Events and Information	Remarks and references to Appendices
PERUWELZ	12th		Training as on 9th. Bombing Class completed	
"	13th		Training as on 10th. New Classes for bombing & Lewis Gunnery formed. 10 O.R. joined from Base.	
"	14th		Training as on 12th. Classes each of 50 N.C.O.s & men under instruction on Lewis Gun and Bombing.	
"	15th	9.30 a.m.	Battalion Church Parade. 148 Other ranks joined from Base.	
"	16th	7.30 a.m.	Training and general routine. Two Companies at Battle practice in known field. One Company at the cover drill & on range & bullets. One Company at range practice and Musketry generally. Lewis Gun and Bombing Classes under instruction.	
		2 pm	Platoon and Company Conferences	
		2.30	Rifle Coys at Musketry. One Coy Tactical Scheme for N.C.Os returning working of Platoon &c.	
		6.15 pm		
		6-6pm	Class of Lewis Gun Officers & N.C.Os at Drill H.O.	
		630 pm	Lecture by Commanding Officer.	

WAR DIARY
INTELLIGENCE SUMMARY
1st Batt. "THE QUEEN'S" Regt.

JULY 1917

Army Form C. 2118.

Place	Date	Hour	Summary of Events and Information	Remarks and references to Appendices
PEDUISY	17th	7.30am 6pm	As on 16th. 1st Day of Divisional Horse Show.	
"	18th	7.30am & 9.30am	Platoon training and musketry. Lewis Gun & Bombing Classes under instructors. Remainder of the day a Holiday. 2nd Day of Divisional Horse Show.	
"	19th	9.15am & 1pm	Battalion paraded at 9.15am and marched to Cone Road NE corner of Bois de Caillon thence through 152d & N of road in attack formation to track across E of CROUY-CANNON Road where it formed into Columns of route & marched towards SOUES, halted at Cone Road, took part in a Bde demonstration by Divisional Gen. afterwards resumed march 10.45am via CANNON-BODENOY. Arriving in Bidulle at 1pm.	
		5pm 6pm & 6.30pm & 7pm	N.C.O.s Class under instruction. Tactical Scheme carried out just W of village – all Officers took part.	
"	20th	7.30am 6pm	As on 16th – Major T. WEEDING as C.O. & Capt. R. HANKINS as Adjutant attended Divisional Exercise without troops over ground between LONGPRÉ and AMIENS approximate duration 7½ hours.	

WAR DIARY
INTELLIGENCE SUMMARY

Army Form C. 2118.

Place	Date	Hour	Summary of Events and Information	Remarks and references to Appendices
PICQUIGNY	21st	9.30am / 6.30am	Three Companies training in the field. One Company at Range Practice & Musketry generally. 2/Lt W.F. CLENSHAW joined from 3rd Batt. Lewis Gun and Bombing Classes continued.	
	22nd	10.30am	Battalion Church Parade.	
"	23rd	9.30am to 2pm / 2-3.15 / 6.30 / 7pm	Bombing Class commenced under instruction. Musketry Drills. Young Officers & NCO Class at work 5pm to 6pm. Conference - Company Commanders under instruction. Lecture to all Officers by Commanding Officer.	
"	Sept 24th	9.30am / 6.15 / 6.30pm	Battalion in Attack Practice. Lecture to Young Officers by Commanding Officer. No. 9752 Cpl J. BETTS and 5986? Pte H. KIRBY accidentally drowned in the River Somme.	
"	25th	9.30am / 6.15pm / 5pm	Recon. 23rd. Inquest of the late 9752 Cpl J. Betts and 5986? Pte H. Kirby. Burial in Amiens yesterday. 10 other ranks reported from Base.	
"	26th Jan	9.30am / 11am / 2pm / 6pm	Battalion Route March Route St to Cross Roads N of Sav. & in FURDRINOY - BREILLY - HILLY - ST SAVIOUR - LA CHAUSSEE. Inspection Conference + C. Tactical Exercise in which all Officers took part. Warning Order Brigade will move forward tomorrow on 21st Instant received.	

Army Form C. 2118.

WAR DIARY
INTELLIGENCE SUMMARY.
(Erase heading not required.)

JULY 1917

1st Batt. "THE QUEEN'S"

Instructions regarding War Diaries and Intelligence Summaries are contained in F.S. Regs., Part II. and the Staff Manual respectively. Title pages will be prepared in manuscript.

Place	Date	Hour	Summary of Events and Information	Remarks and references to Appendices
PICQUIGNY	27th March	Noon	Two Companies at Battle Practice in the Hills. The Company Musketry Competition.	
		2pm to 3pm	One Company at Range Practice & Musketry generally. Conference Coys Comdg & Musketry generally.	
Ditto	28th	7.9 am	Route march via CROUY, thence a wood attack to the South & East towards PICQUIGNY. Lieut L. McBROOK M.C. assumed the duties of Assistant Adjt.	
"	29th	11.15 a.m.	Battalion voluntary Church Parade. Swimming, diving & fishing competitions in the evening. Brigade orders for move of Brigade to the Army sent received.	
"	30th	7 am to noon	Three enhanced Platoon & company training. One company at range practice. Bombing class under separate training. Conferences under Coys Commanders.	
		5 pm	Swimming Competition – Finals. Battn Orders for move to TETEGHEM area 3 mile SE of DUNKERQUE issued.	G.O. 1428.
"	31st	7.30pm 6.15am	Two Conferences on Platoon Training – One Company at Range Practice & Musketry. "B" Coy at disposal of Commandant. "B" Coy marched at 6 p.m. to DUNKERQUE where it arrived at 11.15 to entrain in accordance with orders Bn. 2. Batt. Orders M128. Conferences were held under Company & Commander's arrangements.	S.O. 1428.

Lt Col
Comdg 1st Bn The Queen's Regt

SECRET   Battalion Order No: 138   COPY No: 14
by Lieut: Col: L.M. CROFTS. D.S.O.
Comdg 2nd "The Queen's" Regiment.   Monday 30th July 1917

1. The Division will be transferred to 4th Army by rail on July 31st and Aug: 1st.

2. The Battalion will entrain at LONGPRE on 1st August, and will march there as follows:—
   Train No 16.   "B" Coy, accompanied by its cookers, pack pony, & officer's charges tomorrow 31st inst: after dinners, under Command of Capt: R. FAULKNER. M.C. by whom orders for march will be issued. 2/Lieuts J.R.G. COWAN & J.E. SHIPTON and Pioneers will accompany this party.
   This party will billet for the night 31st/1st at LONGPRE, and will be at station ready for entrainment at 5.10 am 1st August.
   Train No 18   The remainder will assemble on Wed: 1st August in the following order, head of column at N. end of village, ready to move off at 4.40 AM.   H.Q. C. DRUMS D. A.   DRESS – F.S.M.O. Steel helmets to be worn.
   Transport, less cookers & mess cart which will march at 4.0 AM, will march under orders of Capt: H.E. HARRISON. M.C. so as to arrive at LONGPRE Station by 6.30 AM.
   Reveille will be at 2.45 AM. Breakfasts 3.30 AM.

3. Officers Valises to be at Q.M. Stores by 3.0 AM 1st Aug: Those not required for use, night 31st/1st, will be loaded on evening 31st not later than 8.0 pm. Mess Kits to be loaded at H.Q. mess by 3.40 am.

4. Billeting Party, consisting of 2/Lt: K.M. EAST, 1 Sergt per Coy, 1 N.C.O H.Q. will start on bicycles at 6.0 am and 1 N.C.O, Q.M. Stores, 1 N.C.O, Transport, 1 Servant and Interpreter will parade at Battn: H. Address at 5.15 AM tomorrow 31st instant and proceed by 5.42 am train to LONGPRE — and entrain on No: 2 TRAIN with details 98th Inf: Bde. 2/Lt: K.M. EAST will report to O/C Entrainment by 7.30 AM.

5. Entrainment is to be carried out rapidly and in SILENCE.

6. Marching Out States will be prepared and rendered to the Adjt,
   "B" Coys by 1.0 pm remainder by 6.0 pm tomorrow.
   States are to account for all ranks on strength, TOP LINE shewing "ON PARADE" i.e. entraining with Coys. etc.

7. During the journey all ranks are to be warned that water must not be drunk or water bottles filled except from source which will be pointed out, as necessary.

8. On arrival in 4th Army Area, Division forms part of XVth CORPS.

9. On detraining Battalion will march to and be accommodated in TETEGHEM Area, 3 miles S.E. of DUNKERQUE.

10. During march from detraining station, Coys will move at 200x interval.

11. O's C. Coys etc, will ensure all ranks are cautioned to take steps to keep the sand out of their various weapons. Sand will penetrate into mechanism of a Rifle, Revolver, or Machine Gun very easily and oil should not be so plentifully used as ordinarily since it helps to collect the sand and clogs the mechanism.

12. O's C. Coys, etc, will take such steps as will ensure all claims for damage to billets etc, are settled prior to departure and that Billets are left clean and sanitary, and inspected prior to moving off. A report that this has been done will be made to the Adjt: on parade.

(Sgd) R.H. Nevins Lieut & Adjt.
2nd "The Queen's" Regiment

Copies issued:—
1. C.O.   2. O.C No:1
3. O.C No:2   4. O.C No:3
5. O.C No:4   6. Q.M.
7. T.O.   8. Sigt Off.
9.   10. R.S.M.
11. Adjt.   12.
13. War Diary 14. Spare.

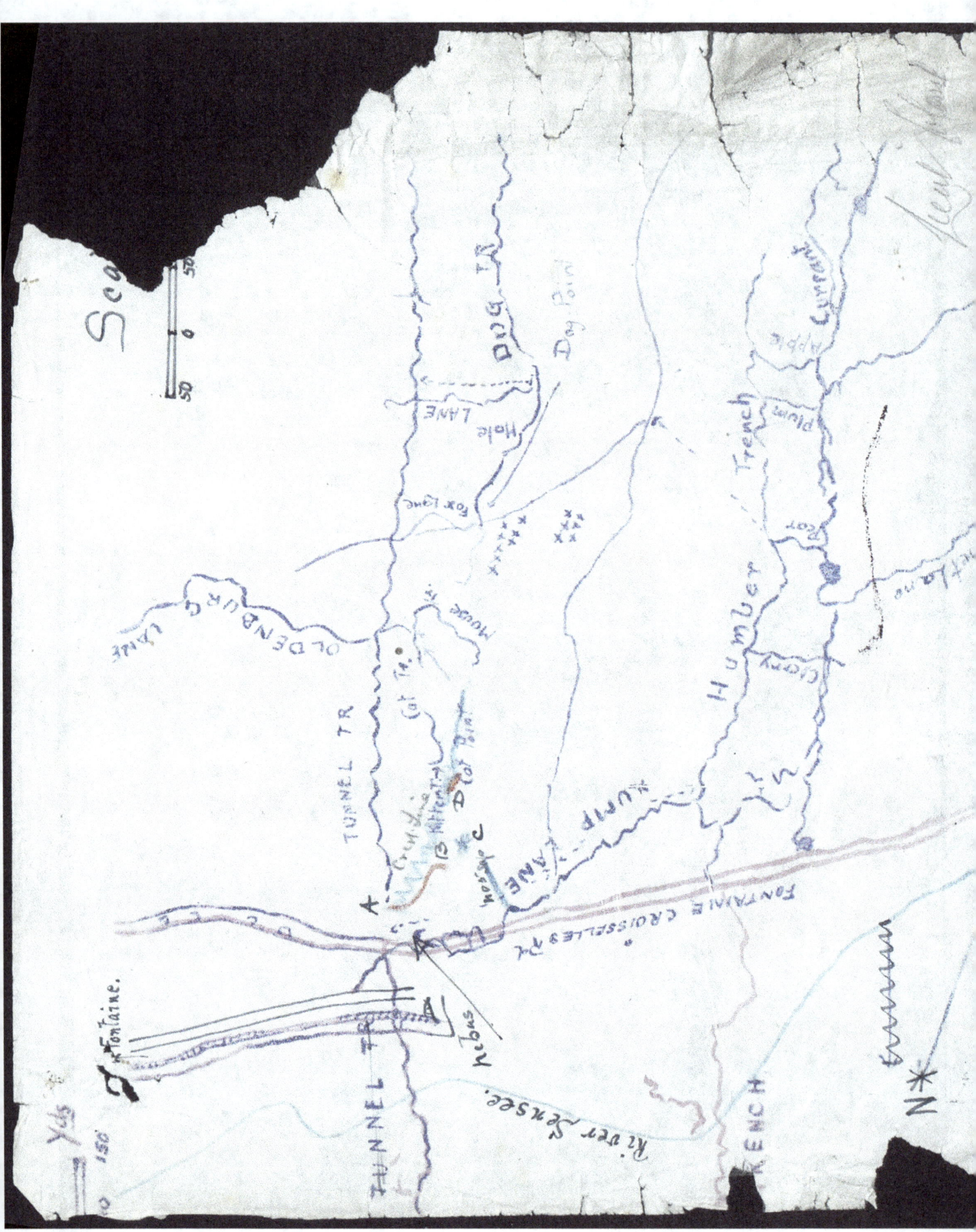

Nitro

	Party	Tools	Party	Tools	Right of Ridge Party	Tools	Party
1st Wave	Left Flank Bombers 1 N.C.O 8 men	—	Bay-net sentries 1 N.C.O 10 men	—			
2nd Wave	Left Lewis Gun ?	4	1st Block 1 N.C.O 10 men ®	4	Bombers 1 N.C.O 8 men	—	
3rd Wave	Right Lewis Guns ? Bombers 1 N.C.O 4 men	4	2nd Block 1 N.C.O 10 men ®	4	Carriers 1 N.C.O 12 men	10	Right Lewis Guns 1 N.C.O 4 men (tools et) ®
4th Wave	Demolition 1 N.C.O 2 T.M. Signallers	6 men 2				10	
5th Wave	Consolidation 1 N.C.O 12 men						
6th	Carrying Party 4 N.C.O.s 30 men ©						

Page 1

19 1/1310S.

Army Form C. 2118.

WAR DIARY
3rd Battn. The Queens Regt.
INTELLIGENCE SUMMARY.
August 1917

(Erase heading not required.)

Instructions regarding War Diaries and Intelligence Summaries are contained in F. S. Regs., Part II. and the Staff Manual respectively. Title pages will be prepared in manuscript.

JW/34

Place	Date	Hour	Summary of Events and Information	Remarks and references to Appendices
1917 En frequing	Aug 1	2.45 a.m.	Battalion roused.	Battⁿ Orders 129
		4.40 a.m.	Battalion marched to LONGPRÉ arriving at 8 a.m. Entrained & left at 9.40 a.m. Passed through ABBEVILLE, ETAPLES, BOULOGNE, CALAIS.	
		8 p.m.	Arrival at DUNKERQUE (DOCKS). Marched into billets a mile away at COUDEKERQUE-BRANCHE.	
COUDEKERQUE-BRANCHE.	Aug 2		Battalion at disposal of company commanders.	
		3.9.30 a.m.	Battalion marched to GHYVELDE arriving at noon. Accomodated under canvas.	
GHYVELDE.		4 a.m.	Battalion undergo company training. 2/Lt A.R. Hastings joined Battn.	
Do.	5	10.55 a.m.	Church Parade.	
		2.15 p.m.	Battalion marched to see show at BRAY DUNES & bathed.	
Do.	6	8–12 noon	Company training. Shooting. Training of bombers, scouts, runners etc.	
		2–3.30	Conferences & lectures.	
Do.	7	8–12 a.m.	Battalion attack practice in vicinity of Belgian Frontier: three companies attacking + one defending.	
		2.45 p.m.	Conference of officers. Discussion of morning's scheme.	

Page 2

WAR DIARY 1st Battn. The Queens Regt.

Army Form C. 2118.

INTELLIGENCE SUMMARY.

Place	Date	Hour	Summary of Events and Information	Remarks and references to Appendices
GHYVELDE	9/8/17	8-12 noon	Battalion route march to HOLIE KOUKE and LES MOERES.	
Do		2.15 p.m.	Battalion bathing or above.	
Do	Aug. 9	8-12	Company & Platoon training. Runners, bombers, machine gunners & scouts were in separate classes.	
		2-3.30 p.m.	Conferences. Night operations were cancelled owing to bad weather.	
Do		10.9-1 p.m.	Route march & attack tactics in vicinity of Belgian frontier.	
			Bathing parade cancelled.	
		6-7.30 p.m.	Tactical scheme for officers.	
Do	11	8-12 noon	Company & Platoon training. Scouts, bombers, signallers & machine gunners under specials.	
			training.	
		3 p.m.	Companies bathed.	
Do	12	9.2.5 a.m.	Divine Service in the open. Band & drums attended.	
		5-6 p.m.	Bathing. 2/Lt. H. Brown & one sergeant departed to attend course at 4th Army School. 2/Lt. S. M. Honeycroft rejoined Battn. from Base.	
Do	13	8-noon	Company & Platoon training	
		2-3.30	Coolerele	

Page 3

Army Form C. 2118.

WAR DIARY
or
INTELLIGENCE SUMMARY. 1st Battn, The Queens Regt.
(Erase heading not required.)

Place	Date 1917	Hour	Summary of Events and Information	Remarks and references to Appendices
GHYVELDE	Aug 14	8-noon	Two companies field firing on beach. One company trained under R.E. supervision.	
		3 p.m.	One company carried Stationary company training. Bathing.	
			1st East left for fortnights M.G. course at LE TOUQUET.	
Do	-15	8-noon	Battalion Attack scheme. C. Coy. defended. Remaining companies attacked.	
		noon	Lecture by Lt Col. Clark XV Corps M.G. officer on machine gun tactics.	
		10 p.m.	2nd Worcesters signal S.O.S. M.G. Coy. to prove safety of overhead fire, to prove	
Beach near frontier.	16	5.30 a.m.	Demonstration by Brigade M.G. Coy. to prove safety of overhead fire, to prove that M.G. barrage can be made on S.O.S. signal.	
GHYVELDE		8-1 p.m.	Brigade Attack Scheme. 16th R.R. & 1st H.L.I. acqd first objective. 1st Queens and 2nd Worcesters sipped 2nd objective, consolidated positions won. Casualties were properly evacuated and signals made to contact aeroplanes.	
		4 p.m.	Company football at BRAY DUNES	
			Lt Allan 1st R. Scots promoted acting captain as from 20-7-17. (G.R.O. 2494)	
			Lt & Adjutant R.H. Nevins ranshd ditto as from 3-8-17 (G.R.O. 2507)	
			Warning order received to relieve 32nd Division in NIEUPORT sector.	Battn orders No. 142.
Do	17	8-noon	Company training.	
Do	18	8.30 p.m.	Battalion marched via ADINKERKE to COXYDE. (See orders attached.) Battalion obtained in good billets left in very unsanitary condition by previous units. Enemy shelled the Area overnight. No casualties.	Battn orders

A.5834 Wt. W4973/M687 750,000 8/16 D. D. & L. Ltd. Forms/C.2118/13.

WAR DIARY
INTELLIGENCE SUMMARY — 1st Battn. The Queens Regt.

Page 4 — Army Form C. 2118.

Place	Date 1917	Hour	Summary of Events and Information	Remarks and references to Appendices
COXYDE	Aug 19	10 a.m.	Voluntary Church Parade. Morning spent in getting billets clean. 100 men & 2 officers and R.E. all day	R.E. all day
		P.M.	2/Lt WATTS left for LONDON to join R.E.	
Do.	20	8 noon	Bathing at COXYDE-BAINS. in small parties. Company Training. About 20 men brought local farmers in cutting and binding the corn & harvest. R.E. working party as before.	
Do.		P.M.	Bathing in the sea.	
Do.	21	11.30 p.m.	Enemy put about 15 shells into village at each of these times.	
		12.30 a.m.		
		1-15 a.m.		
		8 a.m.	2 officers & 100 men sent as working party under R.E. all day. Company Training.	
			Lt. Wallis given 30 days leave.	
		2 p.m.	Bathing.	
Do.	22	8 a.m.	2 officers & 100 men parade for R.E. Fatigue. Company training. Firing on beach.	
			Two Companies route marched.	
		2 p.m.	Bathing parade.	
Do.	23	9 a.m.	R.E. Fatigue party as before. Coy. Companies carried out route march.	
		6 p.m.	Concert. Brigadier General Band dined at H.Q. Mess. A little shelling took place at night.	
Do.	24	9 a.m.	R.E. Fatigue party as before. A Coy route marched. B. Coy carried out field firing on beach at ST IDESBALD. A & B. Coys carried out company training.	

Page 5

Army Form C. 2118.

WAR DIARY
or
INTELLIGENCE SUMMARY 1st Batt. The Queens Regt.

(Erase heading not required.)

Place	Date 1917	Hour	Summary of Events and Information	Remarks and references to Appendices
COXYDE	Aug 24	5.30 p.m.	Tactical scheme for company & platoon section commanders.	
Do	-25	8 a.m.	A & B Coys found R.E. working party as before. D Coy & Lewis gunners & remaining companies carried out hill firing on the beach. Other companies trained in vicinity of billets. Coast guns in a hollow in the village. Returns attended.	
		6 p.m.	Voluntary church service.	
Do	-26	10 a.m.	Maj. J. WEEDING, LT. C. LENSHAW, 2/LT COOKE & 2/LT COWAN left on bicycles to reconnoitre the sector of the Battn. line prior to the Battn. going in. The party were proceeding the WULPEN- NIEUPORT road, Ladabout reached offshoot to RAMSCAPELLE when a shell burst close to the party on the road killing Maj. Weeding, his horse & slightly wounding 2/Lt Cowan & his horse. 2/Lt Clenshaw & 2/Lt Cooke's horse. Party reported to Coxyde with Maj. Weeding's body. After days at Corps Dressing Station 2/Lt Cowan & St. Clenshaw rejoined Battn. Weeding's body.	
		4 p.m. to 4.30 pm	Move to trenches cancelled. Continuous shelling of the village. Two large shells fell within 50 yards of H.Q. No casualties.	
		12.30 a.m.	Warning orders received to move to GHYVELDE on 27th & to TETEGHEM area on 28th.	
Do	-27	9.15 a.m.	Buried Maj. Weeding with military honours in civilian graveyard nr. COXYDE. Firing party under 2/Lt. SHIPTON, all officers & one platoon from each Coy. attended. Eight officers acted as bearers. 2/Lt PARSONS and PURCHAS joined Battn.	
Do		Noon	Battn. moved to GHYVELDE and was stationed in previous camp. Took over from 17th H.L.I. Arrived 3½ p.m.	

Army Form C. 2118.

WAR DIARY
INTELLIGENCE SUMMARY — 1st Battn. The Queens Regt.

(Erase heading not required.)

Page 6

Place	Date 1917	Hour	Summary of Events and Information	Remarks and references to Appendices
GHYVELDE	Aug 28	8.50 a.m.	Battalion moved to COUDEKERQUE via UXEM - GALGHOECK - BOOMKENS. Arrived 1 p.m. Battn. proceeded to widely scattered billets.	
COUDEKERQUE	29		Companies attended of their commanders. Warning order received to move to EPERLECQUES. Transport less 4 cooks, 2 water carts, 4 chargers, medical cart to move at once by road to WORMHOUDT.	
Do.	30	a.m.	Companies carried out training in vicinity of billets.	
		noon	Transport less vehicles as above moved by road to WORMHOUDT. They will there receive orders to meet Battn. at EPERLECQUES to-morrow.	Battn. Order no. 153
Do.	31	3.30 a.m.	Transport left for DUNKERQUE under Capt. CROOK. This party entrained & left at 7.45 a.m. arriving at AUDRUICQ at noon. Party marched to BAYENGHEM arriving at 3 p.m.	
		6 a.m.	Capt. HARRISON left & proceeded to BAYENGHEM.	
WORMHOUDT		8 a.m.	Battalion marched to DUNKERQUE - DOCKS & entrained. Train started 8.50 a.m. Arrived at WATTEN at noon. Marched to BAYENGHEM & arrived at 1.50 p.m. Accommodated in billets.	
COUDEKERQUE				

J.C. Russell
Comdg. 1st Bn. The Queens

SECRET.   Battalion Orders. No: 129.   Copy No 12
          by Lieut-Colonel: L.M. CROFTS. D.S.O.
          Comdg: Bn The Queen's Regt.   Thursday 2/8/17.

Detail for tomorrow
Subaltern of the Day   2/Lieut L.P. SMITH.

1. The Battalion will assemble in the following order, with head of Column at E. of Road Junction at R. in COUDEKERQUE. ready to move off at 9.28 am.
   H.Q. "D" "A" Drums "B" "C" Transport.
   Dress. F.S.M.O. Caps will be worn. S.B.R. respirators resting on Pack, sling fixed to the Belt.
   300ʳ interval to be kept throughout the march.
   Reveille will be at 6.30 am. Breakfasts 7.30 am.

2. Valises to be at Q.M. Stores by 8.30 am.
   Mess kits to be at H.Q. Mess by 8.45 am.

3. Billeting Party consisting of C.O. M.Sgts, 1 N.C.O. H.Drs, under Lt. L.A. CROOK. M.C. with bicycles, will parade at Bn H.Q. Mess at 5.45 AM.

4. A working party composed from 1st Reinforcements as under. will be in readiness to proceed to 15th Corps. H.A. tomorrow moving on receipt of Orders.
   Captain J.P. COOKSON, A Coy 3 Pks, B Coy 1 Sgt 2 Pks,
   C Coy 1 Cpl 2 Pks, D Coy 3 Pks.

5. Steps are to be taken that Billets are thoroughly cleaned up prior to parade & Coy etc Commanders will inspect them and report to the Adjt on parade, this has been done.

6. C & D Coys will each detail one man for Course in Lewis Post commencing on 6th Inst. Names of men selected to be submitted to O. Room by 9.0 am tomorrow.

7. The Un Officers N.C.O.s & men proceed on leave tomorrow and will assemble at D Coys Billet on Bn marching off:
   Captain N.B. AVERY, Lt. J.R.G. COWAN, Sgt Claridge & Sgt Riggs A Coy, Pte Lawson B Coy, 4131 Pte Edwards, Naylor, & L/Cpl Lawson C Coy, 4008 Pte Simmonds & Cpl Judd D Coy.

8. The following have been issued to Coys this day.
   55th Divn. G.657, G.269, G.282, S.S.172, 4th Army C.B. #85
   The contents of G.657 and G.269 are to be made known to all Ranks by means of Lectures forthwith.

9. 2/Lt J.E. SHIPTON will proceed to Divn H.Q. to draw cash for Bn at 10.0 AM tomorrow.

                                (Sgd) R.H. Nevins Lt & Adjt
                                    Bn The Queen's Regt
Copies issued as under.
No 1. C.O.   2. 2nd. No 1. 3. O.C. No 2.
4. O.C. No 3, 5. O.C. No 4, 6. Bn & I.O.
7. Sig. Officer. 8. H.Q. Mess, 9. R.S.M.
10. Adjt. 11. F Files. 12 & 13. War Diary.

SECRET   Battalion Order No 142   (Copy No 12.)
by Lieut Col L M CROFTS D S O
Comdg Bn The Queens Regt

Friday 17th August 1917

1. The Divn is relieving 32nd Divn in the NIEUPORT Sector.

2. The Brigade will be in Divl Reserve at OOST-DUNKERQUE and Camps at H.18.

3. The Battalion will assemble on the CHYZELDE BRAY-DUNES Road in the following order. Head of Column at Road Junction (B Coy Mess) ready to move off at 5 a.m. & march to COXYDE distance about 7 miles. Route ADINKERKE FURNES Road running E.N.E. through A of ADINKERKE and COXYDE.
   H.Q. A.B. Drums C.D. Transport
   Dress T.S.M.O. Caps will be worn.
   Reveille will be at 3 a.m. Breakfasts 3.45 a.m.

4. Valises of Officers in Camp and South end of Village to be at Q.M. Stores at 4.15 a.m. Those of other officers will be stacked at H.Q. Mess by 4.45 a.m.

5. Men's Kits to be at H.Q. Mess by 4.30 a.m.

6. The following Distances will be maintained throughout the March:-
   Between Battalions 400 yds Companies 200 yds
   and Transport 200 yds
   E of COXYDE between Platoons 100 yds

7. Coys to arrange issue of hot tea on arrival new camp.

8. O.C. Coys to will take the necessary steps to see that Billets Huts & Tents are left clean.
   Tent walls will be left Rolled up.

9. Two working Parties will be furnished daily by the Battn commencing 18th inst from and for use each A & B. Coys to at the 357th A.T. Coy R.E at OOST-DUNKERQUE - OOST-DUNKERQUE BAINS Cross Roads (H.11.A 2.2) and 255th A.T. Coy R.E at H.C.39 respectively at 8 a.m. 19th instant.
   Strength of each Party 1 Officer 1 Platoon (made up to 50 OR)
   Dress Drill order Steel Helmets to be worn
   Haversack Rations and 50 shovels to be carried

Copies issued
1. C.O.
2. O.C. Coys
3.
4.
5.
6. M.H.
7. T.O.
8. Sig officer
9. R.S.M.
10. Adjt
11. Cb
12. Spare

(Sd) R.H. Nairn Capt & Adjt
                    Nairn

L.H. Nairn
Capt & Adjt

Demands made on this sheet should consist of personnel required from the Base only, and should not include any demands for personnel which can be completed by promotions or appointments within the unit.

Perforated Sheet giving detail of personnel and horses waiting to complete, shown on Army Form B. 213.

No. of Report _____

Detail of Wanting to Complete										
CAVALRY	R.A.	R.E.	INFANTRY	R.A.M.C.	A.O.C.	A.V.C.				

R.A.		Drivers
R.E.		
A.S.C.		
Car		
Lorry		
Steam		
Gunners		
Smith Gunners		
Range Takers		
Serjeants		Farriers
Corporals		
Shoeing, or Shoeing and Carriage Smiths		
Cold Shoers		
R.A.		Wheelers
H.T.		
M.T.		
Saddlers or Harness Makers		
Blacksmiths		
Bricklayers and Masons		
Carpenters and Joiners		
Wood		Fitters & Turners (R.E.)
Iron		
R.A.		Fitters
Wireless		
Plumbers		
Ordinary		Electricians
W.T.		
Signalmen		
Loco.		Engine Drivers
Field		
Air Line Men		
Permanent Line Men		
Operators, Telegraph		
Cablemen		
Brigade Section Pioneers		
General-duty Pioneers		
Signallers		
Instrument Repairers		
Motor Cyclist		
Motor Cyclist Artificers		
Telephonists		
Clerks		
Machine Gunners		
Fitters		Armament Artificers
Range Finders		
Armourers		
Storemen		
Privates		
W. O's. and N.C.O's. (in ranks) not included in these columns		

War Diary

Officers	TOTAL to agree with wanting to complete
Other Ranks	
Riding	Horses
Draught	
Heavy Draught	
Pack	

Remarks :—

Signature of Commander. _____

Formation to which attached. _____

Unit. _____

Date of Despatch. _____

P.T.O.

(7422) W⁴ W14775/M1653 1,000,000 2/17 (E934) Forms/B213/8

D.D.D. & L. London, E.C.

Battalion Order No 153   Copy No 11
by Lieut Col L.M. CROFTS D.S.O
Comdg Bn The Queens Regt

Thursday 30th Augt 1917

Detail for tomorrow.
Subaltern of the day   Lieut S. M. Howcroft

1. Move
Ref: Map. DUNKERQUE. 1/100,000.
The Battalion will assemble tomorrow on road running through Q of COUDEKERQUE. BRANCHE, C & D Coy near its present Billets joining the Battalion as it passes. It & A & B Coys will be at Bn Hters ready to move off at 6.0 am and march to DUNKERQUE Stn in the order H.Q, D. C. B. A. where it entrains.

Dress F.S.M.O. Caps will be worn.

Rations for tomorrow including cooked meat portion will be carried on the man. Waterbottles will be filled tonight.

Transport, including Bicycles, will move under the orders of Capt. J. A. Crook. M.C. at 3.40 AM.

O.C Coys will fix their own hour for Reveille.

Sufficient Cooking Pots will be left off the Cookers and an issue of tea made before starting. On arrival at Station, Pots will be put back on the Cookers.

Drivers only are to accompany vehicles.

2. Posting
Cpl. G. Fryer R.A.M.C. is attached to 'C' Coy for one month from this date.

3. Discipline
It is to be impressed on all ranks that to use Green Envelopes a 2nd time is contrary to Censorship Rules.

4. Moves
187 Cpl Wall D Coy has been selected to attend j P Instr Course at G.H.Q. S.A. School assembling on 3rd inst. To report at C. Room for instructions on Saturday 2nd Sept: at 8. 0 AM.

Copies issued as under —   (Sgd) R. H. Nevins Capt & Adjt
No 1 C.O.   2. OC No 1.   Bn The Queens Regt
3. OC No 2. 4. OC No 3
5. OC No. 4. 6. Capt. J. A. Crook M.C.
7. B.S.O.   8. Adjt.
9. R.S.M.   10 & 11. War Diary

War Diary.

WAR DIARY — 1st Battn. The Queens Regt. Army Form C. 2118.
INTELLIGENCE SUMMARY — September 1917.

Place	Date	Hour	Summary of Events and Information	Remarks and references to Appendices
BAYENGHEM	1917 1.	a.m.	Companies at disposal of their commanders.	
		2 p.m.	Conference. Company commanders & specialist officers attended. Programme of training was arranged with a view to offensive action.	
Do	2	11.15 a.m.	Divine Service arranged for this hour was cancelled owing to rain. Voluntary service in School room at 11.30.	
Do	3	a.m.	Company training on training ground S. of CALAIS—ST OMER road.	
		2.30 p.m.	All companies fielded 300 yds. on B range.	
Do	4	8–11 a.m.	B. Coy. practised on short rifle range.	Bombers class under 2/Lt. J.E. SHIPTON.
		afternoon	D. Coy. ditto.	
		6 p.m.	Concert in new P. B. Coys billet.	
Do	5	a.m.	A & C. Coys. practised on short range. Other companies under their own arrangements. Bombers class under 2/Lt. J.E. SHIPTON.	
		2 p.m.	Conference.	

WAR DIARY / INTELLIGENCE SUMMARY

Page 2 — 1st Battn. The Queen's Regt., Army Form C. 2118.

September 1917.

Place	Date 1917	Hour	Summary of Events and Information	Remarks and references to Appendices
BAYENGHEM	2		2/Lt. K.M. EAST rejoined Battalion.	
		a.m.	Company & Platoon training. H.Qrs. at range practice.	
		p.m.	Conference.	
Do	7	10.30 a.m.	Battalion practice attack against imaginary position N.W. of LA RONVILLE. A & B Coys attacked on a frontage of 2 sections each. C & D Coys. in support. A creeping barrage was represented by a line with flags. To cope with hostile enemy tanks, companies were allotted an orderly party carrying flags.	
		5.30 p.m.	Lecture on machine gun tactics by 2/Lt. K.M. EAST who had just completed a course of instruction at G.H.Q. Small Arms School.	
Do	8		Battalion marched to GUEMY 7 miles, carried out an exercise as follows:— Each platoon advanced down the field firing range from 6 a.m to 11 a.m. Each platoon carried out an exercise as follows:— Each platoon advanced down the range in artillery formation & came under machine gun fire. It extended, opened fire with Lewis gun, rifle grenades & rifle men & bombers worked close to their objective, finally taking the gun. Enemy counter attack, represented by falling flakes, was then beaten off.	

Army Form C. 2118.

WAR DIARY
1st Battn. The Queens Regt.
INTELLIGENCE SUMMARY
September 1917.

(Erase heading not required.)

Page 3

Instructions regarding War Diaries and Intelligence Summaries are contained in F. S. Regs., Part II. and the Staff Manual respectively. Title Pages will be prepared in manuscript.

Place	Date 1917	Hour	Summary of Events and Information	Remarks and references to Appendices
BAYENGHEM	Sept 9	10.30 a.m.	Voluntary Divine Service in School Room.	
		2.30 to 6.30 p.m.	Companies fired in turn on B. range.	
			2/Lt K.F. PARSONS proceeded to England on duty under instructions from War Office.	
Do	10	8-noon	Company training in vicinity of billets.	
		2.30 to 6.30 p.m.	Companies fired in turn on B. range.	
Do	11	8.30 to 11 a.m.	Band D. Company fired on A range.	
		2 to 4 p.m.	Battalion bathed in batches at EPERLECQUES.	
		4-4.30	Hd Qrs. fired on A range.	
Do	12	7 a.m. to 11 a.m.	Battalion marched to ground S.W. of NORTLEULINGHEM and took part in Brigade attack scheme. Battalion attacked on a frontage of 260 yards capturing enemy first & second lines or areas conducting two strong points beyond under cover. Later a counter attack was beaten off.	
		3.45 p.m.	Conference of all officers to discuss morning scheme.	

Page 4

WAR DIARY 1st Battn. The Queen's Regt.

INTELLIGENCE SUMMARY. September 1917.

Place	Date	Hour	Summary of Events and Information	Remarks and references to Appendices
	1917			
BAYENGHEM	Sep.13	9 a.m.	Brigade manoeuvres identical to yesterday except that the Army Commander was present at the conclusion, the Brigadier, Divisional Commander and Army Commander	
		3 p.m.	(Second Army) (Gen. PLUMER) addressed all officers, pointing out good & bad points and	
			dwelling particularly on future tactics brought about by enemy not continually changing	
		5.30 p.m.	Battalion event.	
			Warning orders received to move.	
		11 a.m.	Conference held on Arango.	
		4 p.m.	Advance billeting party moved to BUYSSCHEURE.	
Do-	15	8.25 a.m.	Battn. marched via WATTEN to BUYSSCHEURE, about 9 miles & arrived 1 p.m.	B.O. 166
			Billets provided.	
BUYSSCHEURE.	16	6.15 p.m.	Battalion marched to STEENVOODE (about 10 miles). Arrived at 1 p.m. In vest of	B.O. 167
			Battalion in billets.	
STEENVOODE	17	8.45 a.m.	Battalion marched to BERTHEN (9 miles). Arrived at 1 p.m. Accomodated in	B.O. 168

Page 5

WAR DIARY

1st Battn. The Queens Regt.

INTELLIGENCE SUMMARY

September 1917.

(Erase heading not required.)

Instructions regarding War Diaries and Intelligence Summaries are contained in F.S. Regs., Part II. and the Staff Manual respectively. Title pages will be prepared in manuscript.

Army Form C. 2118.

Place	Date	Hour	Summary of Events and Information	Remarks and references to Appendices
	1917.		Tents & Billets.	
			2/Lt. R.L. LEIGHTON joined from 3rd Battn.	
BERTHEN	Sep 18	8 a.m.	Companies at disposal of commanders for instructions.	
			2/Lt S.F. PRIOR left for attachment to 100th Trench Mortar Battery. 2/2Lt L.P. SMITH left for attachment to R.F.C.	
Do.	19		Battalion marched 7 miles via WESTOUTRE to a camp 1500 yards S.E. of RENINGHELST. Left at 2 p.m. Arrived at 5 p.m.	Batln O.171
NEAR RENINGHELST	20	11 a.m.	Battalion rested by orders of Army Commander. Conference of company commanders. Camps vicinity were shelled during night. One man was killed & seven wounded.	Eg+x
Do.	21	a.m.	Companies at disposal of commanders. Conference of all officers when forthcoming operations were explained & discussed in further detail.	

Page 6

WAR DIARY 1st Battn. The Queens Regt.   Army Form C. 2118.

INTELLIGENCE SUMMARY. September 1917.

(Erase heading not required.)

Place	Date	Hour	Summary of Events and Information	Remarks and references to Appendices
	1917			
Near RENINGHELST	Sept 22	am	Minimum reserve under Captain DENMAN, paraded at 7 am & proceeded to join Sub Depot No. - BEGHIN. Practical operations to take place in the near future - Conferences were held.	
"	" 23rd	pm	Order received that the 1st Battalion would march to Ridge Horse Area (Sect E) I.26.a). During Coy parade moved off at 5.30 pm, arrived in their area at 6.C. D at 10 minutes interval. Move was completed at 8.30 am. Battalion in bivouac. Lieut Col L.M. CRAPPS reconnoitred FRONT LINE with a view to making dispositions for pending operations. Lieut I.T.P. HUGHES and 1 N.C.O. per Coy proceeded to FRONT LINE to take over stores in position preparatory to Battalion Relief. Lieut Col M.M. GIMMALL reported from leave.	
"	" 24th		Orders received Battalion would relieve 8th BN. K.O.Y.L.I. in Right Sub Sector on night 24th/25th. "B" Echelon established at SCOTTISHWOOD. E of DICKEBUSCH.	B.O. 175
			Report of operations 24th to 27th attached.	
"	" 28th	6 am	Lieuts T. CROMPTON and J.E. CORRY joined from 2nd Battalion. Transport proceeded by road to BLARINGHEM area under Bde T.O. (Capt HARRISON, M.C.).	

WAR DIARY
INTELLIGENCE SUMMARY.

1st Bn "THE QUEEN'S" Regt Army Form C. 2118.

SEPTEMBER 1917

(Erase heading not required.)

Place	Date	Hour	Summary of Events and Information	Remarks and references to Appendices
SCOTTISH WOOD	28th	11 a.m.	Orders received Battalion would march to RENINGHELST extent at worlds entrance	
			to BLARINGHEM area. Battalion paraded at 12.30 p.m. and marched via Cross	
			Country track to RENINGHELST thence by road to SIDING about 2 miles N of village	
			where it entrained. arrived EBLINGHEM 9 p.m. detrained proceeded by march route	
			to Billets at La Belle Hotesse where it arrived at 11 p.m. Hot tea served.	
La Belle Hotesse	29th		Minimum Reveille had marched and were already settled in.	
"	30th		Rest – Cleaning up. Lieuts J. RODKIN, LOPPKER, R.E.DARBY & F.B. DENNY joined	
			from 3rd Battalion.	
			Signal Rates – Refitting etc. Lieut F. ROSSER joined from 2nd Battalion.	

30-9-17

J. W. ?? ? Lt. Col
Comdg 1st Bn The Queen's Regt

Army Form C. 2118.

Report on Operations 24th to 29th September 1917
1st Batt "THE QUEEN'S Regt."

WAR DIARY
or
INTELLIGENCE SUMMARY.
(Erase heading not required.)

Place	Date	Hour	Summary of Events and Information	Remarks and references to Appendices
	Sept 24th	1.0 p.m.	Battalion commences leaving vicinity of BEDFORD HOUSE for the relief of 8th K.O.Y.L.I. in front line trenches on the MENIN Rd near VELDHOEK	
			Front line position with battles round of our Regiments moving at the same time and very considerable artillery fire of enemy being incessant. No battle with artillery fire.	
			A Company + C Coy in reserve in KANTIN E cab't (F) and JASPER TK (G) Batt H.Q. at appendix (1)
			in trench dug out at (H) Took up their positions by daylight - B + D Coy remained in their	
			pill box dug outs in TUMBRIDGE LANES till dusk -	
		7.30 p.m.	Relief of front line commenced. B had platoon that had lost its way in front line (B - C)	
			with one platoon of D and 3 platoons of D in support at (E) - The remaining platoon	
			of B was left at (F) Whole being in relieve in front line.	
	25th	6 a.m. 12.30	Relief complete.	
			Morning very much - at 5.30 a.m. an enemy predatn barrage commenced	
		5.30	Message received at Batt H.Q. that enemy had penetrated 1st front line - shortly afterwards	
		7.30	2nd with from B Coy advanced wounded with information that front line had been practically	
			wiped out by heavy minnies, but that D Coy was holding out.	
			C Coy advanced to make (1) counter attack - During 1 heavy barrage between H.Q. and front line	

WAR DIARY or INTELLIGENCE SUMMARY

Army Form C. 2118.

Place	Date	Hour	Summary of Events and Information	Remarks and references to Appendices
MENIN Road	Sept 25	am	Bn reported unfit to fit a company this the Barrage.	
		7.48	C. S.M. Tipper D Coy arrived badly wounded & reports all D Coy H Qrs & King out. No communication with Bn. Reference notes for by pigeon.	
near VELDHOEK 		8.45	Barrage slightly slackened — C Coy under Capt Carothers advanced in front order to the N W of the MENIN Road — A Coy were kept in hand whilst things on other brigade Bde to South this is the MENIN Rd — Capt Crole ordered C Coy to push on by Bull rum H Qr	
		10.0	"C" Coy reports that 15th L.L. reached the support line and were being held up & left and Sussex (39th Div) night and were preparing to attack front line held in strength by the enemy	
		11.30	'A' Coy of 11 K.R.R. under Capt Francis received instructions to push on & fill in & hold that line took our reserve line (Blue Stone) & post to MENIN road held by ?? Bde) and A Coy under Capt Barrow advanced (reinforced C.)	
		pm 12.15	11.K.R. reports that we broke thro front line (what follows unreadable) & reached LS	
		12.20	position A-B	
		1.30	2 Coys Garrison N of MENIN Rd in touch with H.L.I. on left (C) 2 Coys K.R.R. in reserve trench	Appendix (2)

WAR DIARY
or
INTELLIGENCE SUMMARY.
(Erase heading not required.)

Army Form C. 2118.

Place	Date	Hour	Summary of Events and Information	Remarks and references to Appendices
VELDHOEK	Sept 25	2.10 p.m	Capt Constable and Burrell both wounded - 2 coys returned to about 100 rifles	
			2nd Hants left with a 2nd Coy reld to R.B.	
		3 p.m	1 coy K.R.R. never found to support the Queens -	
			Dur't ½ Coys of Bn in trench havm back to carried with H.L.I. It was not possible to make further advance this night without much further no. and	
	26	am 12.30	Operation order to relieve organisation at 3.50 am received. 1st Hampshire at No. 1 + 2 of K.R.R. reld Bn H.Q. on return were arranged. Gutton a later left of MENIN ROAD was to R.R. in support. arrangements made with artillery Lawson Officer for staying of 5 minutes w/over origind line for cough H.Q. coys [illegible] at 2.7.6.1.3.2. During then Hampshire will relv of farm age -	
		4.0 am	Messy received from Franklin that had taken into of attacks and were not during anything (3rd Regis in large force across most not little HQR to enemy matter.	

WAR DIARY or INTELLIGENCE SUMMARY

Army Form C. 2118.

Place	Date	Hour	Summary of Events and Information	Remarks and references to Appendices
	Sept	am		
VELDHOEK	26		Before zero 5.50 am. 2 coys K.R.R. and remainder of 2 coys Queens were in position as	Appendix 3
			8 am — took expected photos blew in rooms. 2 M.Gs were in position in KANTINT	
			Cable Tr. nor MENIN Rd.	
		5.50	Barrage opened and a Rough time. Troops advanced in conjunction with Hants 39th Div	
			on South of K.G. Road but were held up by strong point x with M.G. and not until	
			proper work to made on the left main attack but line was consolidated in front	
			by Tahir line — 20 prisoners were taken —	
		8.30	one M.G. and funnel — German aeroplane too much in flames by Lewis gun fire —	
		9.30	On companys arrived and to coy sent as support to front companies —	
			Barbing when a left divinn Off.	
		3pm	Germans repulsed massing for counter attack — Some which a left divinn Off.	
		5pm	S.O.S. but up on left/right — an artillery opened strong barrage which continues	
			for over 2 hours —	
		4.0p	Lieut Redin. Commanders Nyroongon's party of various Rift. and noticed their	
			point of x — capturing 4 M.G. 26 prisoners, killing about 40 Bocke.	
			This advance is original position and H.Q. came up — except cleaned and	

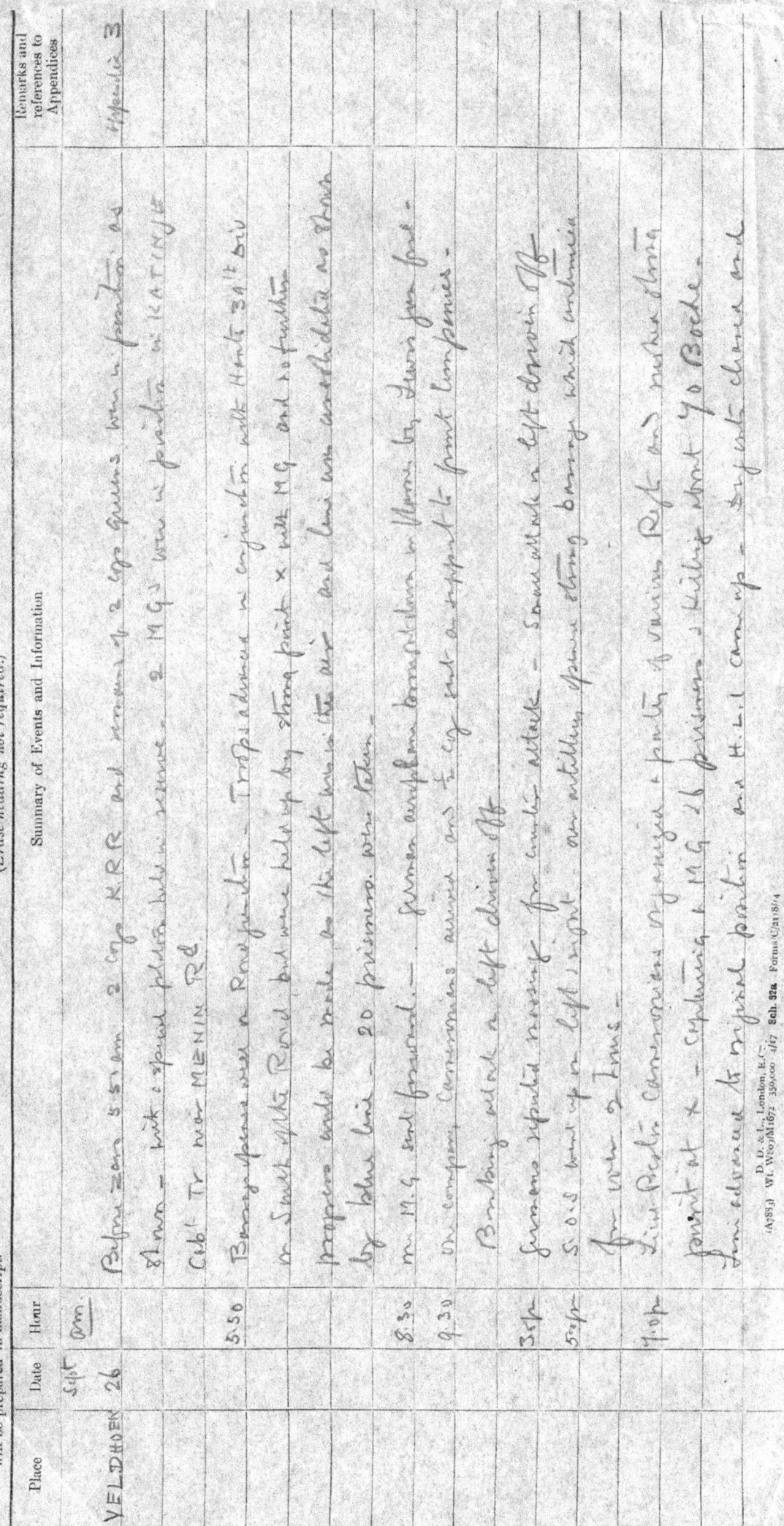

Army Form C. 2118.

WAR DIARY
or
INTELLIGENCE SUMMARY.
(Erase heading not required.)

Instructions regarding War Diaries and Intelligence Summaries are contained in F. S. Regs., Part II, and the Staff Manual respectively. Title pages will be prepared in manuscript.

Place	Date	Hour	Summary of Events and Information	Remarks and references to Appendices
VELDHOEK	Sept 26		Position 28 prisoners secured - Ground being consolidated.	
	27		Most passed without incident.	
		4 am / 5.0	Enemy practise barrage which brought down retaliation. Morning misty and quiet enabling work in connection with consolidation to be carried out. Some of the wounded to be brought down.	
		4.30	2 Coy Cameronians arrived as reinforcements. Casualties sent to forward companies.	
			Remainder of day passed without incident - Continuation reported G.N. & S. late in the day.	
		6.30	Heavy enemy shell which entered Bn HQrs slightly damaging roof.	
		9.30	Relief by 6 K.O.Y.L.I. commenced - parties to relieve returns to Dickebusch.	
	28		Relief completed 1.55 am - Bn proceeded reached camp at 5.0 am. Remarks: All communication during the relief was most difficult. No telephone communication was possible at all to Brigade and company, expending very difficult on account of the broken but bogs - Pigeons were freely used and proved its	

WAR DIARY or INTELLIGENCE SUMMARY

Army Form C. 2118.

Place	Date	Hour	Summary of Events and Information	Remarks and references to Appendices
	Sept 29		Not satisfactory - spasmodic bursts of communication back - communication found	
			to be uncertain from long lines to police phone.	
			The casualties in my own, the two front companies to L.D. during all the	
			Officers & not of other ranks. Steps were set to recover bodies & form a tally	
			[illegible] at the position held by the Queens and a number of men were	
			surrendered and captured.	
			Casualties Officers killed 4 wounded 9 missing 1 total 14	
			O.R. " 59 " 109 " 219 " 387	
			Names of Officers killed. 2/Lieut C.G. KEMP (R.A.) Captain L.A. CROOK M.C. 2/Lieut F.D. TUCKER (25th)	
			2/Lieut G.T. PURCHASE (25th). Wounded. Captain R.C. AVENER M.C. 2/Lieut J.S. MILNER (25th) Captain W.B.	
			CARR-BLAKE. J. BURGGL [?] 2nd Lt P. HUGHES. H.G. TRYTHALL CWG CHARLES. W.H. GAYNES	
			W.L. ATKINSON (25th) MISSING - Lieut W.F. CLENSHAW (25th).	
			Map showing original objectives of Bn. prior to present attack of 25th F	aper (4)/
			Captures from our view of attack	5
			Notes on attack of 30th Sept	6
			Special order of the day by G.O.C. Division & Brigade	7 & 8
			[signature] Lieut Colonel [?]	
			1.10.17	

Secret

Battalion Order No. 166.   Copy No. 14.
by Lieut. Col. J.B. Croft D.S.O.
Comdg Bn The Queens Regt
                                           Friday 14th Sept 1919

1. The Battalion will assemble in the following order, head of column at A Coy's further Billet, ready to move off at 8.25 a.m. tomorrow. – H.Q, A.B. Drums C.D. Transport, and march to – BOYSENGHEM via Route BLEUE MAISON WATTEN – KINDERBRICK. – Dress F.S.M.O. Caps will be worn. Distances to be maintained, between units 500 yds. Between every group of six vehicles 10 yards. With these exceptions the regulation distances will be adhered to.
   O.C "D" Coy will detail an Officer and an efficient N.C.O to collect and bring in stragglers should there be any.

2. Watches will be synchronised at 8 a.m.

3. Breakfasts will be at 7.15 a.m. Officers valises to be at Q.M Stores by 7.30 a.m. Mess Kit at the H.Q Mess by 8.0 a.m.

4. O.C. Coys &c will personally inspect all billets & report to the Adjt on parade this has been done & billets left clean & in a sanitary state.

5. Pioneer Sergt. 2 Pioneers & 1 Sanitary man per Coy will remain behind under Lieut R.M. EAST who will ensure the area is left in a Sanitary state obtaining a certificate from the Area Commandant to this effect.

6. Marching out states will be handed in on parade. These are to account for all ranks on strength – Keep line showing actual number on parade with Coy.

7. O.C. Coys are responsible that there are no claims left unsettled.

                                  (Sd) R. H. Nevin Capt & Adjt
                                            The Queens
Copies issued as under.
No: 1. C.O.   No 2. O.C. "A" Coy
    3. O.C. No 2.   4. O.C. No 3.
    5. O.C. No 4.   6. T.O.
    7. B.M.   8. Lieut R.M. East
    9. Bn S.O.   10. Adjt
   11. R.S.M.   12. File
   and War Diary
                                       R. H. Nevin

Secret.   Battalion Order No 167.   Copy No: 13
by Lieut: Col: L.M. CROFTS. D.S.O.
Comdg: Bn "The Queen's" Regt.

Saturday,
15th Sept: 17

Detail for tomorrow
Subaltern of the day   2/Lt G.F.A. ????

1. The Battalion will assemble in the following order, head of Battn at Bn. H.Q. ready to move off at 6·20 AM. H.Q. "B" "C" Drums "D" "A" Transport. (D. Coy will gain its place in the column at Cross Roads at the Church) and march to STEENVOORDE (Central Area). Distance about 14 miles — Dress. F.S.M.O.
Route - ZUYTPEENE, BAVINCHOVE, OXELAERE - Road lane E of CASSEL.
Distances to be maintained - 500 yds between units 10 yds between each group of six vehicles with these exceptions regulation distances will be adhered to.
O.C. "A" Coy will detail an Officer and N.C.O to collect and bring in stragglers should there be any.

2. Reveille will be at 4·30 AM. Breakfasts 5·0 AM. Officers valises and mess baskets - A & C. to be stacked at road junction E. of "A" and S. of "C" Coy. at 5·30 AM. to be picked up by wagon on return journey - remainder at Q.M. Stores by 5·30 AM.

3. Watches will be synchronised at 5·0 AM.

4. O.C. Coys will personally inspect all billets & report to the Adjt on parade this has been done & billets left clean & sanitary.

5. Billeting N.C.Os will meet Capt. L.A. CROOK. M.C. at Bn. H.Q. at 6·15 am with bicycles.

6. Pioneer Sergt, 2 Pioneers, & 1 Sanitary man per Coy will remain behind under 2/Lt. J.E. SHIPTON to hand over billets to Area Commandant.

7. Coys will arrange that their Billet Guards are visited by an officer tonight.

Copies to —
No: 1 C.O. 2. OC No 1.
3 OC No 2. 4. OC No 3.
5 OC No 4. 6. T.O.
7. Q.M. 8. Adjt.
9. ...
10. ...

(Sgd) R.H. Nevins Capt. & Adjt.
The Queen's Regiment

SECRET   Battalion Order No 168   Copy No 13
                  by Lieut. Col. L. M. CROFTS. D.S.O
                      Comdg Bn "The Queens" Regt
                                                    Sunday 16 Sep. 1917

Detail for tomorrow.
Subaltern of the day.   Lieut. S. F. PRIOR

1. The Battalion will assemble in the following order, head of Column at entrance to Bn. H. Qr. Field, ready to move off at 8.45 a.m.:—
H.Q. C. D. Drums A. B. Transport and march to FONTAINE HOUCK about 10½ miles — Dress, F.S.M.O. Caps will be worn.
Route, ABEELE — BOESCHEPE — BERTHEN.
Distances to be maintained 500ˣ between units, 100ˣ yds between Coys and Transport. Intervals between groups of vehicles will not be kept.
O.C. "B" Coy will detail an Officer and N.C.O to collect and bring in stragglers should there be any.

2. Reveille will be at 6.45 a.m. Breakfasts 7.30 a.m. Officer's Valises and mess kits except "B" & H.Qr. to be ready for loading on roadside outside billets at 7.45 a.m. Those of "B" & H.Qr to be at Q.M. Stores by 8.0 a.m.

3. A watcher will be sent round at 8.0 a.m. for synchronisation

4. O.C. Coys will personally inspect all billets and report to the Adjt: on parade that this has been done and that Billets have been left clean and sanitary.

5. Billeting N.C.O's will meet Capt. L.A. CROOK. M.C. at Bn. H. Qrs at 7.30 a.m. with bicycles.

6. Pioneer Sergt, 2 Pioneers, and 1 Sanitary man per Coy. will remain behind under 2/Lt. J.R.G. COWAN to hand over billets to Area Commandant.

7. Coys. will arrange that their Billet Guards are visited by an officer tonight.

8. A F.G.C.M. will assemble at H. Qrs, 16ᵗʰ K.R.R.C. at 10.0 a.m. 18ᵗʰ Inst.
The following men will be tried by this Court. { 11609 Pte C. MARROTT. "A" Coy
                                                { 31109 — J. SMITH. "D" Coy
O.C. Coys will arrange all evidence is present.
2/Lieut J.R.G. COWAN is appointed a member of this Court.
Capt. L.A. CROOK. M.C is appointed prosecutor

9. It does not seem to be understood that the Water Cart carries water for drinking purposes: which is not to be used for Cooking purposes except on occasions when special orders are issued

Copies issued as under—   (Sgd) K. H. Nevins Capt & Adjt
1. C.O   2. O.C No: 1   Bn "The Queens" Regt
3. O.C. No 2. 4. O.C. No: 3
5. O.C. No: 4 6. T.O
7. Q.M.   8. 2/Lieut. J.R.G. Cowan
9. Capt. L.A. CROOK. M.C 10. R.S.M
11. Adjt.   12. FILE
13 & 14. WAR DIARY. 15. Bn. S.O.

Copy No. 12

Secret

Battalion Order No: 171
by Lieut: Col: L.M. CROFTS. D.S.O.
Comdg: Bn "The Queen's" Regt.

Wednesday
19th Sept. 17.

Ref. Map: Sheet. 5A.

1. The Battalion will assemble in the following order, head of column at X roads S. of B in BERTHEN, ready to move off at 2.15 pm:— Dress F.S.M.O. Caps to be worn.
  H.Q., D, A, Drums, B, C, Transport, and march to CHIPPEWA. Camp, M.6.A. central. Distance about 7 miles.
  Distances to be maintained 500x between Units, 100x between Unit and it's transport and 100x between Coys.
  O.C. "C" Coy will detail one officer and N.C.O. to collect and bring in stragglers should there be any.

2. Officers valises and mess kits of "C" & "D" Coys to be ready by 12 noon, when they will be sent for.
  Of "A" & "H" Qrs at Q.M. Stores by 1.0 pm.
  "B" Coys valises to be ready by 10.30 am. "B" Coy will carry it's Mess kit on L.G. Limber.

3. 3377 Sergt. Lambert "C" Coy will proceed to England for Infantry Commission on 20th instant.

4. O.C. Coys will ensure Billets are left in order and will personally inspect them prior to marching off reporting them left in a clean and sanitary state.

Copies issued as under:—   (Sgd) R.N. Nevins Capt. & Adjt.
                                                  Bn The Queen's Regt.
1. C.O.   2. O.C. No: 1
3. O.C. No: 2   4. O.C. No: 3
5. O.C. No: 4   6. T.O.
7. Q.M.   8. Bn. S.O.
9. Adjt   10. R.S.M.
11. File   12 & 13. War Diary.

Battalion Order No: 175
by Lieut. Col. L. M. CROFTS. D.S.O.
Comdg. Bn. "The Queen's" Regiment

SECRET

Monday 24th September 1917

1. The Bn: will relieve 8. K.O.Y.L.I. in Front Line Trenches today. Coys will be disposed as follows:—
   RIGHT FRONT Coy. "D".   LEFT FRONT Coy. "B".   Support "A" and "C".

2. Guides on a platoon scale are being provided at Battn: H. Qrs. Coys will move, passing Bn: H.Q. at times as stated:—
   "A" 12.30 pm. "C" 1.0 pm. "D" 3.0 pm. "B" 3.30 pm.
   To move by sections at 100ˣ intervals.
   "A" Coy to Trenches running S. to KANTINTZE. CADE.
   "C" Coy to JASPER TRENCH.   Battn. H. Qrs. — J. 20. b. 6. 5.
   "B" & "D" Coys will remain in Bn. H.Q. area until darkness permits of their proceeding to Front line; the portion to be taken over extends from MENIN Road inclusive to the North.

3. Trench Stores will be drawn prior to moving off.
   12 Shovels per Coy, only will be taken up.

4. Shelters will be struck and packed, and greatcoats & haversacs will be dumped on roadside near Bivouacs prior to marching off and will remain under C.Q.M.S. until collected.

5. All ranks are to be warned they are to carry no papers etc which would be of use to the enemy.

6. Each Coy will take forward its Pack Animal carrying 8 tins of water and 4 Yukon Packs one loaded with 8 tins of water and one Yukon Pack will accompany H. Qrs. Animals proceed as far as TORR TOP where loads are transferred to Yukon Packs and carried on by men. It is believed but has not definitely that water tins can be refilled at TORR TOP.

7. Five copies, "Notes for Subordin. Comdrs. in Action" have been issued to each Coy. The contents to be made known to all ranks.

8. Five H.Q. Signallers will accompany leading Coy. i.e. "A", to take over lines etc. Four Battn. Runners will also proceed with "A" Coy, and will reconnoitre routes Bn. H. Qrs to Bde. H. Qrs TORR TOP, Bn. H.Q to "A" & "C" Coys.

9. In the event of hostile aeroplanes flying over during the relief all troops will lie down and will not move until aeroplanes are out of sight.

10. Battn Aid Post will be established at Bn. H.Q.

11. Relief when complete will be notified to Bde H.Q. by the Code Word "MONDAY."

12. Marching Out States will be handed in before marching off and will contain Headings as under:—
    WITH COY, TRANSPORT, DRUMS, "B" ECHELON, MINIMUM RESERVE, LEAVE TO ENGLAND, SICK 1ST DIVL. AREA, COMMAND.

13. The following officers will join "B" Echelon after Battn has moved forward:
    CAPT. & ADJT. R.H. NEVINS, and 2/Lts. LEIGHTON, RODKIN, HIGGS.

Copies issued as under:—
1. C.O.   2. O.C. No 1.
3. O.C. No 2.   4. O.C. No 3.
5. O.C. No 4.   6. T.O. & Q.M.
7. Asst. Adjt. 8. Bn. S.O.
9. Adjt.   10. R.S.M.
11. File. 12 & 13. War Diary.

(Sgd) R.H. Nevins Capt. & Adjt.
Bn. "The Queen's" Regt.

R.H. Nevins
Capt & Adjt

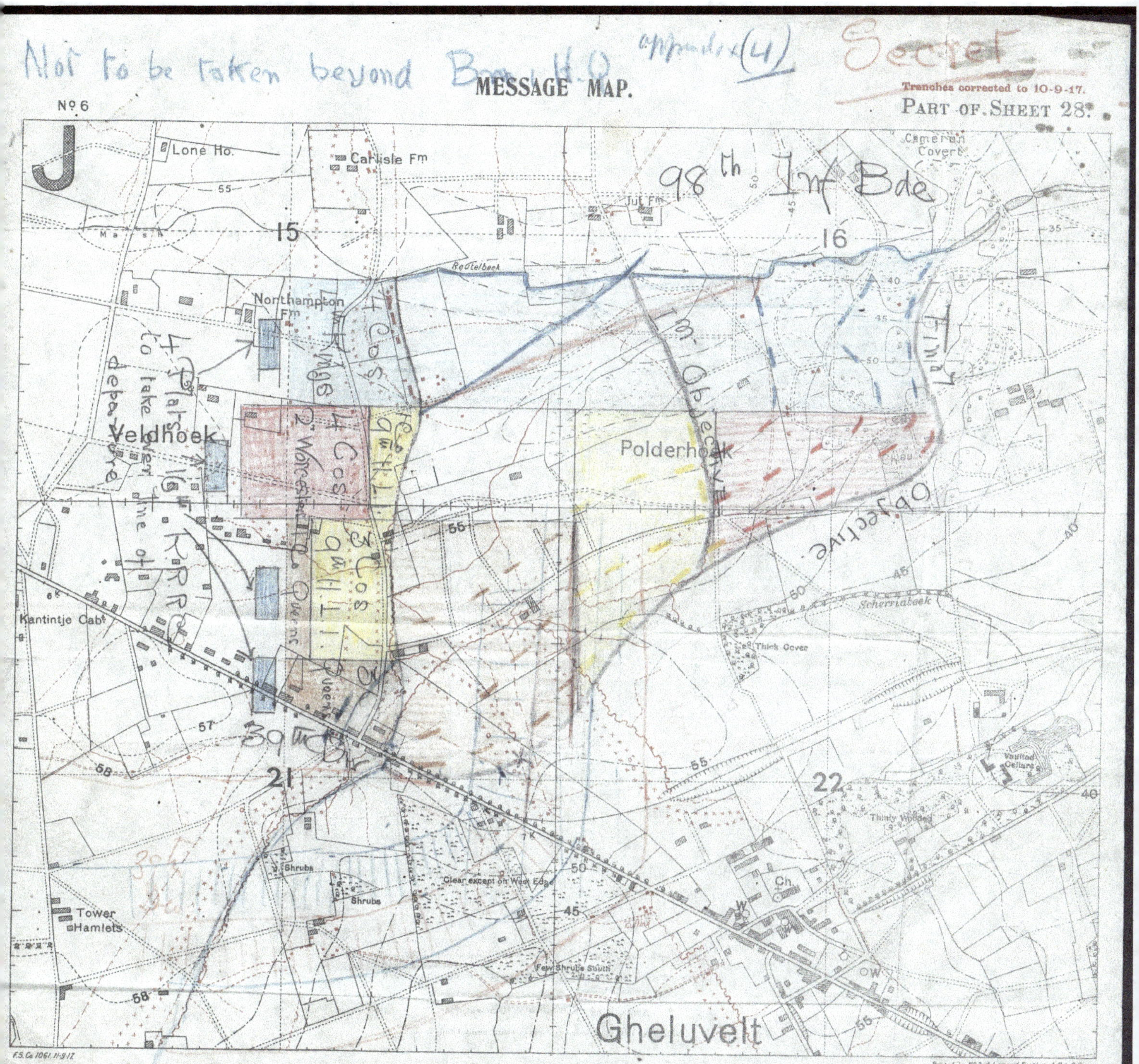

MESSAGE FORM.

To:—   No.

1. I am at........................ Note:—Either give Map Reference or mark your position by a 'X' on the Map on back.

2. I have reached limits of my Objective.

3. My Platoon / Company is at........................and is consolidating.

4. My Platoon / Company is at........................and has consolidated.

5. Am held up by (a) M.G. (b) Wire at............ (Place where you are).

6. Enemy holding strong point........................

7. I am in touch with ....on Right / Left at ....

8. I am not in touch with................on Right / Left.

9. Am shelled from........................

10. Am in need of :—

11. Counter Attack forming at ....

12. Hostile (a) Battery (b) Machine Gun (c) Trench Mortar active at ....

13. Reinforcements wanted at........................

14. I estimate my present strength at .... rifles.

15. Add any other useful information here:—

Time .... m.
Date .... 1917.

Name........................
Platoon........................
Company ....
Battalion ....

(A). Carry no maps or papers which may be of value to the Enemy.

(B). Give no information if captured, except the following, which you are bound to give:—

Name, Rank, (Number) and Regiment.

(C). Collect all captured maps and papers and send them in at once.

WAR DIARY

INTELLIGENCE SUMMARY.

OCTOBER 1917
1st Battn THE QUEEN'S Regt

Vol 36

(Erase heading not required.)

Army Form C. 2118.

Place	Date	Hour	Summary of Events and Information	Remarks and references to Appendices
In Rest Billets			Training and Sport Rates.	
			Captain A Watson returned —	
			Captain A Watson Commd the Reserve Coys reported by to	
			C.O. Batt'n having had no previous Battalion Employment	
			took part in Bourca Divisional Recits.	
			Battalion remained at Huttes in Reserve also to	
			Brigade were sure in as not sub. of an Division etc.	
			Lieut Douglas M.C. arrived at about 11.30am just unreported with the	
			Batt'n. The C.O. noted —	
			Lieut R Burnett, 1/Queens Regt Joined for duty	
			I.M. Crofts DSO Lieut Somerset assumed Command in the C.O. on his absence	
			from me of the Battalion and is to obtain a further instructions yet to attend R36 QMG	
			Went where Countries Captn 16 Dec 1915 to attend R36 QMG	
			Territorial 9629 2/Lt R Covey reverted with the R.M.C. Belgian	
			Assistant Musketry Act the J.C.M. reported for duty	
			M. Cain. G. Wing was not to be it at third Reap and now all-the	

21 1/R
Vol 36

Page 2.

Army Form C. 2118.

WAR DIARY

OCTOBER 1917

INTELLIGENCE SUMMARY. of Batt. THE QUEENS Regt

(Erase heading not required.)

Place	Date	Hour	Summary of Events and Information	Remarks and references to Appendices
Ludd			After moves to Ludding area Battalion allowed to Bath.	
			2.15 p.m the day the Brigadier General announced to all ranks that the C.in C. expressed at the close of the Brigade's great cooperation with the Turn-out had great appreciation of Mode ... in Palestine on the excellent handling of ...	
La Sulle	12th		Water and Company Tournament ... Chief for Young Officers commenced. Having been received - Brigade will ... to T14.Q62 area on 5th instant.	
Hotbose				
	5th		Battalion paraded at 10.4 am in the order "C" "D" "A" "B" Train "H.B" Transport and marched Ruler Gur OO via BELINCHEM - RENESCURE- FORT ROUGE - W ... of STONE T SMARTN an LEIGHT - patrol 18 miles - Move completed in ... Battalion broke in billets.	
			Leaving billets ... Battalion would probably entrain at St Laurent for R. BERWIN area - Transport proceeding by road.	

… Page 3

WAR DIARY
INTELLIGENCE SUMMARY

OCTOBER 1917 — 1st Batt. THE QUEEN'S R.

Army Form C. 2118.

Place	Date	Hour	Summary of Events and Information	Remarks and references to Appendices
ST MARTIN au LAERT	6th		Orders received at 2.45pm Battalion would entrain at WIZERNES Station and proceed to KORTIPYP Area to-day. Transport to proceed by road accordingly. Transport marched at 6am to La Belle Hôtesse where it halted for the day. Battalion paraded at 8.15am and marched to WIZERNES Station where it arrived at 10.15am and entrained immediately. Train left at 11.30am arrived BAILLEUL 1.45pm. Battalion detrained and marched to ALDERSHOT Camp — about 1200 yds SW of NEUVE EGLISE — accommodated in huts. 2nd Lieuts M.M. JAMES, G.F. HINTON, W.S.C. MORGAN, J.A. HUNT, F. de W. GREEN, C.N. ELLIOTT, R.J. BROOKS joined from 3rd Batt. Weather Squally, very cold.	
ALDERSHOT CAMP SW of NEUVE EGLISE	7th		Battalion church parade. Capt. H.E. TREMONGER joined from 6th Batt. and on instruction from Advanced G.H.Q. took up duties as A/Major in Batt. H.Q. Transport marched from La Belle Hôtesse via HAZEBROUCK and arrived in Camp about 2.30 pm.	
"	8th		Company Training — Weather continued squally cold. Lieuts H.E. STREET, C.W. BULL and R.F. RAYNER joined from 8th Battalion — 1 Blanket per man issued.	

WAR DIARY
INTELLIGENCE SUMMARY.

Army Form C. 2118.

OCTOBER 1917 Page 1 1st/4th THE QUEEN'S Regt

Place	Date	Hour	Summary of Events and Information	Remarks and references to Appendices
ALDERSHOT CAMP 3rd of NEUVE EGLISE	9th		Company training – Musketry – Marshall order by L.G.C. X th Corps Reserve X Div Reserve.	
"	10th		Company Musketry training – Weather continued unsettled.	
"	11th		Working Party 1 officer 50 O.R. provided for work under M.G.O. Corps R.E. before WOLVERGHEM. Platoon Training. Afternoon O.A.T. BENTLEY joined from Base. Company Commanders reconnoitred Events posns in N.30.d (Shot 28)	
"	"			
"	12th		Working Party 1 officer 60 O.R. provided as on 11th. Platoon Training. Major T.HOWELL joined from 2nd Battn. Division received Brigade will probably relieve 19th Bde in the line on night 14th/15th. Lt. A. BANCROFT + 55 and Company Commanders reconnoitred portion re of Battalion in Reserve.	
"	13th		Working Party as 12th. 5 New men all available O.R. (60) marched to Railhead near BAILLEUL and entrained, remainder – Weath continued inclement.	

Page 5.

Army Form C. 2118.

WAR DIARY
INTELLIGENCE SUMMARY
OCTOBER 1917
of Both "THE QUEEN'S" Regt

(Erase heading not required.)

Place	Date	Hour	Summary of Events and Information	Remarks and references to Appendices
ALDERSHOT CAMP-SW of NEUVE EGLISE	14th		Working parties as on 13th for R.E. — Battalion Church Parade. Lieut H.F.D. FAULKNER joined from 3rd Entr. Bn. Orders for move of Batt. into RIGHT SUPPORT received. Battalion marched to Bde C. HQ. Battalion members of C'oy's & B Coys proceed into trenches Platoons — Relieves the Companies of Cameronians in T.6.d.7.3. (Sheet 28). — Relief complete by 11.20 p.m.	
BRISTOL CASTLE SE of WULVERGHEM	15th		The Battalion was disposed with three companies A,B,D. in trenches around Bristol Castle and 1 company C in trenches at B6 THECHEM FARM. This latter company was under the immediate command of the O.C. Right Front Battalion for tactical purposes. The day was spent in providing fatigue parties to the R.E. those men not on fatigue being engaged upon improving the trenches.	Batt: D.S.[?]
	16th		Working parties were furnished to R.E. for carrying	

WAR DIARY
INTELLIGENCE SUMMARY.

OCTOBER 1917. 1st Battn. The Queen's Regt.

Page 6

Army Form C. 2118.

Place	Date	Hour	Summary of Events and Information	Remarks and references to Appendices
			and to the Trench Tramway officer during night of 16th-17th a gas shell bombardment was opened on vicinity of PETITE DOUVE DOUR with the result that the men of C Company had taken their box respirators. There was no casualties both the 2/Lt O.R.C. by wounded with a shell splinter. Warning given for relief of 2nd WORCESTER Regiment.	
	17.		Stokers parties were furnished as for preceding days. Improvements to trenches and bomb outs dug outs. Officers proceeded to look over front line. 1 O.R. "A" Company wounded with a shell splinter. Enemy aeroplane very active with reavine shelling of our batteries. Orders received concerning amending previous warning order known nights of 18/19 October	
	18.		Fatigue parties furnished. preparations made to	

PAGE 4

Army Form C. 2118.

WAR DIARY
INTELLIGENCE SUMMARY.

OCTOBER 1917

1st Bn. The Queen's Regt.

(Erase heading not required.)

Place	Date	Hour	Summary of Events and Information	Remarks and references to Appendices
			move up to front line. 3 Companies to relieve the leading platoons started at 5.30 p.m. at an interval of 200x between platoons. Coys marched off in order A, B, C, D, HQ. Being incapable of relief the left front enemy heavily bunch mortared the left front company. This was followed by a heavy fire from our artillery which silenced the T.M. The enemy's artillery then retaliated upon Battn. HQ & reserve lines with his 4.2" at 5.9's. Our artillery was called upon for retaliation. They proceeded to concentrate upon enemy lines and fun. factors & . Relief complete by 12.15 am. It is noteworthy all ranks that the Battalion suffered no Casualties.	
	19		The dispositions of the Battn. were 3 coys in front line A, B + C. 1 Coy in support D. Coy with the	

Page 8

WAR DIARY OCTOBER 1917
INTELLIGENCE SUMMARY. 1st Bn. The Queens Regt.

Place	Date	Hour	Summary of Events and Information	Remarks and references to Appendices
	20		reserve company supplied by the BORDERERS. The trenches being in the valley were waterlogged and the men had knee-deep in water. The only communication trenches on the right sub-sector was incomplete and it was necessary to walk over the open to reach the front line. The enemy shelled Batt HQ. reserve trenches and tracks intermittently during the day and night. 9/Lt. H. HACKETT, EAST SURREY REGT. joined from 3rd Entn. A quiet day's work was carried out on trenches occupied by us and efforts made to drain trenches into DOVE River. 2/Lt S.M. NEWMAN was appointed to a commission in this Regt. Enemy shelled the horse places intermittently	
	21		Work was continued upon the trenches and	

PAGE 9

WAR DIARY
INTELLIGENCE SUMMARY. 1st Bn. The Queens Regt.

OCTOBER 1917   Army Form C. 2118.

Place	Date	Hour	Summary of Events and Information	Remarks and references to Appendices
			and a duck board track was commenced from the forward end of NEW CROSS AV. towards forward posts. About 9.15 pm enemy trench mortars were active upon left company's front and although our artillery retaliated they temporarily silenced them temporarily they recommenced after. They were however finally silenced after a considerable number 2/Lt Wayman went upon reporting from "C" Batth. 2/Lt 17.P. Hughes gassed from fumes of 1.0.R.D. By hundred. Watching being wounded. 10.R.D. By hundred. Watching orders for relief on night of 22/23 received.	
	22		Work on trenches continued - considerable shelling for howitzer over. Fritzes were sent down. Fresh 2/Lt J HOWELLS and the first platoon of the relieving unit reached the front line at 8.30 pm a covering party was	

Page 10

WAR DIARY
INTELLIGENCE SUMMARY. For The Queen's Regt.
OCTOBER 1917
Army Form C. 2118.

Place	Date	Hour	Summary of Events and Information	Remarks and references to Appendices
			sent out to cover relief which passed off without incident except that a few French MotorLorries were fired at C Coy (right Coy) the Company after relief marched to KORTEPYP A CAMP. S of NEUVE EGLISE. Relief was complete by 11.10 pm. The new platoon in camp by 1.30 am. There were no casualties during the relief. Total casualties for the tour 3 OR wounded.	
KORTEPYP "A" CAMP	23		Reveille was at 12 noon & lunch the men & officers had a rest. After dinner a short parade for physical drill was ordered. The remainder of the day was spent in cleaning up. A list of awards was woven today for the attack on Sept 25-26. This resulted in 2 two previous M.M's being attached and 22 M.M's. The C.O. in announcing these awards coupled his congratulations with those of the Divisional and Brigade	

Page 4
October 1917. 1/7 Bn The Queen's Regt.

Army Form C. 2118.

WAR DIARY
or
INTELLIGENCE SUMMARY.
(Erase heading not required.)

Place	Date	Hour	Summary of Events and Information	Remarks and references to Appendices
Bonneville	24		Cleaning up continued today. *A small attack of baths sufficient to bathe 200 men was taken advantage of and N.C. Officers were installed. The companies had Short physical drill parade and games. The H.Q. Companies are officered of Capt and took over command of "A" Coy from Lieut. Fatigue parties consisting of 5 Officers and 230 O.Rs. were furnished at various times from units of MKTSINES.	* Enough time to use to have two clothing issues was no Tallights this is the Battlers Pontoons have been added for our test twice platoons on platoons reserve W.P.
	25		Upon trucks to the young Officers the panhard Gun at 2.15 pm for one hour took main Major WK. Demonym programme work ordinate to perform & conveying portion of west to divid Rent Bath place to 3 hrs notice to improve Divisine front.	
	26		Companies carried out programmes provide as	

Part 2

WAR DIARY OCTOBER 1917 1/5 Bn. The Queens Regt.

INTELLIGENCE SUMMARY.

Army Form C. 2118.

Place	Date	Hour	Summary of Events and Information	Remarks and references to Appendices

submitted. The Young Officers classes continued instruction under Major H.E. Greenup. The C.W. Bubb was attached 4th Transport for instructional purposes from this date. Baths were established near a public line near were in this batty. An O.R. class commenced today for Sgts & 6 R Officers attention.

22. Working Parties were furnished today composed of Officers and 180 O.Rks. they were engaged upon duties similar to those in previous wks. A luncheon class of 25 O.Rks. and a Lewis Class of 8 O.Rks. commenced experiments today. Young Officers class continued under Major H.E. Greenup.
2/Lr V.W. RUDKIN proceed to KINGSMD Bryon kts. WR office from SOS from this date. A draft of 10 O.Rks arrived from particle VA 1, B 1, D 8.

28. The Battalion paraded for Divine Service at 11 a.m.

WAR DIARY
INTELLIGENCE SUMMARY

Page 13
OCTOBER 1917
1/7 Bn. The Queen's Regt.

Place	Date	Hour	Summary of Events and Information	Remarks and references to Appendices
	29		Working parties of 1 officer & 50 O.R. were furnished. Football was played in the afternoon.	
			The C.O. has promised to explain on leave the common alto Battalion guard again. Major D.E. Kempson, who has advertising Clavers continued today. Major Clavers continued with the R.S.M. and C.S.M. Chickakak. Working parties consisting 8 officers and 310 o. Oke was furnished It. Col. S? B R SKADEN now attached to the Battalion from this date. Infantry & Cadet to the C.O.	
	30		Working parties 8 officers and 200 OR were furnished. Lecture on Lewis gun transport by the C.O. Lupis gun and Sniping Clavers continued today. Young officers Clavers continued	

Page 14
OCTOBER 1917
1st Bn. The Queen's Regt.

WAR DIARY / INTELLIGENCE SUMMARY

Place	Date	Hour	Summary of Events and Information	Remarks and references to Appendices
	31		Working parties of 4 Officers and 200 O.Rks furnished. Lewis Gun and Sniping Classes suspended. Young Officers Class continued in the morning only. Battalion played in the afternoon in the afternoon Football. "A" Company paraded as a platoon both by day and by night with a view to a raid taking place during the next tour in the front line.	

H. Jennings Bramly Major
Comdg 1st "The Queen's" Regiment.

SECRET

Battalion Order No 130
by Lieut Col L. M. CROFTS D.S.O.
Comdg. Bn The Queens' Regt.

Copy No 12

Thursday 4 Octr 1917

1. The Battalion will move by march route tomorrow 5th Inst to BILLETS at ST MARTIN au LAERT distance about 13 miles Route RENESCURE - FORT ROUGE - ARQUES. Road Junction 650 yds N of A of ARQUES - Cross Roads 1¼ miles N of ? of WESTROVE - outskirts of ST. OMER.

2. Companies &c will assemble head of column at Cross Roads immediately N of A Coys Billets in the following order ready to move off at 10.15 am - C. D. Dumm A. B. Transport.
   Dress F.S.M.O. - Caps will be worn
   Distances to be maintained between Coys 100 yds. Battn & Transport 100 yds. Between Units not less than 500 yds.

3. The usual halts will be made except that all troops will halt from 11.50 am to 1 pm when Dinners will be served at noon.

4. Officers valises to be at Q.M Stores by 8.30 am - Mess kits to be at H.Q Mess by 9.15 am.

5. O.C Coys will personally inspect all Billets & ground in their Area prior to parade ensuring they are not quitted without being properly cleaned up - reporting to the Adjt on parade this has been done.

6. O.C. Coys will arrange that no claims are left unsettled.

7. Billeting Party C.Q.M. Sgts and N.C.O. H. Qrs and Interpreter under Lieut J.E. Shipton will parade at Bn H.Q with bicycles at 8.am

8. O.C. Coys will report to the Adjt immediately move is complete & troops settled in.

R. H. Nevins Capt & Adjt
Bn The Queens Regt

R.J. Nevins
Capt & Adjt

Copies issued as under:-
1. C.O   2. O.C No 1
3. O.C No 2   4. O.C No 3
5. O.C No 4   6. T.O & QM
7. Lieut JE Shipton 8. Bn S.O
9. Adjt   10. R.S.M
11. File   12. & 13 War Diary.

War Diary

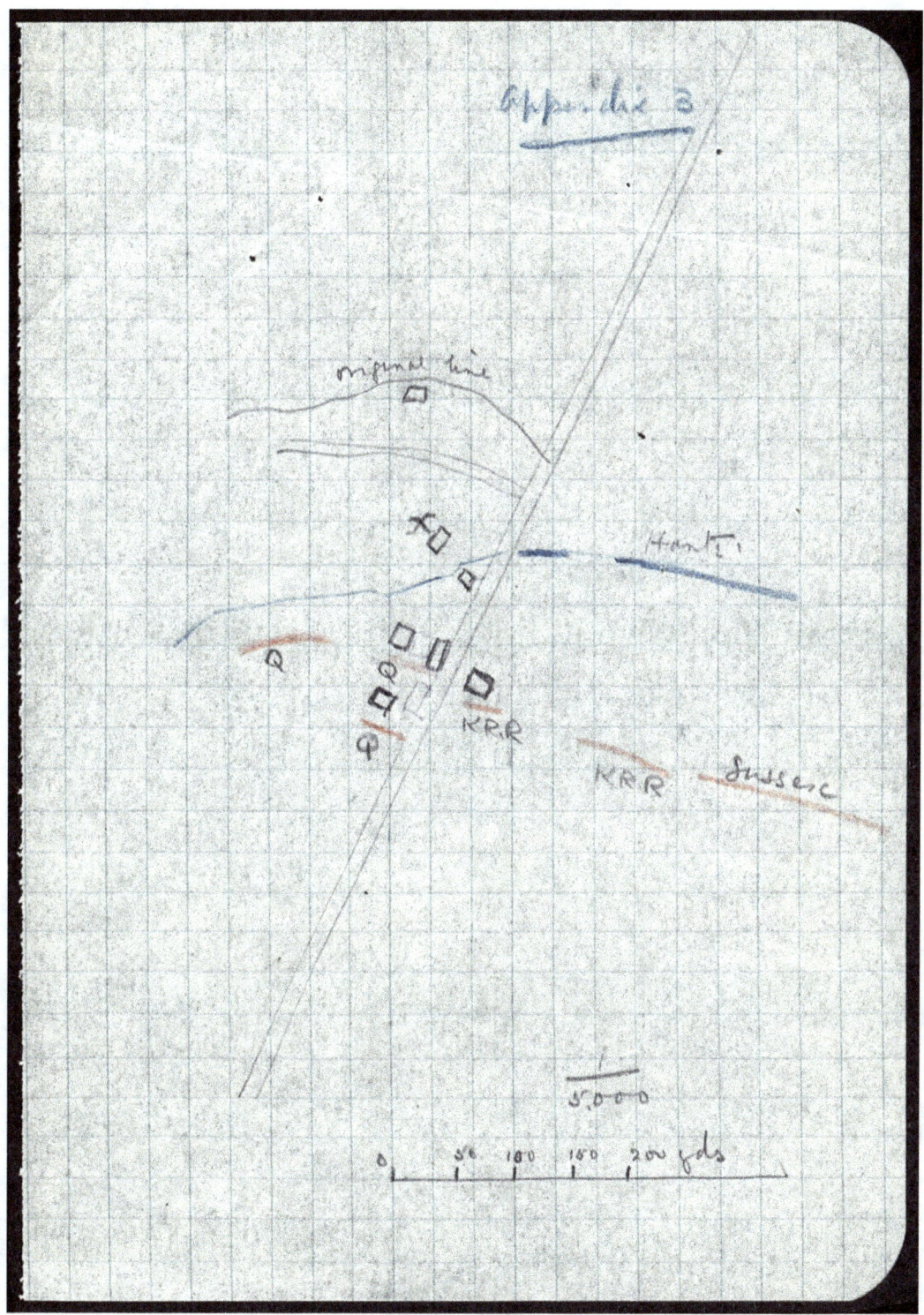

MESSAGE FORM.

To:— No.

1. I am at.................... (Note:—Either give Map Reference or mark your position by a 'X' on the Map on back.)

2. I have reached limits of my Objective.

3. My Platoon / Company is at..................................and is consolidating.

4. My Platoon / Company is at ....and has consolidated.

5. Am held up by (a) M.G. (b) Wire at .... (Place where you are).

6. Enemy holding strong point..................................

7. I am in touch with .... on Right / Left at ....

8. I am not in touch with..........................on Right / Left.

9. Am shelled from........................

10. Am in need of :—

11. Counter Attack forming at..................

12. Hostile (a) Battery
    (b) Machine Gun active at ....
    (c) Trench Mortar

13. Reinforcements wanted at..

14. I estimate my present strength at .... rifles.

15. Add any other useful information here:—

Name.................................
Platoon...........................
Time................m. Company ....
Date .... 1917. Battalion ....

(A). Carry no maps or papers which may be of value to the Enemy.

(B). Give no information if captured, except the following, which you are bound to give:—
    Name, Rank, (Number) and Regiment.

(C). Collect all captured maps and papers and send them in at once.

Nº I Sept. 1917.

MESSAGE FORM.

To :— No.

1. I am at........................ {Note :—Either give Map Reference or mark your position by a 'X' on the Map on back.}

2. I have reached limits of my Objective.

3. My Platoon / Company is at............................and is consolidating.

4. My Platoon / Company is at............................and has consolidated.

5. Am held up by (a) M.G. (b) Wire at............ (Place where you are).

6. Enemy holding strong point............................

7. I am in touch with .... on Right/Left at ....

8. I am not in touch with.................. on Right/Left.

9. Am shelled from............................

10. Am in need of :—

11. Counter Attack forming at ....

12. Hostile (a) Battery (b) Machine Gun (c) Trench Mortar } active at ....

13. Reinforcements wanted at............................

14. I estimate my present strength at .... rifles.

15. Add any other useful information here :—

Time .... m. Name..........................
Date .... 1917. Platoon..........................
  Company ....
  Battalion ....

(A). Carry no maps or papers which may be of value to the Enemy.

(B). Give no information if captured, except the following, which you are bound to give :—
  Name, Rank, ███████████

(C). Collect all captured maps and papers and send them in at once.

Secret.   Battalion   Orders No 169.   Copy No: 14

by Lieut Col. L. M. CROFTS. D.S.O.
Comdg 1st Bn "The Queen's" Regt.
Sunday. 14th October 1917.

1. The Battalion will relieve three Companies of 1st CAMERONIANS in the RIGHT SUPPORT on night of 14th/15th inst:

2. Guides 1 per platoon & to Ors are being furnished at Bde. H.Q. T.6.C.6.7. at 8.15 pm.

3. Companies will move from Camp in the following order "C" H.Q. "D" "A" "B" by platoons at 200ˣ intervals. Leading platoon of "C" Coy moving off at 7.0 pm.

4. One Effective N.C.O. per Coy & H.Q. will proceed in advance moving off from Camp at 4.0 pm.

   A limber with packs of afternoon working party and necessary cooking pots and one cook of each "A" & "B" Coys will also move at 4.0 pm in order that teas can be provided on completion of work.

5. The 4/m officers remaining at "B" Echelon will attend an R.E. Class at 9.0am & 1.0pm daily, near Bde H.Q. at T.6.C.6.7. whilst the Bde is in the line. The servants of these officers will go up with their Coys.
   "A" Coy. 2/Lieuts HOWCROFT, RUDKIN, SWEET.   "B" Coy. 2/Lts ROSSEN & BEATON
   "C" "   "   STEVENSON, LACEY, MORGAN.   "D" " " WATTS, BULL, HOWELL
   A party of 7 Drummers and 1 Coy Cook "D" Coy, are being left behind to act as servants.

6. Sgt Benson "C" & Cpl Kitching "D" Coy will remain at "B" Echelon pending departure to Courses.

7. The 4/m proceeding on leave to England on 16th inst will also remain behind. "A" Coy, 37107 Pte J.C. Hill, 7846 Pte J. Hall, 1356 Pte J. Aldridge.
   "B" Coy, 8941 " A Smales, 165 Pte J. Jordan. "D" Coy, 12848 Pte P.C. Andrews.

8. Valises of Officers going forward to be at Q.M. Stores by 3.0 pm.

9. Beyond those mentioned above no additional personnel is to be left at "B" Echelon.

10. Marching out States will be submitted to O.R. by 3.0 pm. These are to account for the whole strength of the Coy showing in detail how distributed. N.C.Os & men at Bn H.Qrs to be shown under the one head - Bn H. Qrs.

11. "Relief Complete" will be reported to Bde H. Qrs in "B.A.B. Code."

12. Officers accompanying the Battn will wear their "rank & file" jackets.

(Sgd) R. M. Nevins Captain & Adjt.
Bn The Queen's Regt.

Copies issued as follows.
1. C.O.   2. 2nd in C.   3. O.C. No.1.
4. O.C. No.2. 5. O.C. No.3.   6. O.C. No.4.
7. S.M.   8. S.O.   9. Adjt.
10. 2/Adjt.   11. R.S.M.   12. I.O.
13 & 14. War Diary.   15 & 16. Spare.

R M Nevins
Capt & A/A

Appx 5

TRANSLATION OF CAPTURED GERMAN ORDER.

3rd Bn. 229th R.I.R.

24/9/17.

BATTALION ORDER.

1. 3rd Bn. 229 R.I.R. together with the 3rd Bn., 230 R.I.R. will attack the enemy opposite them tomorrow (Sept.25th 1917) and will eject him from his present position.

2. The Sector of the 3rd Bn., 229 R.I.R. will be from the Southern Edge of POLYGON WOOD to the REUTELBACH (REUTELBEEK) the 3rd Bn. 230 R.I.R's Sector will extend from this point southwards.

3. The 229 Bn. will take up position in the front line system with the 11th, 12th and 10th Cos. in three waves which on advancing will follow each other at intervals of 50 metres.
   Breadth of deployment of each Co. - 150 metres.
   10th Co. will keep touch with the REUTELBACH. The Cos. will then move forward into the outpost line. The right wing of the 11th Co. will move along the southern edges of POLYGON WOOD. The 9th Co. 229 R.I.R. will be in second line behind the right flank. Jumping off position in the general line from Hill 727 southwards, the left flank in the neighbourhood of the REUTELBACH. On account of the boggy nature of the edge of the REUTELBACH, patrols from 10th Co. 229 R.I.R. will keep contact with the right flank of the 3rd Bn. 230. Troops to be in position by 4.45 a.m. While moving into position strictest silence must be maintained, every unnecessary noise to be avoided and, finally, equipment (?) to be finally inspected.

4. Light Machine Guns (1908/15 pattern) in the first line heavy Machine Guns (1908 pattern) with the 1st, 2nd, or 3rd wave.
   Each Co. will be allotted one platoon of 1908 heavy machine gunners.

5. As soon as the destructive fire commences, the Cos. will work closer to the enemy. While doing this, touch must be kept in the Bn.
   The flank Platoon Commanders are to be made responsible for this.
   The 9th Co. will join in the advance and keep a look-out to the north, when 3rd or 4th Co. of the 229 R.I.R. will advance with the STORMING TROOP of the regiment.

6. The Cos will attack with strong first waves, immediately the barrage lifts, in order not to give the enemy any time to collect his wits.

7. The WILHELMSTELLUNG is to be taken and to be passed, and a position between 100 and 150 yards in front of it to be taken up when the Cos. must at once consolidate and as soon as possible consolidation in depth will be carried out.
   The STORMING TROOP will take up position in the WILHELM-STELLUNG.

8. On the troops attaining the position from 100 to 150 metres in front of the WILHELMSTELLUNG, they will notify the fact by firing white flares.

P.T.O.

9. The newly won line is to be held as our front line at all costs.

10. The Bn. is to be kept constantly informed as to what is happening; the Intelligence Officer will establish and maintain telephone and runner communication with the B.T.K. 229 (? Bn. Telefon Kammer = Bn. Signal Office.)

11. 20 Stretcher Bearers have been placed at the disposal of the regiment for carrying away wounded.

12. Bomb and Ammunition Store at the B.T.K.

13. First Aid Post on a level with Cemetery to the east of REUTEL about 150 metres south of the road.

14. I am at present at point 727.

15. Prisoners to be brought to the present front line from whence they will be brought to the B.T.K. in the Flandern I line.

(Signed) HETTHEY.

Footnote (in pencil).

March off from the Bn. at 2.10 a.m.
(march order 10th, 12th, 11th Coys., STORMING TROOP 9th Coy.)

Troops must be in position by 4.40
Destruction fire starts at - 5.15
Fall in for the attack - 5.45

Statement that troops are in position, to be sent to point 727.

==*

Appx.6

THE ATTACK ON 33rd DIVISION BETWEEN
POLYGON WOOD and MENIN ROAD,
September 25th, 1917.

1. Orders issued by 50th Reserve Division on the 24th (captured on 26th) indicate that the initial operation was by the Third Battalion of each of the 229th and 230th Regiments of that Division, together with the Assault Battalion of the Fourth German Army. The objectives were in the WILHELM STELLUNG (VELDHOEK Trench - CARLISLE FARM, our front line at that time). The 229th had the Sector between POLYGON WOOD and the REUTELBEEK, and the 230th Regt., south of the BEEK. The Assault Battalion attacked an objective (dugouts, etc.) about the MENIN Road.

2. This attack was to be made at 5.45 in the morning, and was to be supported by a very heavy concentration of artillery with bombardment commencing at 5.15 by 27 Batteries of Field Artillery (of 2 Divisions), 17 Field Howitzer Batteries, 15 Heavy Howitzer Batteries and 5 Batteries of H.V. guns long range. In addition, the neighbouring Divisions were to support by counter-battery work and subsidiary bombardment.

3. The attacks later in the day were doubtless consequent upon the results of this initial attack, and though there is no documentary evidence as yet, it is evident that before the day was out most of the troops of the 50th Reserve Division were engaged in the fighting.

==*

SPECIAL ORDER OF THE DAY

by

MAJOR-GENERAL P. WOOD, C.B., C.M.G.

Commanding 33rd Division.

1. I have received the following messages in connection with the operations in which the 33rd Division took part on September 25th, 26th and 27th, 1917.

I.

From

The Field-Marshal Commanding-in-Chief,
British Armies in FRANCE.

To

General Sir H.C.O. PLUMER,
Commanding 2nd Army.

G. H. Q., 27th September, 1917.

"The ground gained by the 2nd Army yesterday under your command, and the heavy losses inflicted on the enemy in the course of the day, constitute a complete defeat of the German forces opposed to you. Please convey to all Corps and Divisions engaged, my heartiest congratulations, and especially to the 33rd Division whose successful attack following a day of hard fighting, is deserving of all praise."

II.

From X Corps.

To 33rd Division.

G. G. 131. 26th September, 1917.

"Following received from General PLUMER begins AAA Please accept my congratulations on success of to-day's operations, and convey them to the troops engaged AAA The 33rd Division have done fine work under extraordinarily difficult circumstances, and the 39th Division have carried out their task most successfully AAA message ends AAA The Corps Commander adds his own congratulations."

2. In circulating the above messages, I wish to congratulate all Officers, Non-commissioned Officers and men of the Division, on having gained, by their fine fighting qualities, such marks of appreciation from the Commander-in-Chief, and from the Army and Corps Commanders.

P. T. O.

Headquarters,
100th Infantry Brigade,
30th September, 1917.

SPECIAL BRIGADE ORDER.

I wish to express my thanks to all ranks of the Brigade for their gallant behaviour during the recent heavy fighting. They have once more justified my confidence in their valour and my pride in their achievements.

A.V.V. Baird
Brigadier General,
Commanding 100th Infantry Brigade.

C O N F I D E N T I A L.

G.O.C. and All Ranks,
    33rd Division.

    On your departure from Xth Corps I wish to thank you for all your good work while under my command, and particularly for your gallantry and resolution on 25th and 26th September.

    In parting from you, which I do with regret, I wish you all the best of luck in the future.

Ter Morland

H.Q., Xth Corps,
8th October 1917.

Lieut-General,
Commanding Xth Corps.

The following N.C.O's and Men have been awarded the decorations named below in connection with operations on 25th- 26th September 1917.

BAR TO THE MILITARY MEDAL.

1885 Pte G. GILLESBY.   37101 Pte S. HAZZARD.

MILITARY MEDAL.

205269	Pte W. BARRAS.	9243	Pte F. PEPPERCORN.
40018	" A. BECKINSALE.	8436	" A. MORLEY.
441	" F. FOWKES.	13706	L/C W. BATCHELOR.
10138	" W. JARMAIN.	3702	Pte J. GODLEY.
205247	" S. BROCK.	37040	Cpl R. BOSELEY.
14982	Sgt C. HALLX	3335	Sgt G. HODGE.
11066	" R. COBBETT.	245	Pte E. WORSFOLD.
9821	" L. CRIPPS.	10886	Cpl E. TURNER.
30833	Pte J. FERN.	6844	L/C E. BAKER.
9432	Cpl T. JOLLIFE.	6529	Pte H. DILKES.
30701	L/C C. COTTINGHAM.	30029	" A. MOORE.

True Extract.

Army Form C. 2118.

WAR DIARY
or
INTELLIGENCE SUMMARY.
(Erase heading not required.)

NOVEMBER 1917
1st Battn. The Buffs (E.K.) Regt

Vol 37

22 1/RWF

Place	Date	Hour	Summary of Events and Information	Remarks and references to Appendices
HATEPP 1 "N"Camp	1st		Working Parties Retd. 2 officers + 100 O.R. proceeded for R.E. work on forward area. Young Officers Class began instruction. Notification received F.M. Co. C.C. under authority granted by H.M. the K.I.H.G. has awarded decorations as follows for gallantry in the field on dates as noted. MILITARY CROSS Captain W.R. CARSLAKE (acts? 2). Revd J.M. HOWCROFT – 25.9.17. DISTINGUISHED CONDUCT MEDAL 10072 Sergt HATRACEY 24-27.9.17. 29181 Private W.LUFF 26-9.17 MILITARY MEDAL – 74 L/Cpl J SEWELL.	
	2nd		2nd Lieut. C.A.J. BENTLEY from up stats on TOWN MAJOR NEUVE EGLISE. Regd. J.R.G. CONAN proceeded to ENGLAND under instructions from War Office (Regd?). 2/Lieut F.S. PRIOR Coy. 100th T.M.B. Struck off strength. Casualties 1/R killed 1 O.R. wounded (1/LG) Working on working party.	
	3rd		Working Parties Retd. 3 officers + 110 O.R. proceeded for R.E. forward area. Area – An? of A? conducted Land operators by night. Young officers class continued instruction. D.K.?	

Page Army Form C. 2118.

NOVEMBER 1917   1st Battn. The Queen's Regt

WAR DIARY
INTELLIGENCE SUMMARY.
1st Battn. The Queen's Regt
(Erase heading not required.)

Place	Date	Hour	Summary of Events and Information	Remarks and references to Appendices
KORTEPYP "A" Camp			Voluntary Church Service — Lieut G. STEVENSON MARTINEAU, J.A. HUNT, G.F. RAINER, J HOWELLS, A.K. HASTINGS joined Bn. Bath boundistrome Regt. To temporary attachment. Warning Order received. Brigade will proceed to relieve 19th Infantry Brigade in the Line on night 17th and 18th November. Battalion to relieve 20th Royal Fusiliers in RIGHT subsector. Battalion rested.	

C.B. CMG. Dispersal Camps

Army Form C. 2118.

WAR DIARY
or
INTELLIGENCE SUMMARY

(Erase heading not required.)

Wulverghem Vlage
2nd Batt. The Queen's Regt.

Instructions regarding War Diaries and Intelligence Summaries are contained in F. S. Regs., Part II. and the Staff Manual respectively. Title Pages will be prepared in manuscript.

Place	Date	Hour	Summary of Events and Information	Remarks and references to Appendices
Wulverghem (A Camp)	5th	7	Morning Grand Routes. Battalion relieved 20th R.F. in F.1 [sub sector] at 2.30pm and moved up via Hyde Park Corner (where Guns Back Road the Province Morning a field were jumped up by Cpl [illegible] and the Camp and was dropped. RIGHT FRONT C & D to B LEFT FRONT D. POLLARD SUPPORT H: A Cy concentration shells near Reserve. Relief was completed about 10-30pm. Six OR of A Cy were wounded in POLLARD SUPPORT — that 6 OR were put down as follows in connection with a Raid which was carried out by the Enemy about 7pm on extreme left of Left Front Coy of the 2 R.F.	
Trenches	6th		In trenches — Normal Routine — no casualties	
	7th		" " " " " Quiet, nil incident	the
	8th			
	9th			
	10th			

WAR DIARY
INTELLIGENCE SUMMARY

NOVEMBER 1915 [unit heading illegible]

Place	Date	Hour	Summary of Events and Information	Remarks and references to Appendices
[illegible]	11th	2.15 a.m.	Party and O.R. under Lts. L.O. PARKES and A.E. DARBY (one) set out at Rest on the Enemy's line with the object of attacking an identification and inflicting loss on the Enemy — Raid was successful. 11 prisoners were taken. Report attached. 4 O.R. were wounded. Remainder of party normal. 2 O.R. wounded (both injured, but none dangerous) which fell away to first few days. Trenches were in bad state. The Battalion was relieved by Worcestershire (Yeomanry) at 4.5 p.m. completed 9.45 p.m. moving back to Reserve at BRISTOL CASTLE in the R. C Lay on arrival. A.B.C.D. Coys quartered at BRISTOL CASTLE. H.Q. at BETHLEHEM FARM. The Tactical troops under orders of O.C. Worcestershire.	
BRISTOL CASTLE F.6d	12th		Whole Battalion employed in looking out enemy patrols.	

Army Form C. 2118.

WAR DIARY or INTELLIGENCE SUMMARY

NOVEMBER 17

(Erase heading not required.)

Place	Date	Hour	Summary of Events and Information	Remarks and references to Appendices
Bristol Castle Tod	13th		General Routine. Working Party for Rets in front line - 1 Officer. OR's [wounded]. 8pm Rly by 3rd Australian Bath Commenced. Completed 6-10pm Battalion moved by Platoon to Neuve Eglise where it was accommodated in huts.	
NEUVE EGLISE	14th		General Routine - Inventorying up Rets	
"	15th		Enough Parties - Strat Post Not carried out by Company as usual CAT of Entry required from ply on town main Battalion paraded at 3 pm and was inspected by Colonel LOCKHOUSE (0 of he 3)	
"	16th		Company Rout Matches. Evening. Capt. Dr. G. Drewing MC. RAMC. S.R. after 10 months attachment to the regiment proceeded to join FCCS. infantry Battalion. Lieut Sgt of J. Egan Rd enlisted	
"	17th			
"	18th		Due Round read on List of TORONTO Scots (STR & 69) Zampt (Regmt) hand at 12 noon turning on Roup altered 3 Spm Battalion lined out and words for 2.30pm during of troop which are in a very insanitary state.	

2449 Wt. W14957/M90 750,000 1/16 J.B.C. & A. Forms/C.2118/12.

WAR DIARY
INTELLIGENCE SUMMARY

Army Form C. 2118.
Page 6.

November 1917
1/5th Bath. The Queen's Regt

Place	Date	Hour	Summary of Events and Information	Remarks and references to Appendices
TORONTO CAMP	18		Division relieving 1st Canadian Division night 18/19/5 - 100th Inf. Bde.	
			B.Co. in Divisional Reserve.	
	19th		Rest of platoons camp in a sanitary condition continued - whole Battalion employed.	
	20		General Routine - Tramways Camp continued - 1st HASTINGS Hospital (E)	
	21		General Routine - working Camps continued - Whole Battalion left H.Q's S.O. Inspection under Divt. Gas Officer by trying General through Gas Chamber. Respirators found to function - 5 Saturation Inspects B Jul Battn.	
	22		General Routine - Routine given but Battn - Lieut. B. STEVENS R.C.H.143. 5 R.P.UNT HOSTREET. 5 D.W.E.S.W. jun N.Co's full roll at MONT S Est in putting Cork on C HA M.P. 14.R.P. Altspetn received that No Corps Commander has awarded Dev. to Mullary Medal to No 39991 Cpl COTTINGHAM	

WAR DIARY or INTELLIGENCE SUMMARY

Army Form C. 2118

NOVEMBER 1917
7th Battn the Queens Regt
Page 7.

Place	Date	Hour	Summary of Events and Information	Remarks and references to Appendices
	22		Military Medals to 10018 Cpl H.T.ROSS. 10331 Sgt H.C.BATES. 2287 Pte A.GROVES. 14159 Pte A.E.IRONS. 39858 L/Cpl M HOLTHAM for gallantry on night 10/11th November 1917 (Raid). Complimentary letters received from Lt Gen Sir AYLMER HUNTER WESTON K.C.B. D.S.O M.P. with congratulations of the Divisional Commander and Brigadier General. Also Captain and friends of the Six 100 men – 2 Lieut L.O.PARKES and A.E.DARBY on the Raid.	
TORONTO 23 CAMP	23		General Routine – 2 Coys Raid. Work carried out by Coys in preparation for L.S. Will move to the POTIJZE Area in support to the 19 I.L.B. on 24th – 25th inst. Battalion moves in 2.5 to 2.7 pm 8.2.	
	24		Training and Court Kits.	
	25		Battalion moved from LCM, LAA, N. (YPRES) Moves up the BATTLE POSN at 8 am Relief completed at 12 midnight. Relief the Kings Regt merged into Battn Hours.	

WAR DIARY or INTELLIGENCE SUMMARY

Army Form C. 2118.

NOVEMBER 1917

1st Bn "The Queen's" Regt. Page 5.

Place	Date	Hour	Summary of Events and Information	Remarks and references to Appendices
EMFRES	26th	2 Hours	OC working Party in Alberta met Canadian RE Branch to commence improving shelters and Shaft mouth	
"	27th	3 Officers	WELCH provided a covering party to Canadian Engineers Repair Party improving entries at Shaft No 4. Lieut Col K M CROFTS DSO and the other recognised the ground and Lieut S MILNER acquired a copy of Issue received during Operations on 25th September 1917	
"	28th		Battalion at 2 hours notice to move to the Support of the SHERWOODS Brigade	
"	29th	6 Hours	2nd Lt H FORSTER & 14 OR detailed to reconnoitre Reserve Positions. Men of the same Battalion & were detailed to arrange for ? guides rendezvous Lieut L O PARKER, Military Cross, formerly Queen's Regt. Ass No W.5361/2305/7 OR 1417 detailed to return into Right Support on night 31/1st	

WAR DIARY
INTELLIGENCE SUMMARY.
1st Batt. The Queens Regt.

NOVEMBER 1917

Page 9.

Army Form C. 2118.

(Erase heading not required.)

Place	Date	Hour	Summary of Events and Information	Remarks and references to Appendices
E.N.Ypres	30th		General Routine. Hostile Artillery Sentenels in front & moving forward	Batt. Orders No. 220
1923.2			Battalion moved off about 4 pm in accordance with Batt. Order No. 220. Relief complete at 8.45 pm. No casualties occured moving up.	

In left half Corps.
1st Batt. The Queens Regt.

SECRET
Battalion Orders 233.
by Major H. E. TREMONGER
Comdg 1st Bn. The Queens Regt.

Copy No. 13

Tuesday 6th Nov. 1917.

1. The Battalion plus 1 Company 2nd Worcestershires will relieve 20th Royal Fusiliers in the Front line. Right Sub sector on 9th Nov.

2. Guides on a Platoon basis are being furnished at Rd Bn. H.Qrs. U.9.b.9. at 6 p.m.

3. Coys will be disposed as follows:—
Right Front "C" Centre "B" Left "D" Support "A" and will move off from Camp in this order by Platoons at 200x interval 500x between Coys. Leading Platoon of "C" Coy marching off from Camp at 3 p.m. Route HYDE PARK CORNER — DOUVE DUMP — NEW CROSS AVENUE — Dress F.S.M.O. Jerkins in Pack — Waterbottles filled — Great Coats will not be carried but bundled in tens securely fastened & labelled and stacked at Q.M. Stores by 12 noon. Coy of Worcestershires attd will be in Reserve near Bn. H.Q.

4. An Officer and one Effective N.C.O per Coy and Bn. H.Qrs and Signallers who will be employed as such in the line, will proceed in advance to take over stores &c — leaving Camp at 2 p.m.

5. O.C. Coys &c will by means of a Conference ensure that all ranks are acquainted with Trench Standing Orders prior to leaving Camp.

6. Gum Boots are being drawn from Boot Store in Bulk and will be picked up by Coys at RED LODGE — Gum Boots will be carried — not worn until arrival in Front line and then worn only if absolutely necessary.

7. Sergt Broad 4 Cooks 2 Signallers 2 Pioneers will proceed at 2 p.m. with 2 limbers to Tramway Terminus WULVERGHEM with water, Haypacks Cooking Utensils Signalling Stores &c, load on truck at 3 p.m and deliver at Bn. H.Q.

8. "A" Coy will furnish two Lewis Guns and teams to "D" Coy whilst Battn is in the Line.

9. Lewis Guns will be furnished for Anti Aircraft purposes.
A. Coy 1. "C" Coy 2. "D" Coy 1. Coy 2/Worcestershires attd 2.
These Guns will be controlled by an Officer or reliable N.C.O with good Field Glasses.

10. Completion of relief will be notified to Battn H.Q by B.A.B. Code.

11. There is to be as little movement as possible between NEW CROSS AVENUE and POLLARD SUPPORT. There is to be no movement whatsoever in daylight between POLLARD SUPPORT and FRONT LINE.

12. Marching out states will be prepared and rendered to O.R by 12 noon.

13. O.C. Coys &c will inspect huts &c prior to quitting Camp tomorrow ensuring they are left clean & sanitary.

14. Lists showing Trench Stores Defence Schemes Maps Air Photos &c taken over will be forwarded to Bn. H.Q by first runner.

15. Sufficient care has not been taken heretofore in returning Petrol tins. During the Tour Receipts are to be given for the number of full tins and chew Taps received and receipts taken for empties with screw taps sent back.

Copy No 1. C.O
2 O.C. No 1   10. R.S.M
3 " " 2   11 File
4 " " 3   12. War Diary
5 " " 4   13
6 2/Worcesters   14 Bde
7 D.A.A   15 Spare
8 T.O
9 Adjt

(Sd) R. H. Nevins Capt & Adjt

R. H. Nevins Capt & Adjt

Addition to Battalion Order 203, paragraph 9.

Every man is to fire at aeroplanes, which are considered by the Officer of the watch to be 3000 feet or under.

(Sd) R. H. Nevins, Capt & Adjt
"The Queens" Regt

Battalion Orders No 209
by Lieut. Col. ~ ~ Cropper D.S.O.
Comdg. 7th Bn ~~ ~~ Regt.

Saturday 17th Nov 1917

Detail for tomorrow.
Officer of the day   Lieut. H. C. Street
~~ for Monday   2/Lieut. T. J. Newman
~~ of ~~ day

Number reporting Sick
A. Coy 9 B. Coy 2 C. Coy 4 D. Coy 5

The Battalion will move by bus tomorrow to BRANDHOEK
AREA. Transport will move to about noon, by road under
orders of B/de T.O.
Companies will parade in Camp and be in readiness to
move off at 7.30 a.m. Dress F.S.M.O. Steel Helmets on
head. Jerkins will be worn.
Reveille will be at 6. a.m. Blankets to be rolled in ~~
of 10 securely fastened and labelled. Will be ~~
~~ to the stores by 6.45 a.m.
Officers valises to be stacked near H.Q. Mess by 7.~~
Breakfasts will be at 7 a.m.
Mess Kits to be at H.Q. Stores by 7.30 a.m.
Q.O.M. Sergt. and an N.C.O. H. Qrs under Lieut ~~~
will move on cycles at 7 a.m. ~~~ting the S.C. at ~~
Camp (O.19 a 6.5) at 8.30 a.m.
2/Lieut E. RUSSEN for embussing ~~ties will report to the
D.A.Q.M.G. at M.29 a 5.8 at 9.0 am O.C. ~~ ~~
will each detail a Sect. to act as markers will report at
same time and place.
H.Q. Cyclists will proceed by road. No cycles will be taken
on buses.
O.C. Coys H.Q. Parties T.O. & ~~ will render a statement
showing No. of (a) Officers (b) O.R. to be embussed to the O.R.
by 6.30 a.m. tomorrow.
Embussing and debussing will be carried out rapidly
and in silence and while ~~ ~~ to embus Transport
to be kept ~~ of the cookers ~~ to impede the railway
traffic as little as possible.

~~ ~~ Transport will not open. Ration will be issued ~~
~~ O.C. Coys will in the Cookers ~~ ~~
~~ ~~.

O.C. Coys will ensure that their Tent be ~~~
in a clean and Sanitary ~~
Guard Coy. will hand in to Camp and stores ~~
brasses tomorrow ~~.
There will be an Issue of Rum for Coys to ~~ ~~
~~ to pure qual~~ ~~~ ~~
~~ ~~ a.m.

R. M. Newman P/t Adjt

REPORT ON RAID NIGHT OF 10/11TH NOVEMBER.

Prior to Zero, two parties, left party 2/Lt:DARBY and 24 Other Ranks and right party 2/Lt:PARKES and 10 Other Ranks were in position just in front of our parapet.

Stokes Mortars which opened our barrage were good.

Left Party encountered no opposition until they reached enemy's wire, where gap had been reported cut, when machine gun on left opened fire and enemy started bombing vigorously. Wire was uncut and impossible to getn thro', and attempts made to cut it, failed. Party worked to their left towards Sap X and bombed machine gun which was about 20 yds off just South of HIRONDELLE Road and silenced it. Gun and team believed to have been knocked out. Enemy's trench appeared to be strongly held and there is no doubt casualties were inflicted on them by our bombs. After 20 minutes, being unable to get through, the wire, the party returned. Our shrapnel was bursting short behind this party and our front line - appeared to be FROM one gun consistently short - several casualties by our own fire. Four wounded in this party.

Right Party encountered little opposition and no Machine Gun fire. Found gap about 10 yards wide and first four men got into trench and a group of Germans got out behind their trench and started bombing and shooting, except one who was taken prisoner in the trench. Of the others in this group one was shot by Sergt BAYES, one was killed by 2/Lt:PARKES with a revolver, one was bayonetted and a fourth shot. The trench was waist deep in water and impossible to work along it - one man had to be pulled out leaving his gum-boots behind No sign of any other Germans and being unable to get along party returned. No casualties with this party. Our artillery wasbursting well just beyond the enemy trench and barrage on right was very good, about forty yards clear of party.

There was no artillery retaliation except a few T.M's and no rifle or M.G.fire on the return.

Our Verey lights worked well and greatly assisted party.

Both parties found their way back by tapes laid out as they went, which were then pulled in.

11.11.17

S E C R E T.   PATROL ORDER - TO EACH RECIPIENT   COPY No:
OD ORDERS ON RAID ON NIGHT 10/11TH NOVEMBER.

Reference Special Sheet 8150/5 1/10,000 and Aeroplane Photograph
42B 2138. 28U 5d 6c 11b 12a d/21.10.17.

2/Lt:DARBY with 3 N.C.O's from Groups 1,2,and 3, will patrol
the German Front Line opposite Point P between 6.0 p.m. and
7.0 p.m. on the night of the 9/10th November, and
2/Lt:PARKES with 4 N.C.O's from Groups 4,5,6, and 7 will
patrol the German Front Line opposite Point Q between 7.0 p.m.
and 8.0 p.m. on the night of the 9/10th November,
to ascertain condition of Wire - configuration of ground -
exact localities and formation of Saps X,Y, and Z, and Front Line

Brigade has been asked to inform Artillery of these patrols.

                                              Major,
7/11/17.   Commanding 1st Batalion "THE QUEEN'S" Regiment.

Copy No:1....100th Inf: Bde:.
  "   " 2....O.C. "A" Coy.
  "   " 3....C.O.
  "   " 4....War Diary.
  "   " 5....War Diary.
  "   " 6....200th T.M.B.
  "   " 7....100th M.G.C.

BARRAGE TABLE TO ACCOMPANY 14TH D.A. O.O. No.133.

TIME.	GROUP.	No. OF GUNS.	PROCEDURE.
Zero to plus 40.	Right.	All 18 Pdrs (including Wirecutting Guns).	Barrage U.5.d.77.15 - U.5.d.72.23 - U.5.d.85.30 - U.6.c.45.04 - U.6.c.40.60 - U.6.c.45.63.
		One Bty 4.5" Hows.	One Howr on each of points U.12.a.40.70, U.6.c.40.00, U.6.c.67.05 and U.6.d.00.70.
Zero to plus 40.	Left.	Twelve 18 pdrs Remainder 18 pdrs.	Barrage U.6.c.35.55 - U.6.c.58.75 - U.6.a.37.30. Search Tracks V and XIII in U.6.b. and d.
		One Bty 4.5" Hows.	One Howr on each of points U.6.d.15.75, U.6.c.00.65, U.6.a.76.98 and U.6.a.50.47.
Zero to plus 40.	41st H.A.G.	One Bty 6" Howrs.	One Howr on each of points U.12.a.80.85, U.6.d.20.90, Kingsclere, and U.6.a.63.63.
Zero to plus 40.	8th D.A.	One Bty 18 pdrs. do do	Barrage U.12.a.80.85 - U.12.a.12.55 Barrage U.12.a.38.62 - U.12.c.50.97. Barrage U.12.c.00.95 - U.11.d.85.37

RATES OF FIRE.

(Rounds per Gun per minute)	18 Prs.	4.5"Hows	6"Howrs.
Zero to plus 10 minutes...........	3	2	1
Plus 10 Minutes to plus 20 mins.......	2	2	1
Plus 20 Minutes to plus 30 mins.......	3	2	1
Plus 30 Minutes to plus 40 Mins.......	1	1	½

Fires to gradually cease after Plus 40 Minutes.

Copy No:

S-E-C-R-E-T. 14TH DIVISIONAL ARTILLERY OPERATION ORDER No:133
by
LIEUT:COLONEL L.J.OSBORN V.D.

Reference 1/10=000 WARNETON Ed. 2B.

1. (i) The 100th.Inf.Bde. will raid the enemy's trenches on **night**
Novembe r 10/11th.
Zero hour will be notified later.

   (ii) The portion of the enemy's line to be raided will be Saps X,
Y, and Z, and Trench between D. and B.
   Co-ordinates.
   X = U.5.b.03.03.
   Y = U.5.d.99.85.
   Z = U.5.d.85.72.
   D = U.6.c.18.93.
   C = U.6.c.03.78.
   B = U.5.d.99.69.

   (iii) The Raid will be carried out by two parties.
   Party No:1 will enter the German Trench at "C", block the
trench at "C" and "D" and deal with Sap X.
   Party No:2 will enter the German Trench at "B", construct
a block just South of "B" and deal with Saps "Y" and "Z".

   (iv) Bugles will sound a succession of High "G's" as a signal
to return at plus 90 minutes.

   (v) Verey Lights will be fired from Zero plus 3 minutes to
Zero plus 45 mintes to assist the Raiding Party in their Work.

2. (i) From Zero until Zero plus 40 minutes 14th and 8th D.A's and
Heavy Artillery will form a Barrage as shewn in Barrage Table att:

   (ii) Neutralisation of hostile batteries, which normally fire on
the Sector in question, is being arranged by C.B.S.O.

   (iii) Table of rates of fire is attached.

   (iv) Watches will be synchronised at Right Battn:H.Q. (U.10.a.00.65)
at 7.0 p.m. November 10th and 12 m.n.
   An officer of the 8th D.A. will attend at Right Group H.Q.
at 7.30 p.m. Novr 10th to obtain the hour of Zero and to
synchronise watches.

3. O.C.Right Group will detail a Battery Commander as Liaison
officer with Rt.Battn: H.Q. during night Nov 10/11th.
   O.C.Left Group will remain with B.G.C. 100th Inf:Bde during
the raid if desired by the latter.

4. Prior to Zero -
   (i) Wirecutting will be carried out, as arranged, by Right Group
by 41st H.A.G. and also, if necessary by Right Group at U.6.c.03.78)
and U.5.d.99.69.
   (ii) In addition Groups will carry out deliberate wire cutting as
follows - Left Group - North of CINEMA ROAD, Right Group - South
of HIRONDELLE ROAD.
   Two gaps to be made at each of above places.
   Points selected to be reported by Groups concerned.

5. Groups to ACKNOWLEDGE.

(Sgd) H.M.J.ALLEN ? Major R.A.
Brigade Major R.A.
9th Novr. 1917.   14th (Light) Division.

War diary

①

S.S.99.F.1.   ORDERS FOR RAID TO BE CARRIED OUT   COPY N° 4.
              BY 1ST BATTALION "THE QUEEN'S" REGT
                 ON NIGHT 10/11TH NOVEMBER 1917.

Reference Special Sheet 3150/5 1/10,000 and Aeroplane Photo-
-graph 42.B.3130. 38U.5.d.6.e. 14b.15a. d/ 21.10.17.

1. A Raid will be carried out on the night 10/11th November at an
hour to be notified later with a view to obtain identification and
killing the enemy.

2. The portion of the enemy's line to be raided will be Saps X,Y, and
Z, and Trench between points B and B as shewn by co-ordinates.

3. "A"Coy will furnish raiding party consisting of 2 officers (each
accompanied by a Sergt:) and 43 other Ranks told off into parties
as under :-

    Party No:1 consisting of 1 officer and 23 O.Ranks to enter the
German Trench at "C" - Block the Trench at "C" and "D" and deal with
Sap X.
    Party No:2 consisting of 1 officer and 18 O.Ranks to enter the
German Trench at "B", construct a Block just South of "B" and deal
with Saps Y and Z.
NOTE. Two officers will be at P and Q respectively ready to replace
the above two officers if necessary.

4. The whole raiding party is sub-divided into 7 small groups as follows
No:1 1 N.C.O. and 5 men - To construct Block at "C".)
 " 2 1 N.C.O. and 5 men - To construct Block at "D") No:1 party.
 " 3 1 N.C.O. and 5 men - To deal with Sap X.   )
 " 4 1 N.C.O. and 5 men - Reserve Party
 " 5 1 N.C.O. and 4 men - To construct Block just South of "B")No:2
 " 6 1 N.C.O. and 5 men - To deal with Sap Y.   )party
 " 7 1 N.C.O. and 5 men - To deal with Sap Z.
At Zero Party No:1 start from Point "P"
At Zero plus 20 seconds Party No:2 start from Point "Q"
At Zero a T.M. and Artillery Barrage will come down on enemy's Strong
Points just North of "D" and South of "B" and Artillery Barrage will
be placed on enemy Support Line West of Area to be raided.
Machine Guns will fire on approximately same Targets as above.

5. Parties will return at Zero plus 20 minutes. 2 Buglers will sound
a succession of high "C's" at this hour.
Dress Drill order, Steel Helmets, S.B.Respirators, 50 rounds S.A.
A strip of 4 by 2 flannel will be tied on both shoulder straps of men
taking part in the Raid. Any article likely to give an identification will be left behind.
    Bayonet men will carry 4 bombs each.
    Blocking Groups will carry 2 buckets containing 12 bombs in each.
    Reserve Party   "   "   3   "   "   "   "   "   "
Two men each group will have wire cutters affixed to the rifle.
One man per group will carry a sandbag attached to the belt into which
will be put small articles which may be found in the enemy's line,
such as Documents, Maps, etc.

6. Mens faces will be darkened before going over.

7. Gaps in our wire at "P" and "Q" will be cut two hours previous to
Zero.
8. Gaps in enemy's wire will be cut by the Artillery at "P" and "B"
and also at other points in order to deceive the enemy as to actual
intention.

9. Very Lights will be fired by C's C "B", and "D" Coys from Zero
plus 2 minutes to Zero plus 18 minutes to assist Raiding Party in
their work.

10. Prisoners taken and all Documents etc., brought in will be forwarded to Battn: H.Q. as soon as possible by O.C. "A"Coy.

ORDERS FOR RAID CONTINUED - SHEET 2.

11. A tape will be laid by the rear group of each Party to "B" and "C" in enemy's Front Line in order to facilitate return. These tapes will be pulled in on completion of Raid by "B" and "C" Coys respectively.

12. Watches of all concerned will be synchronised at Battn:H.Q. at 7.0 pm and 12 m.n. 10th November.

12a. Co-ordinates.

$$X = U.5.b.93.93.$$
$$Y = U.5.d.20.85.$$
$$Z = U.5.d.35.72.$$
$$D = U.6.c.18.86.$$
$$C = U.5.d.20.80.$$
$$B = U.5.d.89.50.$$

Major,
Comdg:1st Battalion "THE QUEEN'S" Regiment.

Copy No:1 ... 100th Inf:Bde:
  "   " 2 ... O.C."A"Coy.
  "   " 3 ... O.C.
  "   " 4 ... War Diary.
  "   " 5 ...   "
  "   " 6 ... 100th T.M.B.
  "   " 7 ... 100th M.G.C.

S E C R E T.   PATROL ORDER - TO EACH RECIPIENT   Copy No: 4
                OF ORDERS ON RAID ON NIGHT 10/11TH NOVEMBER.

Reference Special Sheet 8150/5 1/10,000 and Aeroplane
Photograph 43B 2138. 28U 5d 6c 11b 12a d/ 21.10.17.

    2/Lieut: DARBY with 3 N.C.O's from Groups 1,2, and 3, will
patrol the German Front Line opposite Point P between 6.0 p.m.
to 7.0 p.m. on the night of the 9/10th November and
    2/Lieut: PARKES with 4 N.C.O's from Groups 4,5,6, and 7 will
patrol the German Front Line opposite Point Q between 7.0 p.m.
and 8.0 p.m. on the night of the 9/10th November,
    to ascertain condition of Wire - configuration of ground-
exact localities and formation of Saps X, Y, and Z., and
Front Line.

    Brigade has been asked to inform Artillery of these patrols.

                                                H.R. Iremonger
                                                 Major,
7/11/17.   Comdg: 1st Battalion "THE QUEEN'S" Regt.

Copy No: 1....100th Inf: Bde:
  "   " 2....O.C. "A" Coy.
  "   " 3....C.O.
  "   " 4....War Diary.
  "   " 5....War Diary.
  "   " 6....100th T.M.B.
  "   " 7....100th M.G. Coy.

SECRET.   SUPPLEMENTARY ORDERS FOR RAID   Copy No 4.
              ON NIGHT OF 10/11TH NOVEMBER 1917.
              ----

1. Zero will be at 2.15 a.m. 11th inst.

2. Raiding Party will be in allotted positions by 1.30 a.m.

3. On conclusion of raid, party will return to Bn:Reserve Trenches.

4. Gaps in our own wire at "P" and "Q" will be cut by 12.30 a.m. by "D" and "B" Coy and will be mended by "D" and "B" Coys respectively as soon as possible after completion of raid.

5. Coy Sergt.Major of "A" Coy will be at point "P" and Coy Sergt Major of "B" Coy at point "Q" for the purpose of checking number of men returning by name.

6. Very Lights will be fired by Units on our flanks as well as by "D", "B", and "C" Coys from Zero plus 3 minutes to Zero plus 15 minutes.

7. Stokes Mortars will fire at a medium rate of fire from Zero minus 1 minute to Zero hour on the enemy's front line trench between D and B, at Zero they will fire at selected targets.

8. At Zero plus 30 two buglers will sound a succession of high "G's" as a signal for withdrawal. One bugler will be with O.C. "A" Coy the other at point "Q".

9. Hot Tea will be taken up to all Coys, leaving BETHLEHEM FARM at 4.0 a.m. 11th inst. A half issue of rumm will be mixed with the tea for Raiding Party and a half issue will be served out on return to Battn:H.Qrs.

10. O.C. "A" Coy will furnish one officer at points "P" and "Q" respectively who will be in readiness to take charge of parties in the event of either raiding officer becoming a casualty.

11. Watches of "A","B","C","D" Coys and all concerned will be synchronised at 7.0 p.m. and 12 m.n. 10/11th inst at Bn:H.Q.

12. O.C. "A" Coy will be in telephonic communication with Bn.H.Q. from his position in the Front Line. Arrangements are being made

13. O.C. "C" Coy will clear his line 50 yards NORTH & South of U.5.d.45.25 from Zero minus 30 minutes till raid is over and situation again normal.

                                                 Major for Lt:Col:
              Comdg: 1st Battalion "THE QUEEN'S" Regiment.

Copy No:1
       2
       3
       4
       5

Vous êtes
9 espece No 45.

SECRET   Battalion Order No. 216.   Copy 12.
                 by Lt. Col. J. R. M. CROFTS. D.S.O.
                 Comdg. 2nd "The Queen's" Regt.
                        Saturday 24th Nov 17.

1.   The Battalion will move to the POTIJZE Area tomorrow 25th inst. (the Bn. being in support to 19th Infy. Bde.) and will parade on Coy etc. parade grounds ready to move off in the following order at 10.25.a.m.
    H.Q. D.C. B.A. TRANSPORT.   Dress — S.M.O. Steel Helmets will be worn.

2.   The following distances will be maintained on the march. Between platoons 100x, Unit & Transport 200x, between Units 500x.

3.   The Battn. will take over Camp — I.9.a.3.2. vacated by 4th Kings.

4.   "B" Echelon will be at Camp No. 7. H.Q.C. central.

5.   Caps & P.H. Helmets will be packed in bags tied & labelled and handed in at Q.M. Stores by 9 a.m. Blankets & Jerkins will be taken to the POTIJZE Area. To be rolled in bundles of 10 securely fastened & labelled and stacked at Q.M. Stores by 7.30 a.m. Mens Kits at Q.M. Stores by 9.30. Officers Valises at Stores by 9 a.m.

6.   Cookers, Water Carts only will remain with Battn. remainder of Transport will return to "B" Echelon. Horses for water carts only will be kept in POTIJZE area.

7.   On arrival in POTIJZE area the L.G.O. will make the usual arrangements for protection of Camp against enemy Aircraft.

8.   All ranks are forbidden to use water from shell holes for any purpose, owing to the probability of the fresh ones being formed by the shell are still containing the liquid.

9.   Coy etc. Gas N.C.O. are to be released from other duties and should be accommodated at Coy etc. H.Q.

10.   Schlonds of lime if available will be kept in readiness for use.

11.   C.Q.M.S. etc, one N.C.O. A.D. and 1 Gas N.C.O. per Coy & H.Q. will parade under Lieut. H. M. East at 9.30.a.m. tomorrow proceeding in advance to take over Camp etc.

12.   O.C. Coys etc. will report to the Adj. immediately they have got their men settled in in Camp tomorrow.

13.   The western boundary of the "ALERT ZONE" is a line drawn through C of Central — C.28 Central. I.4.a, I.3.d, I.9.b.
       I.4.c, I.15.a, &c, I.14.d, I.20 & I.10, I.6.a.o.
                                                                            (Sgd) R. S. Morris Capt & Adjt
Copy No:1. Col. 2. 2/C.No1. 3.O.C.No2.   The Queen's
        4. " No3. 5. " No4. 6. Adj.   R S Morris Capt & Adjt.
        7. I.O. 8. R.S.M. 9. Regt.
       10. H.Q. Coy. Orderly Room.   one missing.

SECRET.   Battalion Order No. 290   Copy No. 12
                      By Lieut: [?] [?] [?] [?]
                      Comg. [?] The Queen's Regt.
                      Thursday 29th Nov: 1917

1. The Brigade will relieve 19th Infy: Bde in the line on 29th November and night of 30th Nov/1st Dec: as follows:—
   Nov. 29th. 2nd Worcesters relieve 5th S.R. in Right Support
              Battn. H.Q. at D.16.c.15.40.
              16th K.R.R.C. relieve the Cameronians in Left Support
              Battn. H.Q. at D.15.a.40.25.
   Night of 30th Nov/1st Dec. 2nd Worcesters relieve 20th R. Fus: in Right
              Sub Sector. — Battn. H.Q. at D.16.b.50.65.
              16th K.R.R.C. relieve H.L.I. in Left Sub Sector
              Battn. H.Q. at D.16.b.7.14.
   The positions vacated by 2nd Worcesters and 16th K.R.R.C. will be occupied by 1st Queen's and 9th H.L.I. on the afternoon 30th.

2. The Battn. will move off tomorrow in the order H.Q. B.D.A.C. leaving at 2-0pm. by Platoons at 100x Interval. Dress. F.S.M.O except that greatcoats will not be taken — jerkins will be carried in the pack. Three days rations will be carried. While in Support one days ration will be consumed and one received each day so that on moving into front line all ranks will be in possession of 3 days ration.

3. Trench stores will be issued and taken up tomorrow.

4. Blankets will be rolled in bundles of ten securely fastened and labelled — Great Coats ditto — and handed over to a representative of the Q.M. at house on Cross Roads immediately beyond the Cemetery. Officers valises at the same place by 12 noon.

5. Guides are being furnished by 2/Worcesters at junction of H & K Tracks (D.21.a.3.6) at 4.40pm. on a scale of 1 per Coy. H.Q. and 1 per Coy.

6. Coys will relieve completed Coys of 2/Worcesters i.e. "A" relieves "A" and so on.

7. "B" Echelon will be established in the near vicinity of Cross Roads (N. side) I.8.b.6.4.

8. Completion of relief will be reported in writing to Bn. H.Q. by runners. Reports of the journey up being sent at the same time.

9. Gumboots are not being used in the line but 100 pairs have been drawn up and will be kept at "B" Echelon as a reserve.

10. Hot food and water will be brought up each morning while in Support. It is again impressed on Coy O. Comdrs that unless haversacks & dixies are sent back complete daily, the supply of hot tea etc must fail. — All ranks must be made acquainted with this fact.

11. All stretcher bearers will attend at the Aid Post at 11.45am tomorrow.

12. Twenty men of H Coy will be accommodated with "D" Coy while in Support.

13. The following officers will be left with "B" Echelon tomorrow:—
    Major H.E. Jemmett. Lieuts J.S. McLeod, D.V. Bernard, F.L. Leighton 2/Lieuts L.M. East, J.A. Talbot, M.W. James, J. Ruskin, J.E. Covey, G.E. Rayner.

                                                    (Sgd) R.H. Nevins Capt & Adjt.
                                                          "The Queen's" Regt.

Copies issued as under:—
1. C.O. 2. O.C. No.1. 3. O.C. No.2.
4. O.C. No.3. 5. O.C. No.4. 6. T.O.
7. Q.M. 8. Adjt. 9. R.S.M.
10. File. 11 & 12. War Diary.
13 & 14. Spare.

                                                    R.H. Nevins Capt & Adjt.

WAR DIARY   DECEMBER 1917   Army Form C. 2118.

INTELLIGENCE SUMMARY. 1st Batt. "The Queen's" Regt.   Page 1.

(Erase heading not required.)

Vol 38

Place	Date	Hour	Summary of Events and Information	Remarks and references to Appendices
SEINE	1st		Battalion in Brigade Support — Working under R.E. supervision on the construction of shelters — Reliefs by Divisions on left — No Casualties.	
"	2nd		Continued in Bde Support. — Work on shelters re-continued	
"	3rd		Continued in Bde Support. Casualties: Other ranks Killed 2, Wounded 11. Battalion relieved 75 & Runs Regt here (D.12.b.0.6. to D.18.C.8.8.) and on completion was disposed as under. Right front "D" Coy, Left front "A" Coy, Support B Coy Reserve C Coy. Relief was completed at 1.55 am. Situation normal.	
Front line 5th Miscellaneous DAMES	4th		Continued in Front Line which consists of a series of Posts requiring much work which was commenced immediately on taking over. No movement possible by day. During night St.A. Roads to Wire carried forward. Casualties: 1 signal J.E. CORRY Wounded. 2 O.R. Killed 4 O.R. Wounded. Shelters improved	3 1/1/20
"	5th		Continued in Front line — Situation Normal — Casualties 2 O.R. Killed.	

Army Form C. 2118.

WAR DIARY
INTELLIGENCE SUMMARY

(Erase heading not required.)

DECEMBER 1917
1/8th Bn. The Queen's Regt.

Page 2.

Instructions regarding War Diaries and Intelligence Summaries are contained in F. S. Regs., Part II. and the Staff Manual respectively. Title pages will be prepared in manuscript.

Place	Date	Hour	Summary of Events and Information	Remarks and references to Appendices
FRONT LINE STROOMBEZELE	6th		Continued in front line. Orders that Bde would be relieved in the line by the 98th Infy Bde received. Battalion to be relieved by 4th Battn Suffolk Regt. Relief commenced at 12 M.N. completed at 4.45am. 2nd Lt. To Casualties. Lieut Col H.M. CROFTS D.S.O acting Brigadier, Brig Genl A.W.F. BAIRD CMG D.S.O. having been wounded. Major H. ETREMONGER in command of Battalion.	
FYNES Iya22	7		The relief Battalion marched to K.07.5.2.E Area. Bn arrived in Trenches Hot water was in readiness all ranks had foot baths after which haversacks & French Hot breakfast was served out. Hot Meal provided. At 10.15am Battn paraded and marched to ST JEAN and entrained at 11am. Detrained at BRANDOEK marched to TORONTO Camp (G.18.a) move completed 12.50pm. Brigade is rest in Divisional Reserve. Regtl P.J. JAKES joined from 3rd: Battn.	
TORONTO CAMP G.18 a 6.5.	8		Rest and cleaning up generally. Capt C.G. KICK D.L.I joined Infantine. Orders received that Brigade will be relieved in Divisional Reserve by the 160th Infy Bde and moved to WINNEZEELE area on 10th instant.	
	9		Voluntary Divine Service. Battalion had Hot Baths, also change of underclothing.	

WAR DIARY
INTELLIGENCE SUMMARY
(Erase heading not required.)

Army Form C. 2118.
DECEMBER 1917
2/4 Batn. The Queen's Regt.
Page 3.

Place	Date	Hour	Summary of Events and Information	Remarks and references to Appendices
TORONTO CAMP	10th		Battalion paraded at 8.50 a.m. and marched to WINNEZEELE Area via POPERINGHE - ST JANSTER - BISKEN - WATOU & Billets N of STEENVOORDE in Squares K.13.19 and 25. Move completed 8 p.m. Draft of 96 O.R. joined from En Raid. Captain L.A. McLean R.A.M.C. joined on attachment relieving Captain G. GANNON R.A.M.C.	BO 222
N of STEENVOORDE K.25.C.9.9.	11th		Rest and cleaning up generally —	
"	12th		Ditto Warning ord. to be prepared to move YPRES and POPERINGHE areas on 13th instant.	
"	13th		Battalion marched to POPERINGHE move completed 3 p.m. Billeted in Billets.	A.O. 224.
POPERINGHE	14th		General Routine Working Party 1 Officer 50 O.R. furnished (for work must N/R)	
"	15th		8 Officers 275 O.R. working party paraded at 8 a.m. entrained 11 a.m. detrained at WIELTJE where guides met them. Worked under 50th Dvn. Art. Sigs.	

WAR DIARY

INTELLIGENCE SUMMARY

DECEMBER 1917   Army Form C. 2118.

2/Batt. "The Queen's" Regt.   Page 54

Place	Date	Hour	Summary of Events and Information	Remarks and references to Appendices
POPERINGHE	15th		Returned WIELTJE aftn. noon. entrained 12 noon for POPERINGHE. Arrived in Belks 1.15 pm. 2 Officers 27 O.R. commenced L.G. course under Sgt. KNIGHT. Brigadier to Leave 14th Lieut. Col. L.M. CROFTS D.S.O. temporarily in command of Brigade.	
"	16th		4 Officers 150 O.R. working party under 50th Divn. Arty. Group furnished. 45 O.R. joined from England. Frost set in.	
"	17		5 Officers 255 O.R. working party under 50 Divn. Arty. Group furnished. (Frost continues)	
"	18		4 Officers 210 O.R. working party under C.R.E. on pipe line finished. Frost continues.	
"	19		— ditto —	
"	20		— ditto —	
"			Orders received for move of Brigade back to WINNEZEELE area on 21st	

WAR DIARY
INTELLIGENCE SUMMARY
1st Batt. The Queen's Regt.

Army Form C. 2118.
DECEMBER 1917
Page 5

Place	Date	Hour	Summary of Events and Information	Remarks and references to Appendices
POPERINGHE	21st		Battalion paraded 10.30am and marched to N. of STEENVOORDE via Rd. Q31	
N. of STEENVOORDE	22nd		ABEELE STEENVOORDE to billets in & near DRAGLANDT. March completed 1.45pm. Divine Service.	
K25C9.9	23rd		General Routine - Cleaning up billets &c.	
"			Voluntary Divine Service.	
"	24th		General Routine - Platoon and Coy Training	
"	25th		Voluntary Divine Service - Band 'B' Coy Xmas Feast & Entertainment. 'A' Coy Batt HQrs	
"	26th		General Routine - Platoon & Coy Training - Bombing Class Commenced. Coy S.L. SHIPTON. Transport, C & D Coys Xmas Feast & Entertainment. Lieut Genl Major Genl Rhoney C.B. delivered a lecture on the Battle of CAMBRAI. Officers and Serjts. to attend.	

Army Form C. 2118.

WAR DIARY
INTELLIGENCE SUMMARY.
(Erase heading not required.)

DECEMBER 1917
1st/5th THE QUEEN'S
Page 6.

Place	Date	Hour	Summary of Events and Information	Remarks and references to Appendices
N. of STEENVOORDE K.25.c.9.9	27th		General Routine – Platoon & Coy Training – "A" Coy Armentières Entrenchment Front.	
	28th		General Routine – Platoon & Coy Training etc. Lecture by Sir Aylmer HUNTER-WESTON Comdg VIIIth Corps. Officers and Sergeants attended.	
	29th		General Routine. Platoon & Coy Training etc. Lt Col KM CROFTS D.S.O. (acting Brigadier) Wounded (both hands) during T.M. demonstration near WINNEZEELE. 2nd Lt S.F.PROB also wounded and 1 O.R. Killed.	
	30th		Voluntary Divine Service. Warning orders received Brigade probably move to BRANDHOEK 4th and POTIJZE area on 5th January 1918.	
	31st		General Routine. Platoon & Coy Training. Organ Platoon Comdrs attended a Brigade lecture on "Intelligence".	

K. Henworthy Major
Comdg 1st/5th Bn "The Queen's" Regt

SECRET.

Battalion Orders No 222
by Major H. E. IREMONGER
Comdg The Queen's Regt

Copy No 11

Sunday 9th Decr 1917

1. The Brigade will be relieved in Divl Reserve by the 150th Inf Bde and proceeds to the WINNEZEELE Area.
The Battn will parade and be ready to move off in the following order at 8.50 a.m tomorrow and march to WINNEZEELE Area distance about 12 miles - Route Cross Roads G 5 d 1.2 POPERINGHE ST JANSTER BIEXEN WATOU
H.Q A.B Drums C. D Transport - Dress Fighting Order Haversacks with W.P. Sheet under flap and Steel Helmets being hung over all by passing Chinstrap under attachments fastening to braces.

2. Reveille will be at 6.30 a.m Blankets rolled in bundles of 10 securely fastened and labelled, to be stacked at Q.M Stores by 7 a.m. Packs (with Jerkins inside) No. Name & Coy of owner plainly marked on bottom edge to be at Q.M Stores by 7.30 a.m.
Coy Mess Baskets at Q.M Stores by 8. a.m.

3. See B.O. 15 of 8th Inst.
Erase 13514 Pte W. Eggar "C" Coy
Add 10262 " A. England "B".

4. Extract London Gazette of 21.11.17.
E. Surrey Regt To be Lieut Lieut H. Mallett 1.7.17.

5. Distances as under will be maintained during the march tomorrow.
Between Coys 100 yds - Battn Transport 100 yds - Between Units 500 yds.

6. Officers Comdg Coys Sections of H.Q. will personally inspect Huts and the lines prior to marching off & will report to the Adjt on parade that they have been left in a clean and sanitary condition. Lieut Denny will hand Camp over to relieving Unit or to Camp Warden in case relieving unit is not represented and obtain a Certificate that the Camp has been left in a clean and sanitary condition.

7. Names of men unfit to march have been given out to Coys. Party will parade under the Regt Sergt Major at the Guard Room at 8.15 a.m.

8. The latest date of posting for delivery in British Isles by Xmas have been fixed as follows :-
London   Letters   Parcels
              19th   17th
Elsewhere   18th   16th

9. The u/m proceed on leave to England tomorrow - Parade at O.Room at 4 p.m. To be paid before leaving & period of leave entered in their A.B Bks. Period of Leave 11/12/17 - 25/12/17.
7945 Pte. J Cockerton "B"

(Sd) R. H. Nevin Capt Adjt
The Queen's

Copies issued as under.
1. C.O 2. O.C N o.1   3. O.C No 2
4. O C No 3. 5. O.C No 4 6. T.O
7. Q.M 8. Adjt 9. R.S.M
10. File 11. 12. War Diary
13 & 14 Spare.

R.W Nevin Capt Adjt

SECRET.   Battalion Orders No: 224   Copy
          by Lt.Col. L.M. CROFTS. D.S.O   No:
          Comdg: Bn. The Queen's Regt
          13th December 17.

1. The Bn will move from WINNEZEELE Area to-day.

2. The Bn will assemble on STEENVOORDE — DROGLANDT Road, in the following order, head of Column at track leading into B Coys Billet ready to move off at 11.45 AM this morning.
   "B" "C" "D" "A" TRANSPORT. Dress — F.S.M.O
   Steel Helmets on Packs and march to POPERINGHE

3. Blankets and Jerkins to be rolled separately in bundles of 10 securely fastened and labelled to be stacked on roadside
   B at J.12.d.9.2.   A.C.&D at J.24.b.9.5.
   H Qrs at QM Stores by 9.30 AM.
   The QM will detail Guides to conduct 2 parties to places where Blankets are to be loaded.

4. Officers valises and mess baskets to be at places for stacking of Blankets by 9.30 AM.

5. C.Q.M.Sgt & 1 NCO H.Q under 2/Lieut K.M.EAST will assemble at Bn H.Q at 8.15 AM proceeding in advance for Billeting. 2/Lt East will report to TOWN MAJOR POPERINGHE at 10.0 AM.

6. The only Transport to accompany Battn will be Cookers, Water Carts, L.G. Limbers, Baggage Wagons, Riders. — remainder will remain.

7. Surplus kit will be left behind at QM Stores.

8. The Drums will remain in present Billets but will play the Battn out.

9. O.C Coys will take the necessary steps to ensure Billets are left in a clean & sanitary state, and will report to Adjt on parade this is so. It was clear on the last move, that in all cases Billets, Cookhouses, Latrines etc had not been inspected.

10. Distances to be kept. — Between Coys 100x
    Bns & Transport 100x   Units minimum 500x.

11. A Coy will detail an Officer & 2 NCO. to collect stragglers should there be any.

12. Mess kits in excess of Blankets will be carried on L.G. Limbers.

Copies to
1. C.O.   2. O.C.No1
3. O.C.No2 4. O.C.No3.
5. O.C.No4 6 Q.M.
7. T.O.   8. 2/Lt K.M.EAST.
9. Adjt   10. R.S.M.
11. File   12.&13. War Diaries.

(Sgd) R.H Nevins Capt & Adjt
                The Queen's Regt

R.H Nevins Capt & Adjt

SECRET

Battalion Orders No. 231
By Major H. E. IREMONGER
Comdg Bn The Queens Regt

Detail for tomorrow.   Thursday 20 Dec 1917
Subaltern of the day.   2/Lieut J E Shipton

1. **Move** — The Bde returns to the WINNIZEELE Area tomorrow occupying same billets.
The Battn will assemble in Rue DE BOESCHEPE in following order, ready to move off at 10.35 a.m — head of column just beyond entry to B. Coy Billets.
H.Q. C. D. Drum A. B.
Dress F.S. M.O. Steel Helmets on packs.
L.G. Limbers & Cookers will accompany Companies.
Companies &c will not move out on the road until necessary to gain their position in the Column.
Distance to be maintained — Between Coys 100 yds. Battn and Transport 100 yds. Units not less than 100 yds.
The Strictest March Discipline will be observed.
Blankets & Jerkins rolled separately in bundles of 10 securely fastened and labelled to be at Q.M. Stores by 7.30 a.m.
Officers Valises 9 a.m — Mess Baskets at H.Q. Mess 9.30 a.m.
Mess Kits and excess of Baskets will be carried on L.G. Limbers.

2. **Billeting** — C.Q.M. Sgts & 1 N.C.O. He Qrs will assemble at Q.M. Stores at 8.45 a.m proceeding in advance on Cycles. The Senior will be in charge.

3. **Working Parties** — No Working Parties are being furnished tomorrow.

4. **Sanitation** — Pioneer Sergt & Pioneers & 1 Sanitary man per Coy will remain behind under Coy O.C. of Coy to hand over Billets to incoming unit (or Town Major).
O.C Coys will take steps to see every billets are left clean every billet occupied by the Coy &c are to be inspected prior to marching off and a report to this effect made to the Adjt on Parade.
Capt KILLICK will obtain a Certificate from the incoming Unit (or Town Major) that Billets have been handed over clean and Sanitary.

5. **Courses** — 10465 Capt R. Kitching has been selected to attend B Course of Instruction at the Lewis Gun Branch of the G.H.Q Small Arms School assembling on the 27th inst. Further instructions will be issued later.

6. **Sick** — Number reporting Sick - A Coy 3 B Coy 1 C Coy 3 D Coy 4 Sgt R 2
Sick parade at 8.30 a.m tomorrow

7. Orders will be at 9-45 a.m tomorrow

L. H. Nevin Capt & Adjt
The Queens

War Diary

Army Form C. 2118.

WAR DIARY
INTELLIGENCE SUMMARY. 1st Batt. "The Queen's" Regt

(Erase heading not required.)

Page 1.

JANUARY 1918

Vol 39

Place	Date	Hour	Summary of Events and Information	Remarks and references to Appendices
N.h STEENVOORDE K23 c9.9.	1st		Day observed as a Holiday. Lieut. Col. S. B. R. SLADEN assumed command of the Battalion on instructions from Division.	
—	2nd		Training and general routine. Brigade Boxing Tournament Open.	
—	3rd		Training and general routine. Orders received to move to TORONTO CAMP.	Ad.1914
—	4th		The battalion marched to the entraining point on WINNEZEELE - DROGLANDT at 11 a.m. Entraining was completed 16/15:30 and column proceeded to the outskirts of VLAMERTINGHE. Upon de-braining the Battalion marched by companies to TORONTO CAMP. Orders received to proceed to relief of 20th Bn. R.F. on night of 5th/6th.	24/1/RN

Army Form C. 2118.

WAR DIARY
JANUARY 1918
INTELLIGENCE SUMMARY. 1st Bn "The Queen's Regt."

PAGE 2

(Erase heading not required.)

Instructions regarding War Diaries and Intelligence Summaries are contained in F. S. Regs., Part II. and the Staff Manual respectively. Title pages will be prepared in manuscript.

Place	Date	Hour	Summary of Events and Information	Remarks and references to Appendices
TORONTO CAMP G/8 a 6.5.	5th		The battalion paraded at 8 am & entrained for YPRES & marched thence to camp at THAOT. where dinners were served. At 3.45 pm battn marched by platoons via ZONNEBEKE road to relieve 8th K. SR. INF. Relief completed by 9 pm. The route was most trying. Stopping of 19th Inf Bde. The area was shelled intermittently by 4.2" guns. 3 O.R. wounded	to M.O. No 5
SR.INF.	6th		Doncast & shelling 10 R killed, 30 R wounded from 6 am & during day air abnormally quiet. 16 Officers & 330 O.R. furnished for working & carrying parties. Officers & N.C.O's reconnoitred forward areas.	
"	7th		6 Officers 205 O.R. furnished for working parties. Situation normal. Officers & N.C.O's reconnoitred forward areas in view of action to be taken in event of enemy attack	

WAR DIARY JANUARY 1918

Army Form C. 2118.

INTELLIGENCE SUMMARY. 1st Bn. "The Queen's" Regt PAGE 3

(Erase heading not required.)

Place	Date	Hour	Summary of Events and Information	Remarks and references to Appendices
			Year seems khaki out in. Quiet night. About 4:30 a.m. heavy shelling by the North apparently on front of Coys on left. Capt. C. G. KILLICK proceeded to join 18th J.L.I. on posting. Orders received that 100th J.B. will relieve 19th J.B. in the line on 8th and night of 9/10th inst. Battalion to relieve 20th R.F. in right subsector on night 9/10th.	
SEINE	8th		Situation normal - snow fell heavily during day. SEINE area intermittently shelled. Working parties as on 7th furnished. C.O. + Adjt. visited 20th R.F. and arranged details for relief taking place on night 9/10th.	
SEINE	9th		The battalion relieved 20th R.F. in front line right subsector just north of PASSCHENDAELE. Commenced at 5:45 p.m. Coys were deployed as follows - Right C. Centre "D" Left "B" Support "A" Relief completed 12:30 a.m. 10th inst. M few casualties occurred during	W.O. M.G.

Army Form C. 2118.

WAR DIARY
INTELLIGENCE SUMMARY.
(Erase heading not required.)

JANUARY 1918.

1st Bn. The Queens Regt.   PAGE 4

Place	Date	Hour	Summary of Events and Information	Remarks and references to Appendices
HAMBURG	10th		Relief. Nowt and snow. 2/Lt J.E. Carry rejoined from hospital. Situation during night normal. Shew Chandlers wounded O.R. 8.	
HAMBURG	11th		At about 1.30 a.m. a Germen fighting patrol numbering from 10 to 15 men which had clearly left our rifles advanced into 4 D Coy pushed the listening post covering point Inner who opened fire but not before the patrol however had got to within about 200 yards in front of the listening post. Two men had entered the listening post itself. The latter immediately defends there own fire to the post. (Gunner 8170 G.C. Mc Cluskie) and rifle fire on the Germans who were charging among the two men in the listening post. (Pte Purdie and Bryson.) The fire caused casualties to the patrol which Pte Purdie saw falling + firing a flare with his last match at the German who were left in the line and searched 6 total which went out. 6 to discovered the bodies of 2 of the	

WAR DIARY JANUARY 1918.
INTELLIGENCE SUMMARY.

(Erase heading not required.)

Army Form C. 2118.

1st Bn "The Queens" Regt PAGE 5

Place	Date	Hour	Summary of Events and Information	Remarks and references to Appendices
			Subsequent enquiries shewed that further casualties were caused. Pte Dinsmore was reported missing after this action. Casualties P.R. wounded 1, but under a/hrly 3. Missing 1. Situation continued normal. Found no further trace of missing.	
HAMBURG	12th		Situation normal. Ground very wet & muddy. Casualties P.R. Killed 3. Wounded 3. Gas rough that battalion will be relieved on night 13/14th inst by 4th Suffolks.	
HAMBURG	13th		Situation normal. No casualties. Relief by 4th Suffolks commenced 5.45 pm. Completed 8.25 pm. As relief Companies moved to BECK JUNCTION where 'bus were waiting. Battalion proceeded by 'bus to POTIJZE – SEAHAM CAMP where all Companies attended hot food but breakfast had to be issued	[Ap. O. O. 7]

Army Form C. 2118.

WAR DIARY
or
INTELLIGENCE SUMMARY.
(Erase heading not required.)

JANUARY 1918.

1st Bn 7th Queens Regt PAGE 6

Place	Date	Hour	Summary of Events and Information	Remarks and references to Appendices
TORONTO CAMP	14th		Entrained at 8.30 am and proceeded to BENDHOEK area. Billetted in TORONTO CAMP. General outer anti-aircraft up.	
TORONTO CAMP	15th		General routine cleaning up, refitting and baths	
TORONTO CAMP	16th		Training (including shoot on to march) and General Bn Duties	
"	17th		143 O.R. joined from Base. Battalion entrained at BRANDHOEK on the Hans Cleart railway at 2pm which proceeded to vicinity of ST JEAN. Battalion proceeded to ST JEAN Camp "B" below menioned at BENDHOEK. Men employed 6.30pm. Battalion under orders of C.R.E. VIII Corps took over from 18th.	
ST JEAN Camp T.8.b.3.6.	18th		Three Coys furnished for work forward. One Coy working on improvement of Camp.	
"	19th		As on 18th	

Army Form C. 2118.

Page 7

WAR DIARY

JANUARY 1918

INTELLIGENCE SUMMARY

2/Bn. "THE QUEEN'S" Regt.

(Erase heading not required.)

Instructions regarding War Diaries and Intelligence Summaries are contained in F. S. Regs., Part II. and the Staff Manual respectively. Title pages will be prepared in manuscript.

Place	Date	Hour	Summary of Events and Information	Remarks and references to Appendices
ST JEAN Camp I.3.b.3.6.	20th		Three Coys furnished for work forward in vicinity of FREZEN BERG. One Coy working on improvement of camp. Voluntary Ch.E service in camp 5pm.	
"	21st		Work as on 20th.	
"	22nd		Ditto.	
"	23rd		Ditto.	Captain H.S Carpenter attached to Heavy Artillery for 48 hours.
"	24th		Ditto.	
"	25th		Ditto.	2/Lieut Ede W. Green attd to R.F.A for 48 hours " L.O Parks }
"	26th		Ditto. H.Q. S.B. & R.S.M. DIEN.to FIRECOURT. Battn in Bde. conference at 9th Army Cadet. Battn to be relieved by 50th Divn. & on relief moved to THIEVES Area. 27/1/18 Orders received from Divn.	
"	27th		Work as on 26th. Transport & Coy to Transport & Lim by rail, remainder by road proceed to rendezvous, voluntary Cdp. C. of E. Service.	

Army Form C. 2118.
Page 8

WAR DIARY
JANUARY 1918

INTELLIGENCE SUMMARY. 1st Bn. THE QUEEN'S Regt.

(Erase heading not required.)

Instructions regarding War Diaries and Intelligence Summaries are contained in F. S. Regs., Part II. and the Staff Manual respectively. Title pages will be prepared in manuscript.

Place	Date	Hour	Summary of Events and Information	Remarks and references to Appendices
ST JEAN Camp L.3.b.3.b.	28th		Battalion moved to SISTAJES. Move completed 2.30pm. H.Q. & C/O.	Ref. App. D. 22.
			Coys occupying huts in village. A Coy in Fillets at FLESINGHEM about a mile distant.	
SISTAJES	29th		Cleaning up. Arms. Equipment & Clothing also Billets.	
"	30th		Ditto	
"	31st		Drawing and General Routine.	

Murray Major
Comdg 1st Bn. The Queen's Regt.

SECRET Battalion Orders No. 12 Copy No. 12
by Lieut Col B. R. Lladen
Comdg The Queens Regt   3D January 1918

1. The Brigade will move to the BRANDHOEK Area tomorrow 4th Inst. will by Bus Transport by road under the orders of Capt. H. E. Harrison M.C.

2. The Battn will march to N.E. of WINNEZEELE tomorrow as under Embussing 400 yds. S.W. of Cross Roads J.12.A.73 H.Q. Drums A.C.&D Coys assemble at Cross Roads J.24 b 8.4 ready to move at 11.30 a.m.
"B" Coy to be at Fork Roads WINNEZEELE J.18 b 7.9 at 11.40 a.m
Dress F.S.M.O Steel Helmets on packs — Jerkins will be worn

3. Transport will move under orders of the Transport Officer. G. Limbers & hookers to be ready to draw out at 8.15 a.m

4. Blankets rolled in bundles of 10 securely fastened and labelled to be stacked together with Mess Baskets Valises as under:
"B" Coy by roadside at about J.12. D.8.2. by 7.45 a.m
C & D Coy   "   Cross Roads J.24 b 8.4 by 8. a.m
A Coy & H.Q. at Q.M Stores by 8.15. a.m

5. Battn will march to TORONTO Camp on debussing probably moving to POPERINGHE on 5th Inst

6. C.Q.M. Sergt 1 N.C.O. H. Ors. billetting party will parade at Bn H.Q under 2/Lt East at 9. a.m

7. O.C. Coys &c will ensure billets are left in a thoroughly clean and sanitary state prior to quitting them reporting to the Adjutant at Parade this has been done.

8. 100 yds distance will be kept between Companies during the march.

9. Busses allotted to Battn each hold 20 men.

10. 2/Lieut Shipton will act as embussing officer to report to Staff Captain at Cross Roads J.12 a 7.3 at 12 noon

11. Bicycles will not be taken on busses.

12. Debussing takes place on road between H.7.c.3.6 and H.8.a H.2 whence Battalion march to Camp by shortest route.

1. C.O.   8. 2/Lt East
2. O.C.No 1 9. R.S.M
3.   "   2   10. O.O.J
4.   "   3   11. File
5.   "   4   12. 3 war Diary
6. T.O.   13.
7. T.M.   14. Spare

J. L. McKergow Capt & Adjt
The Queens

SECRET.

Battalion Order
by Lieut. Col. St B. K. Slader
Comdg. The Queen's Regt.

Friday 11th Jan 1918.

1. The Battalion will be ready to move off at 8 a.m. in the Order H.Q. A. B. C. D. and march to H.8.a.5.3 where it will embus, proceed by bus to Square YPRES; debus and march by platoons at 100 yds interval to SEAHAM CAMP. I.4.a.0.9 whence the move forward to SEINE in relief of 20th R.F. takes place late afternoon. Dress Fighting Order – Packs being worn.
Three days rations will be carried.
Cookers & water carts will proceed under the Orders of T.O. in time for Dinners to be served about noon.
Reveille will be at 6 a.m. – Breakfast 7.15 a.m.

2. Blankets & greatcoats rolled separately in bundles of 10. fastened & labelled to be at Q.M. Stores by 7 a.m.
Caps & P.H. Helmets in bags also tied & labelled to be at Q.M. Stores by 7.15 a.m. – Valises to be at Q.M. Stores by 7.30 a.m.
Mess Baskets at H.Q. Mess by 7.30 a.m.

3. Advance Q.M. Stores will be at T.3.d.8.8 taken over from 4th Yorks.
Transport remains in position now occupied.
Drums will remain with Transport.

4. Coys will move from SEAHAM Camp in the Order H.Q. A.B.C.D at 100 yds. interval – Leading Platoon moving at 3.45 p.m. Guides on the scale of 1 per Bn H.Q. and 1 per Coy are being provided at FREEZENBERG Cross Roads at 5.15 p.m. – who will relieve same Coys 20th R.F.

5. Following officers will remain at B Echelon with Transport
   A. Coy   Capt. K. A. Brown
   B. "   2/Lt. T. Crompton   2/Lt. P. Hughes
   C. "   2/Lt. H. MALLETT   2/Lt. J. W. C. MORGAN
   D. "   2/Lt. H. B. DENNY   2/Lt. M. M. JAMES
   H.Q. Major H. E. IRONMONGER Lieut. J. E. SHIPTON. K. M. EAST.
   Lieut. D. V. BERNARD.

6. Coys will leave Camp clean & sanitary.

7. 1 N.C.O. per Coy & H.Qrs will parade at H.Q. at 8 a.m. under Lieut Shipton proceeding in advance on Bicycles to locate SEAHAM CAMP meet Battn and guide Battn in.

9. Lieut M. M. James will report to Capt Hanson at 8 a.m. for duty with Transport.

10. 2/Lt J.W.C. Morgan, 6409 Sgt Dalton, 10816 Cpl Twines are detailed to attend a Course of Instruction commencing at LOVIE CHATEAU on ?...
Further instructions will be issued.

(Sd) R. H. Ty... Capt & Adjt

SECRET Battalion Order No 6   Copy No 5
by Lt Col S. B. Rawlinson
Cmdg The Queen's Regt
Tuesday 7 January 1918

1. The Battn will relieve 20th R.F. in Ribot Subsector
on night 7/8th January 1918.
Present position will be occupied by 1, 2, & 3 Coys.
Coys will be disposed in the line relieving opposite
numbers. No 2. LEFT. No 1. CENTRE. No 3. RIGHT. No 4 in
                       No 4. SUPPORT
Major H.E. TREMONGER will be in command of front
line and Support Companies.
Guides on a scale of 1 per platoon & sec
On Coy H.Q. will meet Coys at R. TALK Dbh 6.7.3.
Coys will relieve in the order No 2. 1st No 3. 2nd.
No 2 moving from present position at 6.45 pm
Platoons will move at 100 yards interval.
2. An important life — Batt will Coys
Bn will observe tel: bund 19th Jan
3. A Relay Depot and Runners Station will be
installed at HILL 190 Farm.
4. A power Buzzer is installed at Right
Front Coy H.Q.
5. Carrying to Front line is done by Company
of Pioneer Battalion
6. Attention — Drums to front to be changed
in light Brig — Battn Hqrs issued w/
these orders.

7. Each Coy will detail a NCO to remain at Bire Dump to receive rations - Hot food on its arrival and to conduct carrying parties to their Coy HQ. Empty Ray packs & Salt tins e must be handed over to carrying parties to bring back to Dumps on return. Every arrangements must be made that carrying parties are not delayed.

8. Each Coy and B&n HQ will detail 1 Guide for A & B Echns to arrive at Battn HQ at 8pm.

9. All Trench Stores S.O.S. Rifles Sniping Scopes & c. will be handed over & list of stores to be handed over will be rendered to Battn HQ by return runners list of same taken over in exchange will be sent to Battn HQ together with Intelligence Summary on morning 10th inst.

10. Completion of relief will be notified to Battn HQ by A.A.A.A. code.

Copies To -
No 1. A Coy dismounted
" 2. B C " 2
" 3. " "
" 4. " " 3
" 5. " " 4
" 6. " " Lewis
" 7. " " Diary
" 8.

R.N. Stern Capt M.G.
The Queen's Regt.

Secret: Battalion Orders No 7. Copy No 7
by Major A.B.? ......N
Comdg Old Queens
SATURDAY 12th January 1918

1. The ...... will be relieved in the .... by ...... Infy Bde on Jan 12th and night 13th 14th

2. The Battalion will be relieved in reverse .... Order

3. The relief not ..... to......... up to 6 PM on ......

4. Relieving ..... parties of 1 per ..... and ..... 1 NB .... nurses & kitchens & cooks, will take over & will be sent transport in Batt HQ at ....

5. Coy Comdrs will reconn. line their Coys on relief to Major H E MONGER at HH H Q by 2 PM Jany 11 Line to be by N.C.Os and they will be ordered, in not personally at Batt H.Q.

6. All French stores maps ...... sketches, maps .... of .... will be handed over and receipts taken. Lists will ... be in by ...... at Coys HQ ...... 11th.

7. On relief for .... at RFQ, ... for .... being .... will ...... NB .... for .... also ... extra .... just which is to ...... before all men with clean & .... Blankets and valises will be .... On 14th Bn entrains for BRANSMER. Transport by road

8. All Coms North ...... to be brought out
...   R.J. ...... Capt & Adjt

test ? out

1. Truck
2. Truck
Allie C Truck
(scores will be not pass first ca)
Bruce Truck

Copa C

1. L Major
2.
3.
4. B
5.
6. TO

7.
8.

SECRET   Battalion Order No 22   Copy No 10
                      by Major H.E. TREMONGER
                      Comdg The Queens Regt

                                                              Sunday 27 Jan: 1918.

Detail for tomorrow
Subaltern of the day   2/Lieut G.T. Ashpitel
Detail for Tuesday
Subaltern of the day
                                                    2/Lieut W. Ellen

1. Command. Lieut Col S.B.R. Sladen V.D. having proceeded on Temporary duty the Command of the Battn devolves upon Major H.E. Tremonger.

2. Relief. The Divn will be relieved by the 50th Divn between 27th & 30th January.
The Brigade on relief moves to ESQUERDES Area

3. Move. The Battn will parade. Dress F.S.M.O. Steel Helmets & Jerkins to be worn in readiness to move off at 12.50 p.m tomorrow 28th Inst in the Order H.Q. A. B. C. D. and march to St JEAN Station where it entrains for WIZERNES.
Entrainment will be carried out rapidly and in Silence
2/Lieut T. CROMPTON will report to Entrainment Officer at Station at 1 p.m to arrange train accommodation on detrainment Battn will march to SETQUES where it goes into Billets.

4. Discipline. The following distances will be maintained on the march
Between coys 100 yards.
This applies throughout 4th Army Area.

5. Sanitation. O.C. coys &c will take necessary steps to ensure Huts & Tents are left in a thoroughly clean & sanitary state - ground in vicinity also to be absolutely clear of rubbish.

6. Blankets. Blankets rolled in Bundles of 10 fastened & labelled & Officers light Kits to be ready for loading by 8.30 a.m.
O.C. coys &c will ensure Blankets are rolled tightly - Mess Baskets to be outside O.Room by 8.30 a.m.

7. Sick. Sick men will be sent on by coys under an Officer so as to arrive at Station not later than 1.15 p.m. - On detrainment the same procedure will be followed Party marching in rear of the Battn

8. Leave Party. The Leave Party will parade at Bn HQ at 7.15 a.m tomorrow under 2/Lieut Rayner who will report to the Adjt for instructions this evening.

9. Cleaning. On Tuesday 29th the day is to be spent in cleaning up arms & equipment & clothing - Inspections to take place in the afternoon - O.C. coys will report personally at Bn HQ at 7 p.m.

10. Sick. The Sick will be seen at 9. a.m tomorrow - On Tuesday at 9.30 a.m

11. Books &c. Silhouette - DE HAVILLAND 9. - is issued herewith 2 copies to each coy

12. Gum Boots on charge of coys will be tied in pairs ready to be handed over at 9. a.m tomorrow.

13. P. Day 4737. Pte T. Edwards D Coy granted P.P. class II @ 3d per diem will off from 16/2/17.

14. Sick. Number reporting Sick.
A. 19. B. 25. C. 17. D. 20.

                                          R. Morris Capt & Adjt   H. Nevins Capt & QM
                                                                   The Queens

www.ingramcontent.com/pod-product-compliance
Lightning Source LLC
Chambersburg PA
CBHW080844010526
44114CB00017B/2368